D0561838

HOTELS AND COUNTRY INNS
of Character and Charm
IN SPAIN

Hunter Publishing, Inc.
www.hunterpublishing.com

HUNTER PUBLISHING, INC.
130 Campus Drive, Edison NJ 08818
(732) 225 1900, (800) 255 0343; fax (732) 417 0482

IN CANADA
Ulysses Travel Publications
4176 Saint-Denis
Montreal, Quebec H2W 2M5 Canada
(514) 843 9882, ext. 2232; fax 514 843 9448

ISBN 1-55650-903-0
Third Edition

For complete information about the hundreds of other travel guides offered
by Hunter Publishing, visit our website at **www.hunterpublishing.com**

**Hotels and Country Inns
of Character and Charm in Spain**
Translator: Derry Hall, and Anne Norris
Front cover photograph: El Morrito (Gerena, Andalucia)
photo by Fabrice Camoin
Back cover: Fuente de la Higuera (Ronda, Andalucia)

Special Sales
Hunter Travel Guides can be purchased in quantity at special discounts. For
more information, contact us at the address above.

Printed in Italy by Litho Service
10 9 8 7 6 5 4 3 2 1

HUNTER RIVAGES

HOTELS AND COUNTRY INNS

of Character and Charm

IN SPAIN

Project editor
Michelle Gastaut

Conceived by
Michelle Gastaut
and Fabrice Camoin

This is a problem. The translation is not well done. The first three paragraphs should read as follows. I will e-mail this to you as well so you dont have to retype:

This new edition details 299 hotels. The inns and hotels selected range from simple comfort to grande luxe. We have made sure that our readers can always easily identify the category of each inn or hotel, independent of its star rating.

You should also note that **the prices are those quoted to us at the time we went to press** and some of them may since have changed. The paradors, notably, adjust their prices in the month of March.

When making your reservation by phone or fax, you should ask for the latest detailed rates. Most hotels quote rates to us **without including VAT** (value-added tax), which is 7% or 15%, depending on hotel category. You should understand that rates quoted for half board (one meal) and full board are often in addition to the room rates given.

In this new edition we have also given a selection of restaurants and cafés grouped by major tourist areas. The prices shown are for a full meal, but exclude drinks.

How to use this guide
We have classified hotels by regions in alphabetical order, and within each region by town or locality in alphabetical order. The number of the hotel page corresponds to the hotel number used on the regional maps, in the Contents pages and in the index of hotel names.

Please let us know...

If you are attracted by an inn or small hotel not listed in our guide, and you think it worthy of selection, please tell us so that the author may visit it. In like manner, if you are disappointed by any of the selections, please let us know.

Mail can be sent to:

Michelle Gastaut
Editions Rivages
10, rue Fortia
13001 Marseille - FRANCE

You can also contact us on the Guides Rivages' website at:
http://www.guidesdecharme.com

Or get in touch via our US website at
http://www.hunterpublishing.com

CONTENTS LIST

Contents

Contents restaurants

Essentiel information

Calendar of festival 'corridas' and fairs

Map of Spain

Road maps

CONTENTS RESTAURANTS

Restaurants in Spain:

ESSENTIAL INFORMATION

AIRPORTS

ANDALUSIA

– **Almeria**: Tel. 951-22 19 54 - 12 km.
– **Gibraltar**: 2,5 km.
– **Granada**: Tel. 956-27 33 22 - 17 km.
– **Jerez de la Frontera**: Tel. 956-33 42 32 - 11 km.
– **Málaga**: Tel. 952-32 20 00 - 9 km.
– **Melilla**: Tel. 952-68 35 64 - 4 km.
– **Sevilla-San Pablo**: Tel. 95-451 61 11 - 14 km.

ARAGON

– **Saragosa**: Tel. 976-32 62 62 - 9 km.

ASTURIAS CANTABRIA

– **Bilbao - Sondica**: Tel. 94-453 06 40 - 11 km.
– **Fuentarrabia**: Tel. 943-42 35 86
– **San Sebastian - Fuentarrabia**: Tel. 943-64 21 67 - 20 km.
– **Santander**: Tel. 942-25 10 09 - 7 km.
– **Vitoria**: Tel. 945-27 00 00 - 8 km.

BALEARIC ISLANDS

– **Ibiza**: Tel. 911-30 03 00 - 9 km.
– **Menorca - San Clemente à Mahón:** Tel. 971-36 15 77 - 5 km.
– **Palma de Mallorca**: Tel. 971-26 42 12 - 11 km

CASTILLA LEON

– **Valladolid**: Tel. 983-56 01 62 - 14 km.

CATALUNYA

– **Barcelona** : Tel. 93-317 10 11 - 12 km.

EXTREMADURA

– **Badajoj**: Tel. 924-44 00 16 - 16 km.

GALICIA

– **Coruña - Alvedro:** Tel. 981-23 35 84 - 10 km.

MADRID

– **Madrid - Barajas**: Tel. 91-205 40 90 - 13 km.

NAVARRA

– **Pamplona**: Tel. 948-31 72 02 - 7 km.
– **Reus**: Tel. 977-30 37 90 - 3 km.

VALENCIA

– **Alicante**: Tel. 96-528 50 11 - 12 km.
– **Murcia - San Javier**: Tel. 968-57 00 73 - 50 km.
– **Manises**: Tel. 96-379 08 50 - 12 km.

TIME DIFFERENCES

Spain is 6 hours later than EST; 1 hour later than GMT

TELEPHONE/FAX

To call Spain from the USA:
International 00-34 - Town code - Number (omitting the first number between brackets, which is used only for calls within the country).

WEIGHTS AND MEASURES

1 meter (m) = 1.09 yards   1 yard = 0.92 m
1 kilometer (km) = 0.62 mile   1 mile = 1.61 km
1 gram (g) = 0.04 ounce   1 ounce = 25 g
1 liter = 1.6 quarts   1 quart = 0.94 liter

CALENDAR OF FESTIVALS, 'CORRIDAS' AND FAIRS *

March
- 'Fallas' Festival of bonfires at Valencia
- 'Semana Santa' (Holy Week). The best-known are those of Seville, Valladolid, Toledo, Murcia, Lorca and Cuenca

April
- Seville fair

May
- Horse Fair at Jerez de la Frontera
- Festival of 'Córdoban patios' at Córdoba
- Fair of San Isidro at Madrid
- 'Romerio de Rocio' (Gipsy festival) at Huelva (no 'Corrida')

June
- Corpus Christi (Catholic festival celebrated throughout Spain). The best-known are those of Granada, Toledo, Málaga.
- 'Hogueras' of San Juan, Burgos fair

July
- Pamplona fair ('Encierro' (Bull-running) and 'Corrida')
- San Jaíme fair at Valencia (Second week of July)

August
- Málaga fair (end-July, early-August)
- Burgos fair
- Flamenco festival at Jerez de la Frontera

September
- 'Corridas' of Valencia
- Salamanca fair
- Grape harvest fair of Logroño
- 'Corridas' of Barcelona

October
- Fair of the feast of the 'Virgen del Pilar', closing the 'Corridas' season

* This list naturally cannot be exhaustive and only mentions the major events in Spain. Verify dates with the Spanish tourism office, which can also give you a copy of its complete listing of hundreds of local events.

CONTENTS

In Spain the I.V.A (7%) will be added to these prices

A N D A L U S I A

A R A G O N

A S T U R I A S - C A N T A B R I A

C A S T I L L A   L E O N

C A T A L U N Y A

E X T R E M A D U R A

G A L I C I A

M A D R I D

N A V A R R A

P A I S   V A S C O

PRINCIPALITY OF ANDORRA

VALENCIA

* Prices shown in brackets are prices for a double room, sometimes with half board or full board.
For precise details, go to the page mentioned.

MAPS

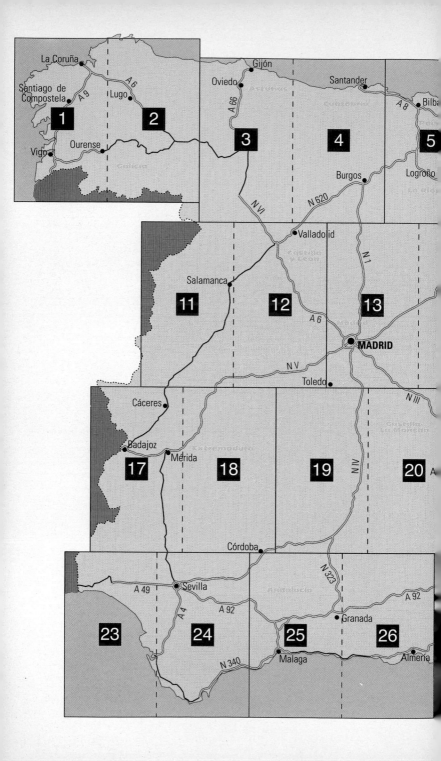

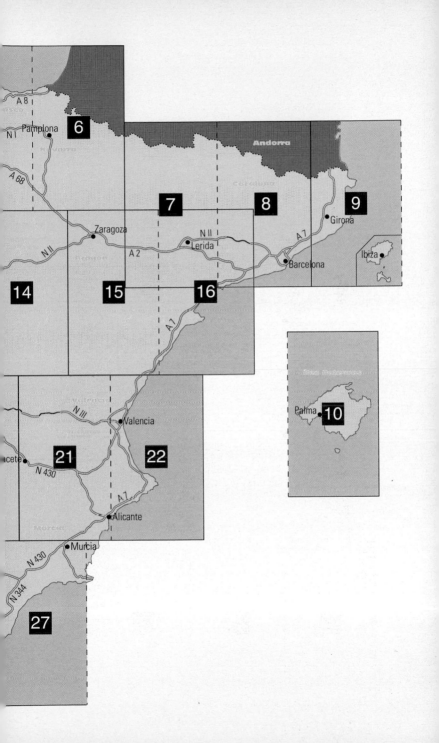

KEY TO THE MAPS

Scale : 1:1,000,000
maps 26 and 27 : scale 1:1,370,000
maps 28 : scale 1:1,250,000

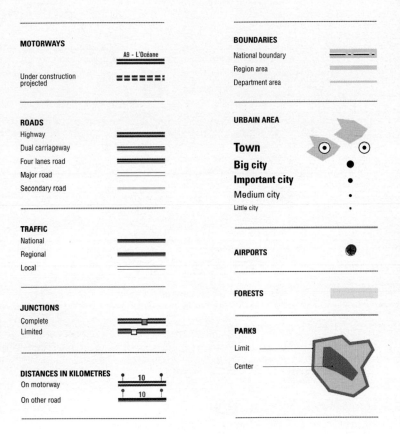

MOTORWAYS

A9 - L'Océane

Under construction
projected

ROADS
Highway
Dual carriageway
Four lanes road
Major road
Secondary road

TRAFFIC
National
Regional
Local

JUNCTIONS
Complete
Limited

DISTANCES IN KILOMETRES
On motorway
On other road

BOUNDARIES
National boundary
Region area
Department area

URBAIN AREA

Town

Big city

Important city

Medium city

Little city

AIRPORTS

FORESTS

PARKS
Limit
Center

Created by

90, rue Nationale
75 013 PARIS
01 45 84 30 84

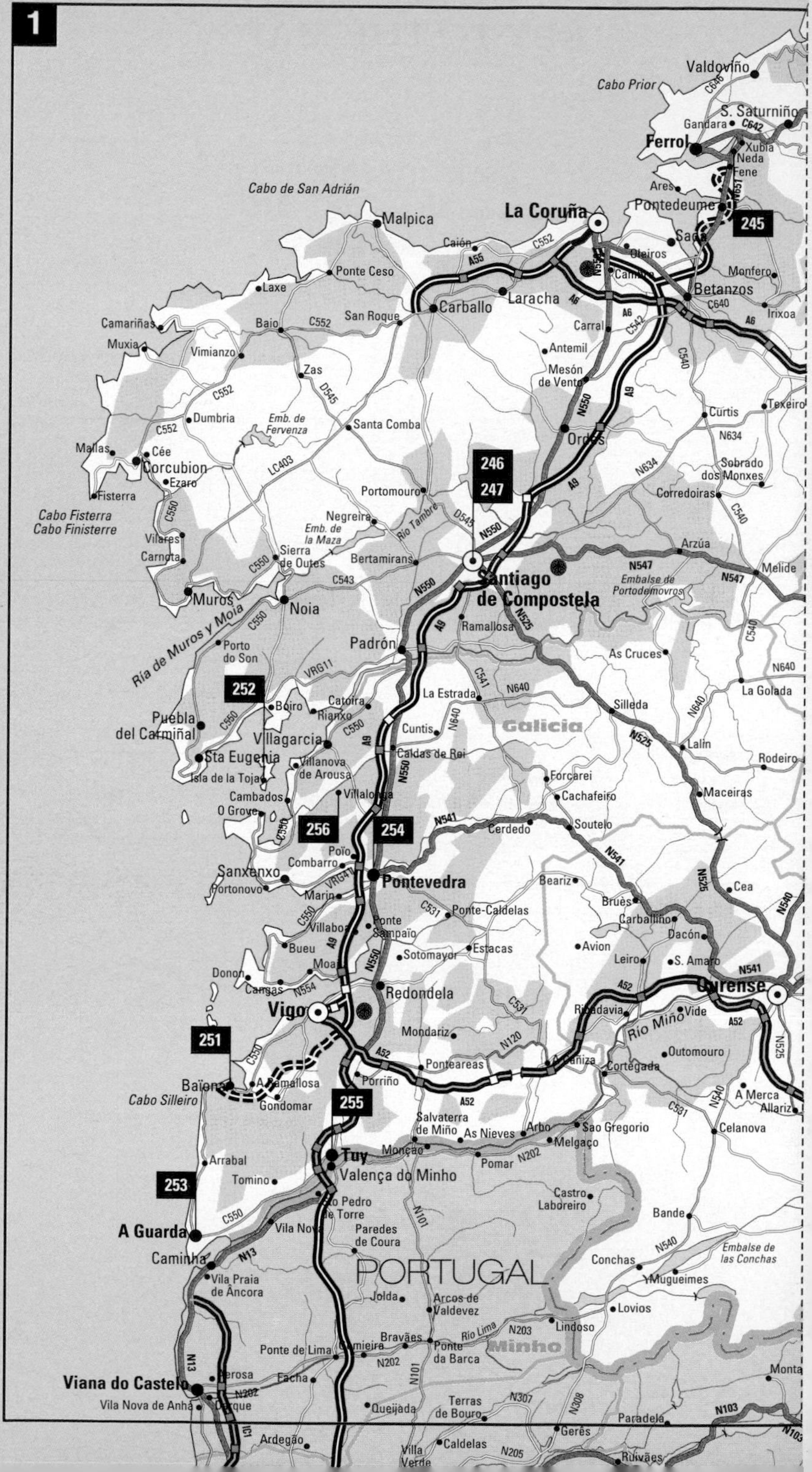
1
Valdoviño
Cabo Prior
S. Saturniño
Gandara
Ferrol
Xubia
Neda
Fene
Ares
Pontedeume
245
Cabo de San Adrián
Malpica
La Coruña
Sada
Caión
Oleiros
Monfero
Ponte Ceso
Laxe
Laracha
Betanzos
Carballo
Camariñas
Baio
San Roque
Carral
Irixoa
Muxia
Vimianzo
Antemil
Zas
Mesón de Vento
Texeiro
Curtis
Dumbria
Emb. de Fervenza
Santa Comba
Mallas
Cée
Corcubion
Ordes
Ezaro
Sobrado dos Monxes
Fisterra
Portomouro
246
247
Corredoiras
Cabo Fisterra
Cabo Finisterre
Negreira
Emb. de la Maza
Río Tambre
Vilares
Carnota
Sierra de Outes
Bertamirans
Arzúa
Melide
Santiago de Compostela
Embalse de Portodemouros
Muros
Noia
Ría de Muros y Moia
Ramallosa
Padrón
Porto do Son
As Cruces
252
La Estrada
La Golada
Boiro
Catoira
Rianxo
Silleda
Puebla del Carmiñal
Cuntis
Galicia
Villagarcia
Caldas de Rei
Lalín
Sta Eugenia
Rodeiro
Villanova de Arousa
Isla de la Toja
Forcarei
Cambados
Villalonga
Cachafeiro
Maceiras
O Grove
256
254
Cerdedo
Soutelo
Poïo
Combarro
Sanxenxo
Pontevedra
Portonovo
Marin
Beariz
Brués
Cea
Ponte-Caldelas
Carballino
Ponte Sampaïo
Villaboa
Dacón
Bueu
Sotomayor
Estacas
Avion
Donon
Moaña
Leiro
S. Amaro
Cangas
Redondela
Ourense
Vigo
Ribadavia
Vide
Río Miño
Mondariz
251
Outomouro
Ponteareas
A Cañiza
Cortegada
Baïona
A Ramallosa
Porriño
A Merca
Allariz
Cabo Silleiro
Gondomar
255
Salvaterra de Miño
As Nieves
Arbo
Sao Gregorio
Celanova
Melgaço
Tuy
Monção
Arrabal
Pomar
Valença do Minho
253
Tomino
Castro Laboreiro
S. Pedro de Torre
Bande
A Guarda
Vila Nova
Paredes de Coura
Caminha
Conchas
Embalse de las Conchas
PORTUGAL
Vila Praia de Âncora
Mugueimes
Jolda
Arcos de Valdevez
Lovios
Lindoso
Río Lima
Bravães
Ponte de Lima
Gemieira
Ponte da Barca
Minho
Montalegre
Viana do Castelo
Perosa
Facha
Vila Nova de Anhã
Darque
Queijada
Terras de Bouro
Paradela
Ardegão
Gerês
Vila Verde
Caldelas
Ruivães
C646
C642
N651
A55
C552
N550
A6
C542
C640
C540
D545
A9
N634
LC403
C550
C543
N547
N525
VRG11
C541
N640
N541
VRG41
C531
N554
N120
A52
N540
N202
N13
N101
N203
N307
N308
N205
N103
IC1

Cabo de Peñas

3

Cabo Vidio

80

95

82

81

91

Luarca
Novellana
N632
Cudillero
S. Estebán
de Pravia
Salinas
Luanco
Candás

Canero
Soto
de Luiña
Pravia
N632
Avilés
A8
A8
Gijón
Tazones
Lastres
N632
La Isla

N634
Soto del Barco
N634
Posada
AS18
Villaviciosa
Amandi
Ortigueira
92
Ribadesella

AS216
Salas
90
Cornellana
Lugones
Noveña
Pola de Siero
Cabranes
N634
Collía
Arriondas
N634

La Espina
Grado
N634
Oviedo
El Berrón
Nava
Sebares
Infiesto
Cangas
de Onís

AS15
Soto de
los Infantes
Trubia
79
Fresanta
Covadonga

Tineo
Belmonte
Proaza
AS111
Sontrodio
N625

Corias
AS227
Castro
89
Mieres
Pola
de Laviana
AS17
Soto
de Sajambre

Cangas
del Narcea
Asturias
La Plaza
Pola de Lena
Cabañaquinta
Campo
de Caso
AS17
Oseja
de Sajambre
N625

AS15
Campomanes
Puente de
los Fierros

AS221
Piedrafita
S. Emiliano
Puebla de Lillo
Embalse
del Porma
Embalse
de Riaño

Villager
C631
Villablino
C623
Cabrillanes
C623
Rodiezmo
N630
Riaño
N621

Palacios
del Sil
Emb. Barrios
de Luna
N621

2
Murias
de Paredes
A66
La Pola
de Gordón
Matallana
C626
Boñar

Páramo
del Sil
Vegarienza
La Magdalena
C626
La Vecilla
Sabero
Cistierna

Boeza
La Magdalena
La Robla
N625
C611

Folgoso de
Ribera
Rioseco
de Tapia
Cuadros
Garrafe
de Torio
Vegas
del Condado
Almanza

Bembibre
Suéros
Cimanes
de Tejar
A66
C623
Villaquilambre
León
Gradefes
N625

Torre
del Bierzo
NVI
Carrizo
de la Ribera
S. Andrés
del Rabanedo
Valverde
149
La Virgen
del Camino
N601

148
Benavides
Sta Marina
del Rey
N120
Villarente
N601
N625

Astorga
Valdevimbre
Mansilla de
las Mulas
El Burgo
Ranero
C611

Sta Colomba
de Somoza
N120
Veguellino
de Órbigo
C521
Valdevimbre
N630
Santas
Martas

Luyego
Riego
de la Vega
N630
Sahagún
N120

Destriana
Sta María
del Páramo
Villamañán
Valencia
De Don Juan
Melgar
de Arriba
Villada
C613

Justel
C622
La Bañeza
Laguna
de Negrios
N601
C611
C611

Españedo
C622
Castrocontrigo
Castrocalbón
Villaquejida
N630
Mayorga
Villalón
de Campos
Villaramiel

Monbuey
A52
Santibáñez
de Vidriales
La Torre
del Valle
168
Valderas
Becilla
de Valderaduey
N610
N601
Frechilla

Río Negro
del Puente
N525
Morales de Rey
Benavente
N525
Fuentes
de Ropel
Villanueva
del Campo
Villalón
de Campos
Villamayor
de Campos
C611
Villerías

Villardeciervos
Camarzana
Río Tera
Otero de Bodas
Ferreras
de Abajo
Sta María de V.
Pueblica de V.
NVI
Villamayor
de Campos
C612
Villafrechos
Medina
de Rioseco
C611

San Vitero
Emb. del Esla
de Ricobayo
Tabara
Río Esla
La Tabla
Villafáfila
C612
Villalpando
Villabragima
Villalba de
los Alcores
N601

N122
11
Villarín de Campos
NVI
12
Castronuevo
La Mudarra

Fonfria
Carbajales
de Alba
C612
Villardefrades

4

83 ▸85
86
88
102
101
96
103-104
107 ▸109
105-106
110
100
87
98
99
97
151
142
143
144
150
145
12
13
5

N634 • Nueva • Posada
Llanes
Tresgrandas
Colombres
Alevia
Unquera
Pechón
S. Vincente de la Barquera
Comillas
Suances
Cabo Mayor
Santander
Isla
Noja
Cabo de Ajo
Santo
Ajo
Escalante
Oreso
Collnoso

Onis
Carreña de Cabrales
Arenas de Cabrales
Picos de Europa
de Cabrales
AS114
Panes
Villanueva de Colombres
Quijas
Santillana del Mar
El Astillero
Solares
Liérganes
Ramales de la Victoria

La Hermida
Castro
Puentenansa
Cabezón de la Sal
Las Caldas de Besaya
Puente Viesgo
Sarón
Corvera de Toranzo
Villacarriedo

Sta Marina
Fuente Dé
Camaleño
Trevino
Pozes
Espinama
Cosgaya
La Vega de Liebana
Valle de Cabuernlga
Arenas de Iguña
Cotillo
Molledo

Portilla de la Reina
C627
Cantabria
Espinilla
Reinosa
Embalse del Ebro
Corconte
Espinosa de los Monteros
Villasante

Besande
Embalse de Camporre Dondo
S. Salvador de Cantamuda
Barruelo de Santullán
Arija
Cilleruelo
Soncillo
Sanfelices
Villarcayo
Medina de Pomar

Guardo
Santibañez de la Peña
Cervera de Pisuerga
Cantoral de la Peña
Sotillo
Escalada
Valdenoceda
Trespaderne

Villalba de Guardo
Congosto de Valdavia
Emb. de Aguilar
151
Aguilar de Campóo
Santa Maria de Mave
Valdelateja
Oña
Sales de B.

Buenavista de Valdavia
Alar del Rey
Humada
Basconcillos del Tozo
Tubilla del Agua
Poza de la Sal

Saldaña
Herrera de Pisuerga
Sotresgudo
La Nuez de Arriba

Castrillo de Villavega
Villadiego
Briviesca
Monasterio de Rodilla

Osorno
Melgar de Fernamental
Villasandino
Villanueva de Argaño
142 143
Sotopalacios
Villafria
Villafranca Montes de Oc

N120
Carrión de los Condes
Cervatos de la Cueza
Fromista
Castrojenz
Villaquirán
Burgos
Ibeas
Villorobe

Villoldo
Villalumbroso
Paredes de Nava
Amusco
Astudillo
Estepar
Sarracin
Pineda de la Sierra

Becerril de Campos
Monzon de Campos
Villodrigo
Sta Maria del Campo
Cuevas de S. Clemente
Vizcainc

Villamartin de C.
150
Palencia
Quintana del Puente
Villahoz
Covarrubias
Hortigüela

Ampudia
Sta Cecilia del Alcor
Buños de Cerrato
Reinoso de C.
Baltanas
Espinosa de Cerrato
Río Arlanza
Lerma
144
Sales de los Infantes

Dueñas
Cevico de la Torre
Cevico Navero
Villafruela
145
Sto Doming de Silos

Mucientes
Valoria la Buena
Esguevillas de E.
12
Tortoles de Esgueva
Olmedillo de Roa
13
Bahabón de Esgueva
Caleruega
Huerta del Rey

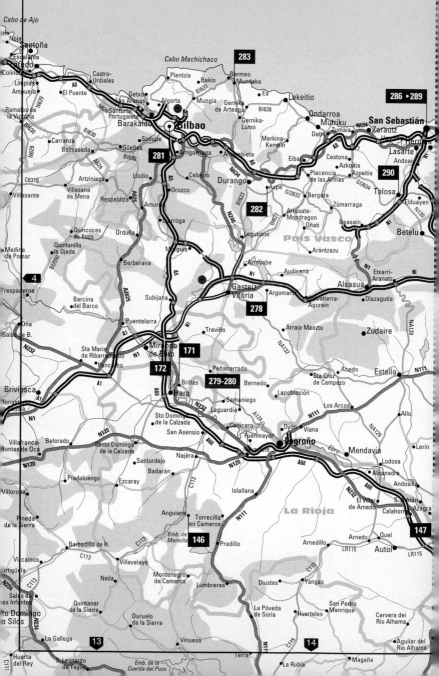

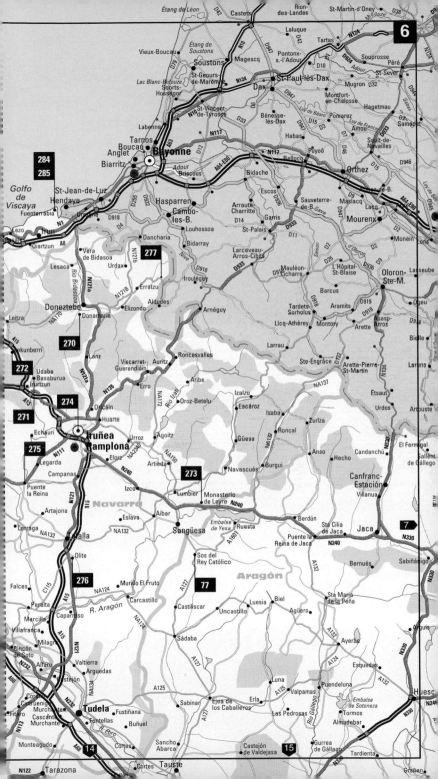

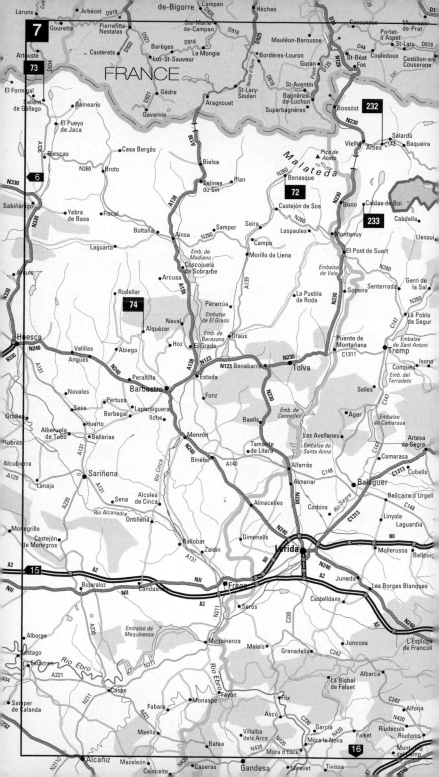

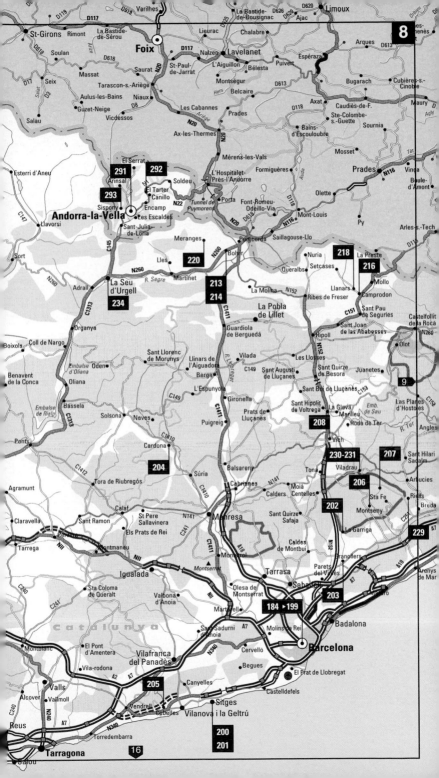

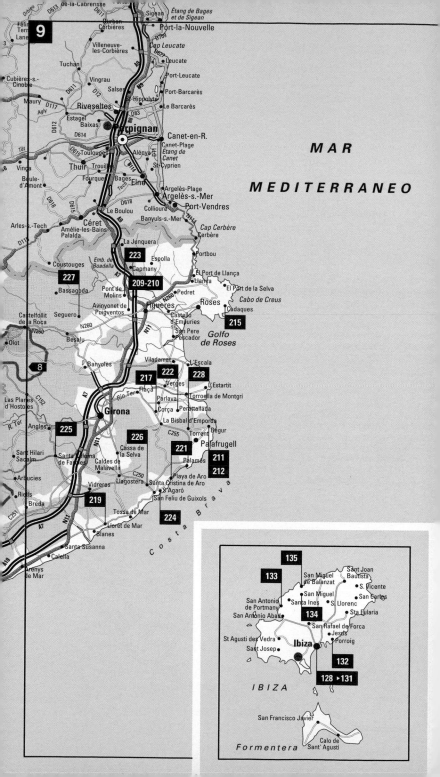

Cap de Formentor

115 **125** **111**
114 **126**
123 **112**
116 **113** **118**

127

124

117

MALLORCA

I. de Cabrera

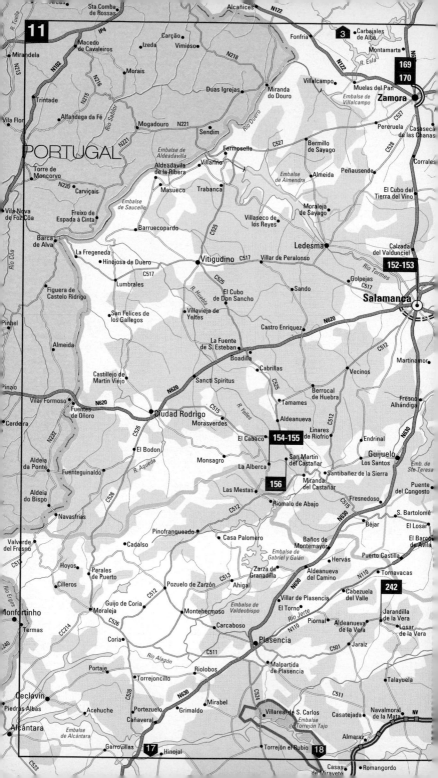

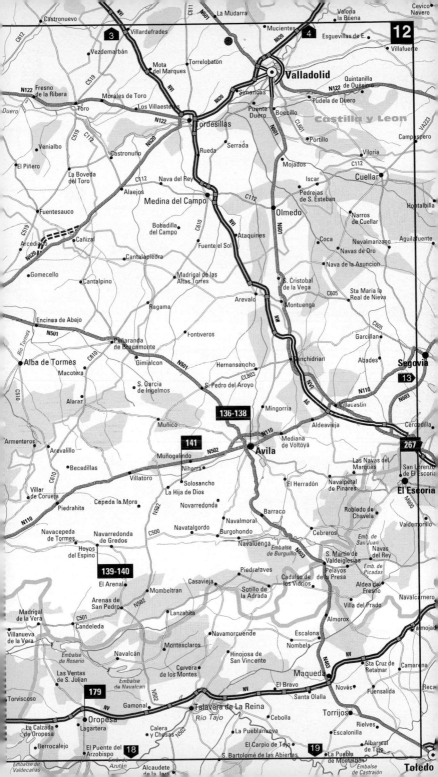

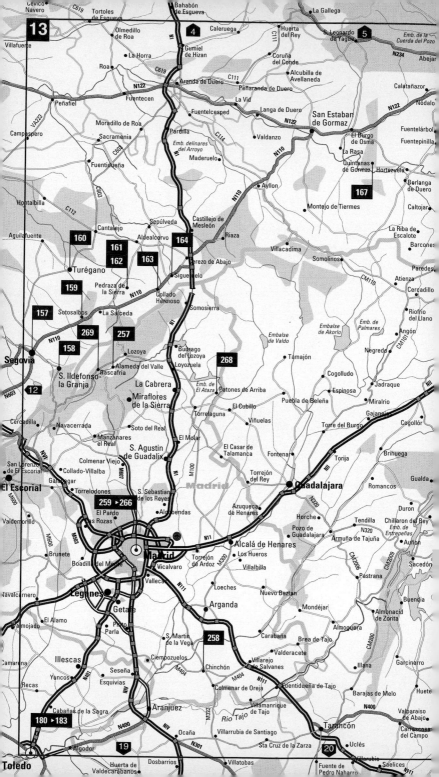

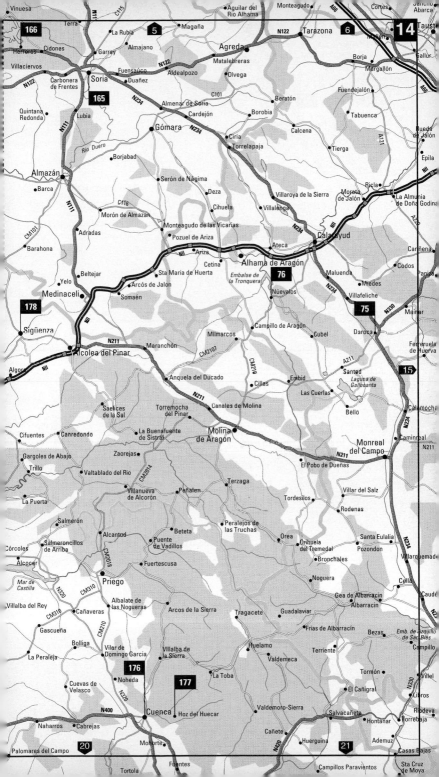

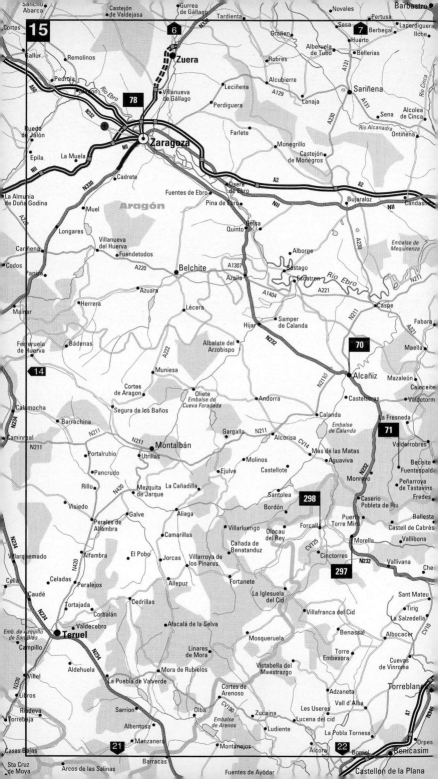

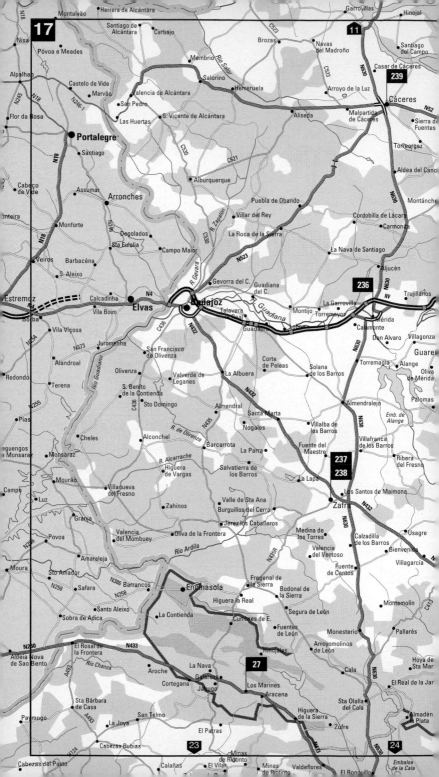

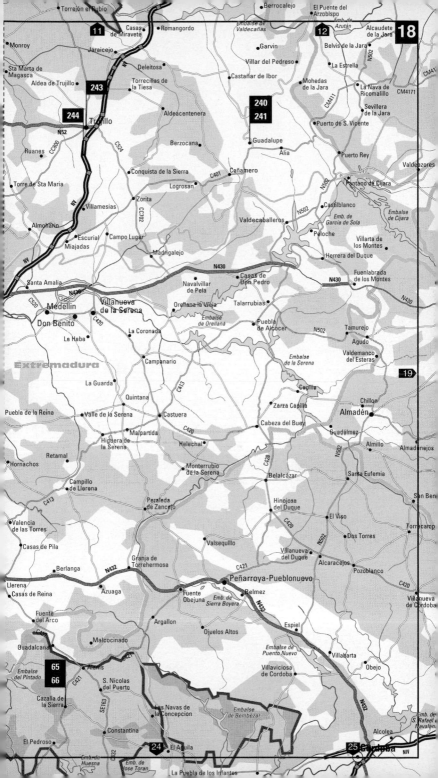

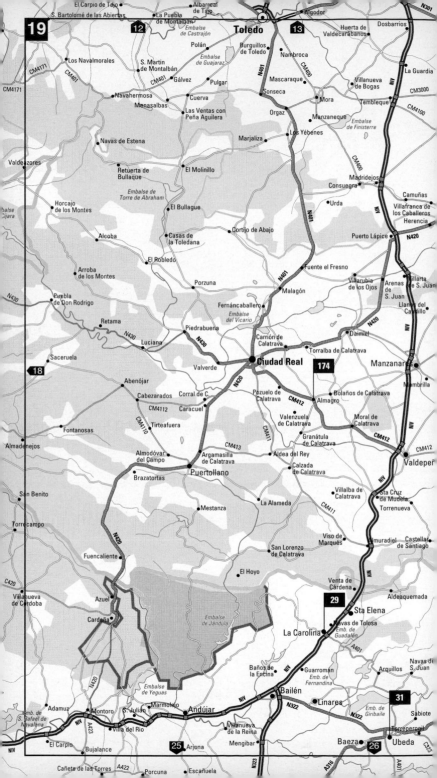

22

16

MAR MEDITERRANEO

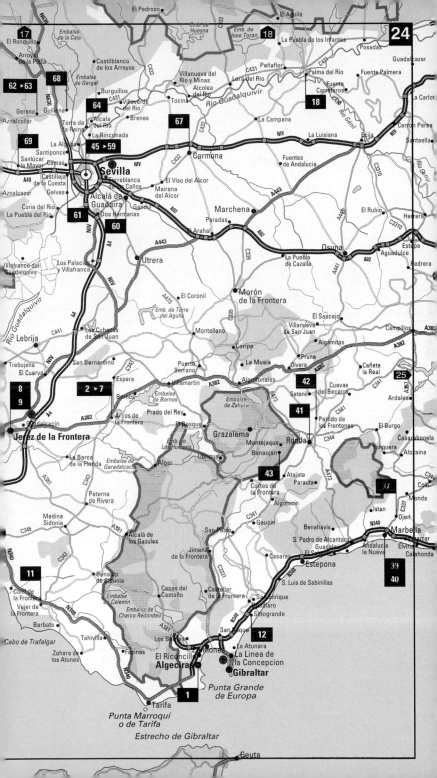

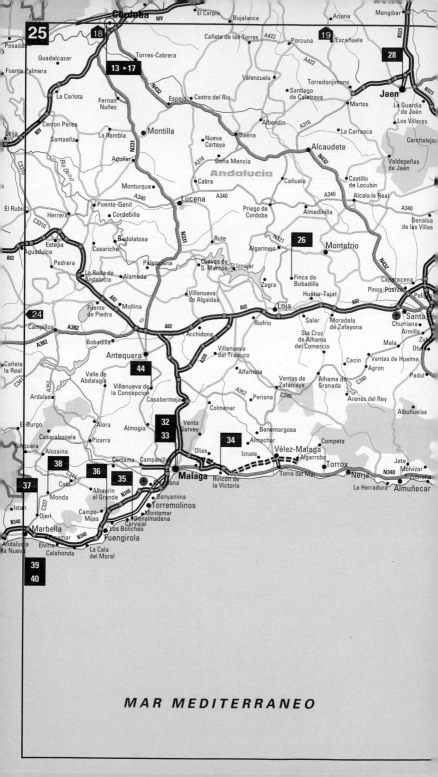

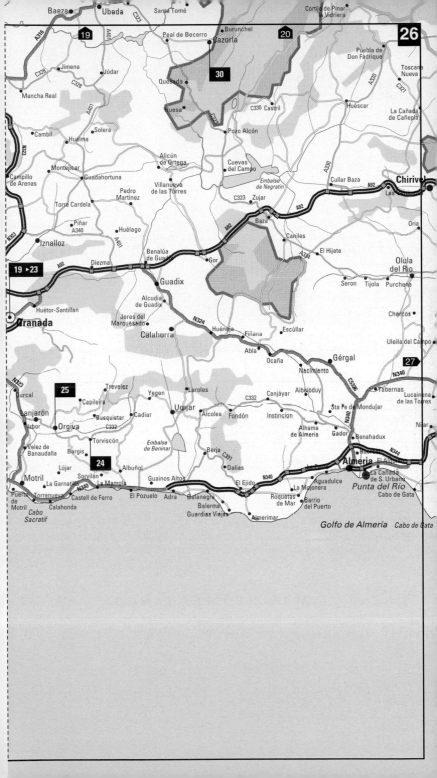

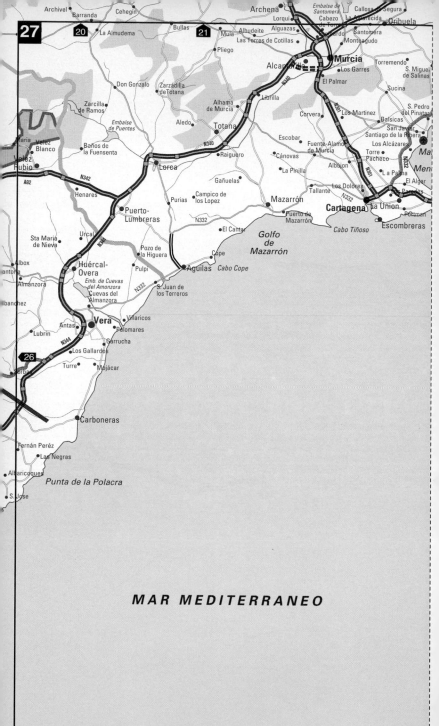

HOTELS AND
COUNTRY INNS

Hotel Reina Cristina

11200 Algeciras (Cádiz)
Paseo de la Conferencia
Tel. 956-60 26 22 - Fax 956-60 33 23
Sr Gonzalez

Category ★★★★ **Rooms** 188 with air-conditioning, telephone, bath, WC, TV. **Price** Double with half board 7,200-11,750Pts (per pers.). **Meals** Breakfast (buffet) included, served 7:15-10:30. **Restaurant** Service 1:00PM-3:30PM, 7:00PM-9:30PM; also à la carte. Regional and international cooking. **Credit cards** All major. **Pets** Small dogs allowed in the rooms. **Facilities** Swimming pool, tennis, minigolf, sauna, parking. **Nearby** Beaches of Getares, Chaparral, Los Ladrillos, El Rinconcillo - Ceuta (2 hours by boat from Algeciras) - Gibraltar - The road from Algeciras to Ronda - Feria the last week of June. **Open** All year.

This hotel is haunted with memories. Its history began in 1890 when the government commissioned a British company to build the railway from Bobadilla to Gibraltar. Lodging in Algeciras during the work, the director was so attracted by the region that he decided to build a hotel here. The setting for the Algeciras Conference in 1906 and a haunt of spies during the war, it has now recovered all its old peace and quiet. Large gardens planted with pine and cypress trees surround the hotel which has retained its comfortable, rather British style. Its principal charm is in the fact that it is a haven in an all too touristic region.

How to get there *(Map 24): 124km southeast of Cádiz via N430; 200 meters from the port.*

Parador Casa del Corregidor

11630 Arcos de la Frontera (Cádiz)
Plaza del Cabildo
Tel. 956-70 05 00 - Fax 956-70 11 16 - D. Perez Moneo
E-mail: arcos@parador.es

Category ★★★ Rooms 20 with air-conditioning, telephone, bath, WC, satellite TV, minibar. **Price** Double 17,500Pts. **Meals** Breakfast 1,300Pts, served 8:00-11:00. **Restaurant** Service 1:00PM-3:30PM, 8:00PM-10:30PM; mealtime specials 3,500Pts, also à la carte. Regional cooking. **Credit cards** All major. **Pets** Dogs not allowed. **Facilities** Parking. **Nearby** Jerez de la Frontera - Bornos - Monastery of the Cartuja - Villamartin (wine cellars of Pajarete). **Open** All year.

Arcos de la Frontera is on the summit of a granite promontory surrounded by the Guadalete River, in the midst of a Mediterranean landscape of vines, orange and olive trees. The hotel is in town but thanks to its location on the edge of a cliff, it forms a natural balcony with a superb view. It is a very old building but has been sumptuously reconstructed while retaining its original architecture. The panorama can be enjoyed from the lounges, bar, dining room and the best rooms which have terraces. Close to Jerez de la Frontera, this is a good center for visiting the bodegas and sherry wine cellars of the region.

How to get there *(Map 24): 65km northeast of Cádiz via A4, exit Jerez de la Frontera, then N342; opposite the Ayuntamiento (town hall).*

Cortijo Fain

11630 Arcos de la Frontera (Cádiz)
Caret. Algar, km 3
Tel. 956-23 13 96 - Fax 956-23 13 96
Sr Jose Luis Jimenez

Category ★★★ **Rooms** 10 with with air-conditioning, bath, WC. **Price** Single 8,000Pts, double 10,000Pts; suite 16,000Pts (2 pers.), 23,000-30,000Pts (4 pers.); extra bed +2,500Pts. **Meals** Breakfast 1,000Pts, served 8:00-11:00. **Restaurant** Service 1:30PM-3:30PM, 8:00PM-11:00PM; mealtime specials 3,000Pts. Regional cooking. **Credit cards** All major. **Pets** Dogs allowed. **Facilities** Swimming pool, parking. **Nearby** Jerez de la Frontera - Bornos - Monastery of the Cartuja - Villamartin (wine cellars of Pajarete). **Closed** Christmas and New Year.

This large property situated 3km from Arcos de la Frontera is not a typical hotel, but ten rooms have been opened in this beautiful 17th-century farm for the use of guests who can also take part in the daily life of the estate. While the rooms are very large and each has a lounge and open fireplace, and all are comfortably arranged and decorated in the best Andalusian style (two have their own private terraces), their upkeep is not always faultless. This is regrettable because the rest of the house is particularly attractive and guests can visit the library, which, with its 10,000 volumes, is one of the finest private collections in Spain. The house, with its white-walled setting covered with bougainvillae, is surrounded by olive trees which make for very pleasant walks. In summer, the swimming pool can also be used while horse riding is available in the Andalusian countryside throughout the year.

How to get there (Map 24): 68km northeast of Cádiz via A4, exit Jerez de la Frontera, then N342 and Algar road for 3km.

Hotel Los Olivos del Convento

11630 Arcos de la Frontera (Cádiz)
Paseo de Boliches, 30
Tel. 956-70 08 11 - Fax 956-70 20 18
Sr J. A. Roldan

Category ★★★ **Rooms** 19 with air-conditioning, telephone, bath or shower, WC, TV, minibar.
Price Single 4,280-5,350Pts, double 7,490-9,630Pts, suite 9,630-11,770Pts; extra bed +2,140Pts.
Meals Breakfast 900Pts, served 8:00-11:00. **Restaurant** See p. 301. **Credit cards** Amex, Visa,
Eurocard, MasterCard. **Pets** Dogs not allowed. **Nearby** Jerez de la Frontera - Bornos - Monastery of
the Cartuja - Villamartin (wine cellars of Pajarete). **Open** All year.

An astonishing small Andalusian town, Arcos de la Frontera aligns its white houses on the crest of the plateau overlooking the Guadalete River. The town has conserved some beautiful remnants of its Moorish past and its magnificent church in the flamboyant Gothic style (Santa Maria de la Asunción) is well worth a visit. Nicely located in the center of town, the hotel is simple but all is arranged in the good taste typical of Andalusian houses: white walls, cane furniture in the lounge-gallery that surrounds the interior patio and rather monastic rooms that are very well maintained. Some rooms overlook the river. Prices are reasonable.

How to get there *(Map 24): 65km northeast of Cádiz via A4, exit Jerez de la Frontera, then N342.*

Hotel El Convento

11630 Arcos de la Frontera (Cádiz)
Maldonado, 2
Tel. 956-70 23 33 - Fax 956-70 41 28
Sra Moreno

Category ★ **Rooms** 11 with air-conditioning, telephone, bath, WC, satellite TV. **Price** Single 5,000-8,000Pts, double 7,000-12,000Pts. **Meals** Breakfast à la carte 300-800Pts, served 8:30-10:30. **Restaurant** Service 1:00PM-4:00PM, 7:00PM-10:30PM or 7:30PM-10:30PM (summer); mealtime specials 3,000Pts, also à la carte. Specialties: Ajo a la comendadora - Sopa de clausura - Pierna de cordero. **Credit cards** All major. **Pets** Dogs not allowed. **Nearby** Jerez de la Frontera - Bornos - Monastery of the Cartuja - Villamartin (wine cellars of Pajarete). **Open** All year.

The Hotel El Convento occupies part of the convent of Monjas de Clausura Mercedarias Descalzas, built in the 17th century. A small hotel with only ten bedrooms in a typically Andalusian style, a simple family atmosphere is found here, along with excellent home cooking. Morevover, recent improvements have further enhanced the comfort. In a historically classified village and completely free from cars, it is just a few paces from several listed national historical monuments. The village is full of charm and the hotel is one of those that one dreams of finding on a journey in southern Spain. Sevilla is just 100km away!

How to get there *(Map 24): 59km northeast of Cádiz via A4, exit Jerez de la Frontera, then N342 to Antequera.*

Cortijo Barranco

El Bosque km 8,2 - 11630 Arcos de la Frontera (Cádiz)
Molino Ntra Sra de la Luz
Tel. 956-23 14 02 - Fax 956-23 12 09
Sra Maria José Gil Amián

Rooms 8 with bath. **Price** Double 10,000-12,000Pts; apart. by day for 1 week 18,000-20,000Pts.
Meals Breakfast 500Pts, served 9:00-11:00. **Restaurant** Service 8:30PM; mealtime specials 3,000-
4,000Pts. Regional cooking. **Credit cards** Not accepted. **Pets** Dogs allowed. **Facilities** Swimming
pool, parking. **Nearby** Jerez de la Frontera - Bornos - Monastery of the Cartuja - Villamartin (wine
cellars of Pajarete). **Open** All year.

Y ou leave the road to Arcos and continue for three kilometers through fields
of sunflowers and olive trees before arriving at an attractive white farm
house nestling on the hillside. An impressive wooden gate opens and you
discover a courtyard resplendent with geraniums, rambling roses and lemon
trees where swallows have taken up residence. If a fine collection of popular
art is displayed on the walls to remind you that you are in a center of "rural
tourism", the rest of the place is no less elegant. The rooms, while not
particularly large, are pleasantly decorated with regional furniture including
wrought-iron beds and colorful printed fabrics. Every room has a view of the
sunflowers and there is an apartment for those who prefer a little more privacy.
The lounge and billiard room are at your disposal, along with a magnificent
swimming pool with an exceptional view overlooking the valley.

How to get there *(Map 24): 3.7km from Arcos de la Frontera on A372 towards*
El Bosque. The dirt road turning off to the left is marked camino privado a la
izquierda.

Hacienda El Santiscal

Lago de Arcos 11638 Arcos de la Frontera (Cádiz)
Avenida del Santiscal, 129
Tel. 956-70 83 13 - Fax 956-70 82 68 - Fransica Gallardo Carrasco
E mail: santiscal@gadesinfo.com

Rooms 12 with air-conditioning, telephone, bath, TV. **Price** Single 7,800-12,900Pts, double 10,000-20,000Pts, junior-suite 14,000-22,000Pts, suite 16,000-24,000Pts; extra bed +4,500Pts. **Meals** Breakfast included, served 7:30-11:00. **Restaurant** at the hotel; mealtime specials 3,500Pts or see p. 301. **Credit cards** All major. **Pets** Dogs not allowed. **Facilities** Swimming pool, parking. **Nearby** Jerez de la Frontera - Vejer de la Frontera - Bornos - Monastery of the Cartuja - Villamartin (wine cellars of Pajarete). **Open** All year.

Lying at the foot of the legendary Andalusian village of Arcos is a vast lake and on one of its banks is El Santiscal, a superb 15th-century hacienda belonging to the Count of Lebrija, owner of a most attractive property close to Sevilla, El Cortijo de Esparragal, which appears in this book. The yellow and white building stands in the center of the field overlooking the lake which is visible from the garden. An impressive doorway opens on a patio offering welcome summer shade and a second door leads to a salon with a high ceiling and beautiful stone floor plus a dining room on the verandah overlooking the countryside. All the rooms are spacious and comfortable with personal and individual touches. We recommend those giving on the garden with a view of the lake as well as the extremely chic no. 2 offering a terrace on two sides. The service is excellent and the food very well prepared. In addition to visits to historical sites, you may also enjoy spending a few days in this region astride a bicycle or a horse.

How to get there *(Map 24): 4km from Arcos. On N342 towards Antequera, turn left upon leaving the village in the direction of El Bosque. After the bridge, follow the signs indicating Santiscal.*

Hotel Jerez

11400 Jerez de la Frontera (Cádiz)
Avenida Alcalde Alvaro Domecq, 35
Tel. 956-30 06 00 - Fax 956-30 50 01/31 95 43
E-mail: jerez@travelcom.es - Web: www.travelcom.es/jerez

Category ★★★★ **Rooms** 121 with air-conditioning, telephone, bath, WC, satellite TV, minibar; elevator. **Price** Single 13,140-15,620Pts, double 16,300-24,000Pts, junior-suite 25,500-32,000Pts. **Meals** Breakfast 1,550Pts, served 7:00-12:00. **Restaurant** Service 1:00PM-4:00PM, 8:30PM-11:30PM; mealtime specials 3,500Pts, also à la carte. Specialties: fish - shellfish. **Credit cards** All major. **Pets** Dogs not allowed. **Facilities** Swimming pool, tennis, parking. **Nearby** Cádiz - Arcos de la Frontera - Bornos - La Cartuja - Sanlúcar de Barrameda - Bodegas de Xéres de Gonzalez Byass, Pedro Domecq, Williams Humbert (tasting, buying) - Feria del Caballo (Horse Fair May 10-16) - Flamenco Festival in August. **Open** All year.

Only 4km from the town center in a modern building in the residential area, this hotel in the Ciga chain offers a wonderfully calm setting. The bedrooms are luxurious and all have a balcony, most of which look onto the garden and its beautiful lawns, palm trees and exuberant plants, all protected from the road by thick hedges. You can also enjoy the large swimming pool at your leisure. The restaurant offers excellent seafood dishes, accompanied by the well-known wines of the area from its world-renowned cellars. Service and comfort are very high quality, but one should remember that prices/rates are marked up by 30% during the Feria.

How to get there *(Map 24): 35km northeast of Cádiz via A4, exit Jerez de la Frontera; 4km from town center.*

Hotel Serit

11400 Jerez de la Frontera (Cádiz)
Avenida Higueras, 7
Tel. 956-34 07 00 - Fax 956-34 07 16 - Sra Acosta Jimenez
E-mail: hotelserit@redicon.es

Category ★★★ **Rooms** 29 with air-conditioning, telephone, bath, WC, safe, satellite TV; elevator - 1 room for disabled persons. **Price** Single 6,000-8,000Pts, double 8,000-12,000Pts. **Meals** Breakfast 500Pts, served 8:00-11:00. **Restaurant** See p. 302. **Credit cards** All major. **Pets** Dogs allowed. **Facilities** Parking (1,000Pts). **Nearby** Cádiz - Arcos de la Frontera - Bornos - La Cartuja - Sanlúcar de Barrameda - Bodegas de Xéres de Gonzalez Byass, Pedro Domecq, Williams Humbert (tasting, buying) - Feria del Caballo (Horse Fair May 14-21) - Flamenco Festival in August. **Open** All year.

Jerez is a town made famous by the wine carrying its name: "sherry" (slightly deformed by the British because of its impossible pronunciation). It also boasts a riding school with a great reputation, as well as the attractions of the vine. The annual Feria in honor of the horse is one of the most important in Andalucia. In a small street close to the center, the Serit is one of those hotels with a discreet facade but whose appeal is apparent once the front door is opened. The comfort, calm and the reasonable rates all appeal. Although rather standardized, the rooms are agreeable and all have a small antechamber separating them from the bathroom. A corner lounge on the ground floor has comfortable sofas and a marble floor, while beautiful photographs on the walls recall picturesque aspects of Jerez life.

How to get there *(Map 24): 35km northeast of Cádiz via A4, exit Jerez de la Frontera; next door to La Plaza de las Angustias.*

Posada de Palacio

11540 Sanlúcar de Barrameda (Cádiz)
Calla Caballeros, 11
Tel. 956-36 48 40 - Fax 956-36 50 60
Sr Navarrete

Category ★★★ **Rooms** 13 with telephone, bath, WC. **Price** Double 7,000-8,000Pts, suite 10,000Pts. **Meals** Breakfast 800Pts, served 8:30-11:30. **Restaurant** Only for residents; mealtime specials 2,000Pts or see p. 304. **Credit cards** Diners, Visa, Eurocard, MasterCard. **Pets** Small dogs allowed. **Nearby** Bodegas (Hijos de A. Pérez, Meijía, Manuel Garcia Monje, Rafael Reig y Cia) in Sanlúcar - Jerez de la Frontera - Monastery of Nuesta Señora de Regla close Chipiona - Beaches of Rota - Feria of the Manzanilla in May - Donaña. **Closed** Jan and Feb.

S anlúcar de Barrameda is an aristocratic town whose reputation is due to its churches and excellent wine cellars, as well as its very beautiful houses. One of these houses has been converted into a posada with a great deal of love and taste by a very attractive young couple who have respected the original architecture of the house. You are immediately won over by the patio and feel comfortable in the welcoming rooms, even though their comfort does vary. The best, strangely, is on the ground floor with a large window onto the street. And as this is a region of superb wines, there is a bar, of course, with a few tables in the white and flowered courtyard.

How to get there *(Map 23): 121km south of Sevilla via A4, to Jerez de la Frontera, then C440.*

Hotel Convento de San Francisco

11150 Vejer de la Frontera (Cádiz)
La Plazuela, 6
Tel. 956-45 10 01/02/03 - Fax 956-45 10 04
Sr Don José Gutiere Murillo

Category ★★★ **Rooms** 25 with telephone, bath, WC. **Price** Single 6,800Pts, double 9,100Pts, extra bed +1,800Pts. **Meals** Breakfast 525Pts, served 8:00-11:30; half board +2,185Pts, full board +3,950Pts (per pers.). **Restaurant** Service 1:00PM-3:30PM, 8:30PM-11:30PM; closed Tues; mealtime specials 2,205Pts. Specialties: Cocina de mercado. **Credit cards** All major. **Pets** Dogs not allowed. **Nearby** Medina Sidonia - Benalup de Sidonia - Costa de la Luz from Cádiz to Tarifa - Holy Week and Na. Sa. de la Oliva (Aug 24) - Campo San Andrés golf course (18-Hole). **Open** All year.

On a steep hill stands an old 17th-century Franciscan convent now transformed into a hotel. One is first of all impressed by the entrance which happily has conserved its multicolored mosaics. The lounges have kept their grandiose aspect, even if the furniture has not. Particular care has been taken with the vast bedrooms where simplicity and the rustic have been melded together, notably with the use of open stonework. The small town of Vejer is classified as a "historical-artistic monument" and has a rather wild charm with its windmills. To lovers of folklore it offers a full calendar of fêtes and fairs.

How to get there (Map 24): 53km southeast of Cádiz via N430.

Villa Romana

Pueblo Nuevo de Guadiaro 11311 Sotogrande (Cádiz)
Calle Altamira, 8
Tel. and Fax 956-79 44 24
Jean and Aloma Lancelle

Rooms 3 and 1 suite with bath. **Price** 2 doubles with shared bath 8,000-10,000Pts, double 10,000-12,000Pts, suite 12,000-15,000Pts. **Meals** Breakfast included; half board +3,200Pts. **Evening meals** By reservation, service 8:00-11:00PM; mealtime specials 3,200Pts. **Credit cards** Not accepted. **Pets** Dogs allowed. **Facilities** Swimming pool, parking. **Nearby** Beaches - Castellar - Sierra de Cádiz - Toros road - Tarifa - Ronda - Gaucin Casares - Valderrama golf course (27-Hole), Real Club golf course (27-Hole), Cañada golf course (18-Hole), Almenara golf course (18-Hole). **Open** All year.

On the always-sunny Costa del Sol with its reputation as a European Florida, the Sotogrande has been a well-frequented residential and sporting center ever since the building of a marina and the creation of numerous stunning golf courses. The village of Pueblo Neuvo de Guadiaro is inland and facing the port. The Villa Romana offers a splendid view of the river, the valley, the mountain and the seaside resort. This is a very pretty house and its interiors as well as its surroundings have been particularly well looked-after by its owners. The garden offers exotic plants and the decoration, consisting of local antiques, lively rugs and souvenirs of world travel, creates an atmosphere both friendly and comfortable. The rooms are also attractively furnished and well-equipped, with those on the ground floor having a communicating bathroom and are ideal for family residency. The other two are upstairs, the suite having a lounge and a private terrace. Dinner in the evening allows you to enjoy the exceptionally friendly welcome offered by your hosts.

How to get there *(Map 23): N340 Cádix-Málaga, exit Pueblo Nuevo de Guadiario (no.132).*

Hotel Alfaros

14001 Córdoba
Calle Alfaros, 18
Tel. 957-49 19 20 - Fax 957-49 22 10 - M. David Madrigal
E-mail: alfaros@maciahoteles.com - Web: www.maciahoteles.com/alfaros

Category ★★★★ **Rooms** 133 with air-conditioning, telephone, bath, WC, satellite TV, safe, minibar; elevator - Wheelchair access. **Price** Single 11,600-14,000Pts, double 14,500-17,500Pts, suite 20,000-21,500Pts. **Meals** Breakfast (buffet) 1,250Pts, served 7:00-11:00. **Restaurant** Service 1:30PM-3:30PM, 8:30PM-11:00PM; mealtime specials 2,000Pts, also à la carte. **Credit cards** All major. **Pets** Dogs not allowed. **Facilities** Swimming pool, parking, garage (1,400Pts). **Nearby** Medina az Zahara - Monastery of San Jerónimo - Las Ermitas de Córdoba - Sanctuary of Santo Domingo de Scala Dei - Fiesta de los Patios (May 5-15) - Feria (May 25-29) - Los Villares golf course (18-Hole). **Open** All year.

One can only know Spain and Andalucia well by visiting Córdoba, the former capital of the Moslems whose cultural and spiritual empire stretched from Rome to Africa, and further to the west. The mosque-cathedral alone is worth the journey but the town with its flowered patios, wrought-iron work and *azuleros* also has a lot of charm. The Alfaros Hotel has sought to transpose all such influences into a modern decor, which has created a luxurious and theatrical hotel. Great comfort reigns throughout the hotel which also offers all the latest technology: fax connection, TV satellite dish and magnetic card access to rooms, etc. All rooms are spacious and light. The swimming pool is worthy of an Arabian Gulf palace. Along with the full-time service, this is a great hotel.

How to get there *(Map 25): In the center of town.*

Hotel Al-Mihrab

14012 Córdoba
Avenida del Brillante, km 5
Tel. 957-27 21 88 - Fax 957-27 12 80 - Sr Antonio Matas Aguilera
Web: www.bd.andalucia.es

Category ★★★ **Rooms** 29 with air-conditioning, telephone, shower, WC, satellite TV. **Price** Single 6,000Pts, double 7,000-11,000Pts. **Meals** Breakfast 1,000Pts, served 8:00-10:30. **Restaurant** Only for residents, 1:30PM-3:30PM, 8:30PM-11:00PM; mealtime specials 2,000Pts, also à la carte. **Credit cards** All major. **Pets** Dogs allowed. **Facilities** Swimming pool, riding tour, parking. **Nearby** Medina az Zahara - Monastery of San Jerónimo - Las Ermitas de Córdoba - Sanctuary of Santo Domingo de Scala Dei - Fiesta de los Patios (May 5-15) - Feria (Sept 25-27) - Los Villares golf course (18-Hole). **Open** All year.

The name of the hotel plainly evokes the period of wealth and splendor this city experienced during its occupation by the Moors. It was at that time that the Great Mosque was built and its presence explains why Córdoba has been classified part of Humanity's Legacy. The Mirhab in a mosque is the holiest of places, the one where the Koran is kept. This Córdoban-style residence dating from the latter half of the 19th century has recently been renovated and transformed into a very pleasant hotel. Located in a residential neighborhood and away from the center of the city, it offers a garden with small palm trees brought from the Canary Islands. The interior is uncluttered and gets its decorative effect from fabrics with brightly colored geometric patterns. The rooms are large and comfortable, the lounge has a fine view of the sierra and the city, and the restaurant, reserved for the guests, gives you an excellent opportunity to try the region's specialties. A truly charming hotel. The prices indicated do not apply to Holy Week.

How to get there *(Map 25): 140km of Sevilla. 5km from the city center, to Plaza de Colón and avenida del Brillante.*

Hotel Conquistador

14003 Córdoba
Calle Magistral González Frances, 15/17
Tel. 957-48 11 02 - Fax 957-47 46 77
Sra Pilar Ruiz Sanchez

Category ★★★★ **Rooms** 102 with air-conditioning, telephone, bath, WC, satellite TV, safe and room-service. **Price** Single 18,000Pts, double 22,000Pts, suite 28,000Pts. **Meals** Breakfast 1,500Pts, served 7:00-10:30. **Restaurant** See p. 301. **Credit cards** Diners, Visa, Eurocard, MasterCard. **Pets** Dogs not allowed. **Facilities** Parking (1,950Pts). **Nearby** Medina az Zahara - Monastery of San Jerónimo - Las Ermitas de Córdoba - Sanctuary of Santo Domingo de Scala Dei - Fiesta de los Patios (May 5-15); Feria (Sept 25-27) - Los Villares golf course (18-Hole). **Open** All year.

This is the former Hotel Adarve which the new owners have baptized the Conquistador. All the amenities however remain the same while the prices, in contrast, have been lowered a little. Adjoining the mosque, this modern hotel was nevertheless built in an Andalusian Moorish style using both mosaics and marquetry to a very successful effect. All the reception rooms give onto a charming patio where there are columns, a fountain and luxurious vegetation. The rooms are designed with elegance and some, such as Rooms 110, 210 and 310, are very luxurious with marble bathrooms, and a view onto the patio. Those on the facade have a view of the mosque that is illuminated at night.

How to get there *(Map 25): In the Old Town.*

Hotel Amistád Córdoba

14004 Córdoba
Plaza de Maimónides, 3
Tel. 957-42 03 35 - Fax 957-42 03 65
Sr Muñoz

Category ★★★★ **Rooms** 84 with air-conditioning, telephone, bath, WC, TV, minibar; elevator. **Price** Single 19,500Pts, double 27,000Pts, extra bed +7000Pts. **Meals** Breakfast 1,500Pts, served 7:30-11:30. **Restaurant** Service 12:00PM-4:30PM, 8:30PM-11:30PM; à la carte. **Credit cards** All major. **Pets** Dogs not allowed. **Facilities** Garage (1,500Pts). **Nearby** Medina az Zahara - Monastery of San Jerónimo - Las Ermitas de Córdoba - Sanctuary of Santo Domingo de Scala Dei - Fiesta de los Patios (May 5-15); Feria (Sept 25-27) - Los Villares golf course (18-Hole). **Open** All year.

The Amistad of Córdoba is a very new hotel in the Barrio de la Judería, the former Jewish ghetto with its white and flowery narrow streets, giving on to the famous Córdoban patios. Do not fail to visit the well-known Mezquita (cathedral-mosque) in this quarter, and also the synagogue, one of the most celebrated in Europe along with that of Toledo. The hotel is close by and even if the buildings are 18th-century, entry is still made via an arch pierced in the ancient Moorish wall. To accommodate the hotel, two former residences have been joined but the interior *mudéjar* patio has been preserved. All amenities are resolutely contemporary but with some references to local style, as with the suite of arcades in the main lounge where decor is elegant and very sober. The rooms are much warmer, spacious and just as refined. Comfort and personalized services are the main priorities, and this is one of the best hotels in Córdoba.

How to get there *(Map 25): In the Old Town.*

Hostal Séneca

14003 Córdoba
Calle Conde y Luque, 7
Tel. 957-47 32 34 - Fax 957-47 32 34
Sra Peignier

Category ★ **Rooms** 7 with basin and 5 with bath (some with air-conditioning with extra charge) **Price** Single 4,200-4,700Pts, double 5,400-5,900Pts, triple 7,800-8,100Pts. **Meals** Breakfast included, served 9:00-11:00. **Restaurant** See p. 301. **Credit cards** Not accepted. **Pets** Dogs allowed. **Facilities** Parking (1,500Pts). **Nearby** Medina az Zahara - Monastery of San Jerónimo - Las Ermitas de Córdoba - Sanctuary of Santo Domingo de Scala Dei - Fiesta de los Patios (May 5-15); Feria de Mayo (last week of May) - Los Villares golf course (18-Hole). **Closed** Dec 15 - Jan 15.

In the heart of old city, this small hotel is run by a very attractive French woman who came here more than twenty years ago after falling in love with Córdoba. Each year she sees the return of a loyal band of devotees won over by the atmosphere of calm and studied simplicity reigning here. Even if the comfort is less than perfect, you will feel relaxed and at ease in the nicely personalized rooms. no. 14 can accommodate four people (8,000 to 11,000Pts) is recommended for its access to the terrace with its view over the roofs and minaret of the Mezquita close by. There is no restaurant but no. 8 on the same street is strongly recommended by the owner. A warm and relaxed ambiance is assured in this house with a soul all of its own.

How to get there *(Map 25): In the Old Town. Put your car aside at the parking Mezquita, the hotel is at 100 meters.*

Hospedería de San Francisco

14700 Palma de Río (Córdoba)
Avenida Pio XIII, 35
Tel. 957-71 01 83 - Fax 957-64 51 46
Sr Iñaki Martinez

Category ★★★ **Rooms** 22 with air-conditioning, telephone, bath, WC, TV. **Price** Single 7,875Pts, double 11,550Pts. **Meals** Breakfast 790Pts, served 8:00-11:00; half board +3,675Pts, full board +5,775Pts. **Restaurant** El Refectorio, service 1:00PM-4:00PM, 8:30PM-11:00PM; mealtime specials 4,000Pts, also à la carte. Regional cooking. **Credit cards** Visa, Eurocard, MasterCard. **Pets** Dogs allowed. **Facilities** Parking. **Nearby** Medina az Zahara - Monastery of San Jerónimo - Las Ermitages de Córdoba - Sanctuary of Santo Domingo de Scala Dei - Fiesta de los Patios (May 5-15) - Feria (Sept 25-27) - Los Villars golf course (18-Hole). **Open** All year.

Palma del Río is an interesting stop located between Sevilla and Córdoba with a number of small and pretty churches and archeological remains. The hotel was once a monastery and has managed to keep the atmosphere of its earlier days. The open-air cloister is painted in shades of yellow and bordeau, the rooms, formerly monks' cells, retain their attractive entrances with reinforced arches. Each one is decorated with antique furniture and religious engravings. The restaurant is in what was once the dining hall, and the manager, who is also the chef, is a Basque who skillfully combines the art of Basque cuisine with that of Andalucia. A very friendly welcome awaits his guests. An excellent address.

How to get there (Map 24): 92km northeast of Sevilla towards Carmona and Palma del Río.

Alhambra Palace ★★★★

18009 Granada
Peña Partida 2, 4
Tel. 958-22 14 66/67/68 - Fax 958-22 64 04
Sr Fernando Maldonado

Category ★★★★ **Rooms** 136 with air-conditioning, telephone, bath, WC, TV, room-service, minibar; elevator. **Price** Single 18,000Pts, double 22,500Pts, triple 30,375Pts, garden-suite 33,500Pts. **Meals** Breakfast 1,500Pts, served 7:30-10:00; full board 9,095Pts. (per pers., 3 days min.). **Restaurant** Service 1:00PM-3:30PM, 8:30PM-11:30PM; mealtime specials 4,600Pts, also à la carte. **Credit cards** All major. **Pets** Dogs allowed. **Facilities** Parking. **Nearby** La Cartuja (Charterhouse), the gypsy quarter of Sacromonte, the Moorish quarter of the Albaicin de Granada - Viznar (Federico García Lorca National Park) - Guadix cathedral - Sierra Nevada (50km via GR420). **Open** All year.

At the top of a small hill inside the Alhambra Gardens, the towers and minaret of this immense building dominate Granada and have a magnificent view from the terraces over the city and the year-round snow on the Sierra Nevada. The decoration of the entrance hall and the living room are new. In addition to comfortable rooms there are some luxurious suites which enjoy the superb panorama. We also appreciated the availability of room service until 11 p.m., the attention of the personnel and the private parking in a city with an almost full-time tourist presence. This is a good and beautiful hotel.

How to get there *(Map 26): Inside the Alhambra Gardens.*

Hotel America

18009 Granada
Real de la Alhambra, 53
Tel. 958-22 74 71 - Fax 958-22 74 70
Sr Garzón

Category ★ **Rooms** 13 with air-conditioning, telephone, bath or shower, WC. **Price** Single 9,000Pts, double 13,000Pts, suite 16,000Pts. **Meals** Breakfast 950Pts, served 8:00-10:00; half board +2,350Pts, full board +4,800 Pts (per pers. 3 days min.). **Restaurant** Service 1:00PM-3:00PM, 8:00PM-10:00PM; mealtime specials 2,200Pts, also à la carte. Specialties: Potajes al pujarreño - Cocidos - Platos de jamon - Serrano - Quesos manchegos. **Credit cards** All major. **Pets** Dogs not allowed. **Facilities** Parking (400m). **Nearby** La Cartuja (Charterhouse), the gypsy quarter of Sacromonte, the Moorish quarter of the Albaicin de Granada - Viznar (Federico García Lorca National Park) - Guadix cathedral - Sierra Nevada (50km via GR420). **Open** Mar 1 - Nov 30.

It is inside the Real of the Alhambra that one will find the pretty white facade and flowered windows of the Hotel America. This modest but attractive place with its fourteen rooms has become a really charming hotel thanks to the care and talents of the owner. One is above all attracted by the relaxed atmosphere reigning here, and the place soon becomes intimate and almost familiar. The small size of the hotel, its simple but personalized decoration, the family cuisine and the warm welcome all mean a lot here and give its clients the impression of being guests in a friend's house. In summer, meals are served under the trellis in the cool green courtyard. A guest will always return here with pleasure.

How to get there *(Map 26): Inside the Alhambra.*

Parador San Francisco

18009 Granada
Real de la Alhambra
Tel. 958-22 14 40 - Fax 958-22 22 64
Sr Gianello Louro

Category ★★★★ **Rooms** 38 with air-conditioning, telephone, bath, WC, TV, minibar. **Price** Single and double 29,500-33,000Pts. **Meals** Breakfast 1,600Pts, served 8:00-11:00. **Restaurant** Service 1:00PM-4:00PM, 8:30PM-10:30PM; mealtime specials 3,700Pts, also à la carte. Specialties: Gazpacho - Tortilla de Sacramonte - Choto a l'alpurrena. **Credit cards** All major. **Pets** Dogs not allowed. **Facilities** Parking. **Nearby** La Cartuja (Charterhouse), the gypsy quarter of Sacromonte, the Moorish quarter of the Albaicin de Granada - Viznar (Federico García Lorca National Park) - Guadix cathedral - Sierra Nevada (50km via GR420). **Open** All year.

Set within the walls of the Alhambra, close to the Arab Alcazar and the palace of Charles V, the parador is housed in a former Franciscan convent founded by the Catholic Kings after the reconquest of the town. In the midst of the famous Alhambra Gardens, there is a superb view over the Generalife, the Albaicin and the Sierra Nevada. One has to wander through the galleries decorated with old Spanish furniture, in the patio and the chapel to be imbued with the serenity and beauty of this unique site. Ideal for idleness, a small Arab lounge recalls the origins of this site. Perfect for relaxation, the convent rooms are comfortable, while Rooms 205, 206 and 207 have terraces opening onto the Generalife. This truly is a real "plus" in your discovery of Grenada, but be warned: 6-months advance reservation's are required in high season.

How to get there *(Map 26): Inside the Gardens of the Alhambra.*

Hotel Palacio de Santa Inés

18010 Granada
Cuesta de Santa Inés, 9
Tel. 958-22 23 62 - Fax 958-22 24 65

Rooms 9 and 4 suites with air-conditioning, telephone, bath, satellite TV, minibar, safe. **Price** Single 12,000Pts, double 15,000-17,000Pts, suite 20,000-35,000Pts, extra bed +5,000Pts. **Meals** Breakfast 800Pts, served 7:30-11:30. **Restaurant** See p. 302. **Credit cards** All major. **Pets** Dogs not allowed. **Facilities** Garage (1,800Pts). **Nearby** La Cartuja (Charterhouse), the gypsy quarter of Sacromonte, the Moorish quarter of the Albaicin de Granada - Viznar (Federico García Lorca National Park) - Guadix cathedral - Sierra Nevada (50km via GR420). **Open** All year.

A delightful small hotel at the bottom of the Albaicin quarter which has been declared part of Humanity's Legacy by UNESCO. The *palacio* which dates from the 16th century is on a small square surrounded by a maze of narrow streets forming a labyrinth between the canal which borders on one side the Alhambra hill and the Albaicin hill on the other. The patio bears witness to this historic past with elegant galleries in sculpted wood on two stories and the remains of a fresco attributed to a student of Raphael on the walls. The Alhambra suite is the second such witness to this Moorish-inspired period with an attractive wood-paneled ceiling in *mudéjar* style. Here, contemporary paintings cover the walls, clearly defining the tastes of the current owner. The rooms are less grandiose, and although small are invariably decorated in excellent taste. The suites have well-equipped kitchenettes and two of them, Morayama and Boabdil, offer a view of the Alhambra. At the height of the season, service suffers some. It is, nevertheless, Granada's Hotel of Character and Charm.

How to get there *(Map 26): From the Albaicin quarter near the Plaza Nueva, take the Carrera del Darro following directional arrows on the left.*

Hotel Carmen de Santa Inés

18010 Granada
San Juan de los Reyes, 15/Placete de Porras, 7
Tel. 958-22 63 80 - Fax 958-22 44 04

Rooms 5 and 4 suites with air-conditioning, telephone, bath, satellite TV, minibar, safe. **Price** Single 12,000Pts, double 14,000-16,000Pts, suite 20,000-28,000Pts, extra bed +5,000Pts. **Meals** Breakfast 800Pts, served 7:30-11:30. **Restaurant** See p. 302. **Credit cards** All major. **Pets** Dogs not allowed. **Facilities** Garage (1,800Pts). **Nearby** La Cartuja (Charterhouse), the gypsy quarter of Sacromonte, the Moorish quarter of the Albaicin de Granada - Viznar (Federico García Lorca National Park) - Guadix cathedral - Sierra Nevada (50km via GR420). **Open** All year.

This recently-opened hotel gives Granada its second Hotel of Charm. It should be pointed out that *carmen* refers to a specific type of architecture, that of 16th-century Andalucia and clearly influenced by Arab philosophy and Islamic law which dictates that interior wealth must not appear on the outside. *Carmen* comes, in fact, from the Arab word Karm, "a small plot of land where trees have been planted and is surrounded by a wall". In Granada, it is in the Albaicin barrio where these very livable buildings stand, offering truly delightful conditions: a patio where side by side you find Gothic and *mudéjar* columns, a Renaissance fountain, a small geometric garden with box-trees and myrtle plus a loggia giving on the street. The interior has been very well redecorated to reconcile comfort, tradition and modern conveniences. All the rooms have beds with attractive designs and antique furniture while the bathrooms feature locally-produced ceramics. The best among them is the Mirador suite and the smaller Albayzin. Access is difficult, but that is the price to be paid for living in this historic quarter; still, there is an elevator for baggage.

How to get there *(Map 26): From the Albaicin quarter near the Plaza Nueva, then the Carrera del Darro following directional arrows on the left.*

Alguería de Morayma

18440 Torvizcón (Granada)
Ctra 332
Tel. 958-34 32 21 - 958-34 33 03 - Fax 958-34 32 21 - Mariano Cruz

Rooms 8 and 5 houses with telephone, bath, TV. **Price** Double 6,500-8,000Pts, apart. for 2 pers. 9,000Pts, house for 4 pers. 11,000-12,000Pts, extra bed +1,500Pts. **Meals** Breakfast 400Pts, served 8:00-11:00. **Restaurant** Service 1:00PM-2:30PM, 8:30PM-10:30PM; mealtime specials 1,800Pts. **Credit cards** Visa, Eurocard, MasterCard. **Pets** Dogs not allowed. **Facilities** Swimming pool, parking. **Nearby** Villages of Cadiar, Bubíon, Trevelez, Yegen. **Open** All year.

Between sea and mountain, between Granada and Almeria lies a truly extraordinary region, Las Alpujarras. This last Moorish refuge is a place where Nature is wild and unspoiled, plentifully irrigated by water from the sierra. The road passes through a multitude of small, white villages in a landscape that is genuinely astonishing. The Alguería's buildings in this impressive setting are nicely integrated into a 35-hectare finca devoted to naturally produced regional products derived from olive, fig and especially almond trees. There is a marked rustic quality to both the environment and the architecture here; the main building houses the shared areas: a dining room where you can discover local *alpujarres* - specialties that contribute to the owner's renown (he is very well known for his Albaicin restaurant El Mirador de Granada); the bodega with its immense wine barrels where you can enjoy wine and tapas; the library devoted to the Sierra Nevada and Alpujarra. A quaint alleyway leads you to the rooms which are, in fact, small houses: La Casa de la Maestra, de Montañero and La Morisca. Each has its own charm inspired by the history and traditions of the region, the most original being the one that was formerly an old chapel. The quality and authenticity of this address invariably contribute to a deeper understanding of Andalucia.

How to get there *(Map 26): 50km southeast of Granada via N323 to Lanjarón, Orgiva and Torvizcón.*

Hotel Taray

18400 Orgiva (Granada)
Ctra Tablate-Albuñol, 18,500 km
Tel. 958-78 45 25 - 958-78 45 31 - Fax 958-34 32 21
Dtor Eladio Cuadros Lara

Category ★★★ **Rooms** 27 with air-conditioning, telephone, bath, satellite TV, minibar; Wheelchair access. **Price** Single 6,675Pts, double 9,318Pts, double with sitting room 12,146Pts, double with sitting room and terrace 14,143Pts; extra bed +2,000Pts. **Meals** Breakfast 600Pts, served 7:30-11:00. **Restaurant** Service 1:00PM-2:30PM, 8:30PM-10:30PM; mealtime specials 1,830Pts. **Credit cards** All major. **Pets** Dogs not allowed. **Facilities** Swimming pool, parking. **Nearby** Villages of Lanjarón Pampaneira, Bubíon, Cadiar, Trevelez, Yegen. **Open** All year.

The village of Orgiva is on the western border of the Alpujarra and here the *pueblos blancos* route begins. The hotel is a kilometer outside of town, situated in a large property surrounded by orchards and olive groves, rose bushes and bougainvillae with the snowy peaks of the Sierra Nevada as its horizon. It also features numerous forms of animal husbandry that include chickens, cows and even trout, all of which finish on the tables of the guests. Three large buildings house not only the restaurant which, in the summer, is extended to include a large terrace but also the rooms which are accessed via a flower-lined gallery. The decoration is not always in the best of taste but the hotel is truly spacious, spotlessly clean and comfortable. Its special quality lies in its large swimming pool with a view of the majestic Sierra mountains.

How to get there *(Map 26): 50km southeast of Granada via N323 to Lanjarón and Orgiva.*

Hotel la Bobadilla

18300 Loja (Granada)
Finca La Bobadilla - Apartado, 144
Tel. 958-32 18 61 - Fax 958-32 18 10 - Sr Klaudius Heckh
E-mail: info@la-bobadilla.com - Web: www.la-bobadilla.com

Category ★★★★★ **Rooms** 60 with air-conditioning, telephone, bath, WC, satellite TV, minibar; elevator. **Price** Single 24,200-37,100Pts, double 34,400-39,500Pts, double with sitting room 45,200-51,800Pts, suite 58,400-111,000Pts, extra bed +8,000-8,700Pts. **Meals** Breakfast included, served 8:00-11:00; half board and full board +6,300Pts. **Restaurant** Service 1:30PM-3:30PM, 8:30PM-11:00PM; La Finca: à la carte 8,000-10,000Pts - El Cortijo: à la carte 6,000-8,000Pts. Regional and international cooking. **Credit cards** All major. **Pets** Dogs allowed except in the restaurant. **Facilities** Swimming pools, tennis, riding, sauna, health center, bikes, garage. **Nearby** Loja - Los Infiernos de Lojas - Antequera - Granada. **Open** All year.

The Bobadilla is a "grand luxe" hotel in a very beautiful residence built in the best Andalusian style, with succeeding patios, flowered terraces, gardens and fountains. The rooms are very comfortable and exquisitely decorated. The two restaurants serve a cuisine of quality. This hotel attracts with all that it offers for a truly relaxing stay: tennis court, swimming pool, horse riding and a fitness center. All this is in a region not lacking in tourist interest, and note that very interesting reduced rates are available in the winter months (Christmas excepted), depending on length of stay.

How to get there *(Map 25): 76km west of Granada via A92 (Granada/Sevilla); exit no. 175: Villanueva, Iznájar, Salinas.*

Finca Buen Vino

21293 Los Marines (Huelva)
Tel. 959-12 40 34 - Fax 959-50 10 29
Sr and Sra Chesterton

Rooms 4 with bath (2 in the room), WC. **Price** Half board (1 pers.) 14,000-16,000Pts, double (per pers.) 13,000-15,000Pts. **Evening meals** Mealtime specials. Regional and international cooking. **Credit cards** Visa, Eurocard, MasterCard. **Pets** Dogs not allowed. **Facilities** Swimming pool (Jun-Sept). **Nearby** Gruta de las Maravillas in Aracena (Cave of Marvels) - Almonaster la Real - Church of the convent of Santa Clara in Moguer - Ayomonte - Isla Cristina - Sevilla (1 hour) - Portugese border (40 mn) - El Romero del Rocio of Huelva (May). **Closed** Dec 16 - Jan 7 and Aug.

At equal distance from Lisbon and Gibraltar, and 50km from the border with Portugal, the Finca Buen Vino will prove a charming stopover. At this residential hotel you must reserve in advance if you wish to enjoy this pretty house with only three rooms open to visitors. The traditional Hispano-Moorish facade is overrun by roses and clematis. The hotel was bought a few years ago by an English couple, and you will find full British charm and comfort in the interior: old furniture, chintzes, pot-pourri, souvenirs of the Empire and so on. The same refinement is found around the guests' tables: linen napkins, silverware, crystal; all of it, however, arranged with a certain simplicity - even if correct dress is required for dinner. Midday meals are served on the terrace in summer. The kitchen garden, mixing flowers, vegetables and fruit, supplies the house recipes. The welcome is cordial.

How to get there *(Map 17): 100km west of Sevilla via N433 (km 95).*

Parador Castillo de Santa Catalina

Oeste 23001 Jaén
Tel. 953-23 00 00 - Fax 953-23 09 30
Sr Jesus Cardenas

Category ★★★★ **Rooms** 45 with air-conditioning, telephone, bath, WC, satellite TV, minibar; elevator. **Price** Double 17,500Pts. **Meals** Breakfast 1,300Pts, served 8:00-10:30; full board +6,375Pts. (per pers., 2 days min.). **Restaurant** Service 1:00PM-4:00PM, 8:30PM-11:00PM; mealtime specials 3,500Pts, also à la carte. Regional cooking. **Credit cards** All major. **Pets** Dogs not allowed. **Facilities** Swimming pool. **Nearby** In Jaén Feria de San Lucas (Oct12-20) - Baeza - Ubeda - Martos. **Open** All year.

Attached to the impressive fortress built at the same period and in the same style as the Alhambra at Grenada, the Parador Santa Catalina has the severe appearance of a fortified castle with its stone outworks and the tiny apertures of its facade. The view however is superb over a valley scattered with olive groves. Most of the rooms have balconies and you can enjoy such a view at your leisure. The reception rooms are very spacious and have been arranged with furniture sometimes very much in the 1960's "designer" style, and decorated with tapestries and canvasses on loan from various national museums. Do not miss the dining room with its lamps created in the spirit of Moorish-Arabic art.

How to get there (Map 25): 4,5km west of Jaén.

Hotel de la Perdíz

23200 La Carolina (Jaén)
Carret. N IV
Tel. 953-66 03 00 - Fax 953-68 13 62
Sr Eufemio Mansilla Garcia

Category ★★★★ **Rooms** 95 with air-conditioning, telephone, bath, WC; elevator. **Price** Single 12,000 Pts, double 13,000Pts. **Meals** Breakfast 1,100Pts, served 7:30-11:00; half board +4,300Pts, full board +6,400Pts. (per pers.). **Restaurant** Service 1:30PM-3:45PM, 8:45PM-11:15PM; mealtime specials 3,500Pts, also à la carte. Specialties: game. **Credit cards** All major. **Pets** Dogs allowed (except in restaurant). **Facilities** Swimming pool, garage, parking. **Nearby** Convento de la Sierra Morena and Palacio de la Carolina - Feria (May 11-15). **Open** All year.

There is a very "hunting lodge" ambiance in this hotel that owes its name to the park close by renowned for its abundant game. The large fireplaces, the hunting trophies and arms collections on the walls, the impressive beams of the ceiling and beautiful old Spanish furniture all contribute to the warm and rustic atmosphere of the lounges. The bedrooms are more simple but are all carefully maintained and pleasant. At the heart of the building is a small enclosed garden planted with palm trees, scented cypresses and fig trees which form a small haven of cool and peace. Most of the rooms have a view of the garden while others have terraces. If you cannot get one of these, go for those looking over the olive groves and the village.

How to get there (Map 19): 44km north of Linares via N322 to Bailén, then N4.

Parador de Cazorla

Sacejo
23470 Cazorla (Jaén)
Tel. 953-72 70 75 - Fax 953-72 70 77

Category ★★★ Rooms 33 with telephone, bath, WC, TV. **Price** Double 12,500-15,000Pts. **Meals** Breakfast (buffet) 1,200Pts, served 8:00-10:30. **Restaurant** Service 1:00PM-4:00PM, 8:30PM-10:30PM; mealtime specials 3,200Pts, also à la carte. Specialties: game, trouts. **Credit cards** All major. **Pets** Dogs not allowed. **Facilities** Swimming pool, parking. **Nearby** Ubeda - Nature Park of Sierra de Cazorla - Quesada - Villages of the Sierra de Segura "Valle del Paraiso": Orcera, Beas de Segura and Segura de la Sierra. **Open** All year.

Arrival at the parador is possible only after an expedition up the mountain road at Cazorla leading to Sacejo. The trip is worthwhile, both for the wild and wooded site and the picturesque villages that you drive through. Visitors come here above all for the walking, fishing or hunting. The source of the Guadalquivir river is close by, and the Sierra de Cazorla is a very beautiful nature park scented by pines, oaktrees and junipers-the home of stags, deer and wild boar. The hotel architecture is inspired by the Andalusian *cortijos*, with care taken to look out over the surrounding nature as much as possible. It is better to go for the rooms looking over the swimming pool side as they have the best view. The decor is sober but comfortable and very well maintained. In the restaurant, a cuisine favoring game, the specialty of the region, is served. To better enjoy your stay, do not hesitate to take part in the excursions (free) organized by the hotel for clients: cultural visits, horse riding and mountain bike trips, all to the natural sites of Andalucia.

How to get there (*Map 26*): *25km east of Cazorla.*

Parador Condestable Davalos

23400 Úbeda (Jaén)
Plaza Vasquez de Molina, 1
Tel. 953-75 03 45 - Fax 953-75 12 59
Sr Munoz

Category ★★★★ **Rooms** 31 with air-conditioning, telephone, bath, WC, satellite TV, minibar. **Price** Double 16,500-18,500Pts. **Meals** Breakfast 1,300Pts, served 8:00-10:30. **Restaurant** Service 1:00PM-4:00PM, 9:00PM-11:00PM; mealtime specials 3,700Pts, also à la carte. Specialties: Ajo blanco - Espiñacas al estilo Jaén - Pimientos rellenos de perdíz - Natillas con borrachuelos. **Credit cards** All major. **Pets** Dogs not allowed. **Nearby** Sabiote - Nature Park of Sierra de Cazorla: Embalse del Tranco and shores of the Guadalquivir - Villanueva del Arrobispo - Jaén - Segura de la Sierra. **Open** All year.

This 16th-century palace boasts a long, Greco-Roman style facade in the historical part of the town, where a number of monuments from the Renaissance period rival its beauty. Renovated in the 18th century, it was converted into a hotel in 1942. The long glazed galleries, a dream patio where in summer a canopy is put up to provide shade and bedrooms with a postcard view all contribute to its delightful charm! To note: The suite on the facade forming the corner is very beautiful, and reasonably priced, while a "taverne" on the ground floor will delight all lovers of good wines.

How to get there (Map 19): 24km east of Linares via N322; nearby the Salvador church and the Ayuntamiento (town hall).

Parador del Golf

29080 Málaga
Tel. 95-238 12 55 - Fax 95-238 21 41
Sr Garcia Alonso

Category ★★★★ **Rooms** 56 and 4 suites with air-conditioning, telephone, bath, WC, satellite TV, minibar. **Price** Double 17,500Pts. **Meals** Breakfast 1,300Pts, served 8:00-10:30. **Restaurant** Service 1:30PM-4:00PM, 8:30PM-11:00PM; mealtime specials 3,500Pts. **Credit cards** All major. **Pets** Dogs not allowed. **Facilities** Swimming pool, tennis, golf, parking. **Nearby** Cártama - Alora and Convento de Nuestra Señora Flores - Tropical gardens of the Hacienda de la Concepción - El Chorro and the Garganta del Chorro - Club Campo de Málaga golf course (18-Hole). **Open** All year.

6km west of Málaga and 4km from Torremolinos, the Parador del Golf will prove a stopping place particularly appreciated by adepts of this sport. At once close to the airport and located on the golf course, the hotel is thus protected from the galloping urbanization that is ravaging the Costa del Sol. Access to the course is free, and hotel guests enjoy a 50% reduction from November 1 to June 30. Those not playing the game can always play tennis or unwind beside the large swimming pool or on the beach close by. The architecture is without much personality but has the merit of being discreet. The bedrooms are quiet and decorated with care. The service is irreproachable. Rather than a hotel of charm, here we have a "de luxe" hotel to spoil all golfers.

How to get there *(Map 25): 6km west of Málaga towards Torremolinos.*

Parador Gibralfaro

Gibralfaro
29016 Málaga
Tel. 95-222 19 03 - Fax 95-222 19 04
Sr Juan Carlo Garcia Alonso
E-mail: gibralfaro@parador.es

Category ★★★★ **Rooms** 38 with air-conditioning, telephone, bath, WC, satellite TV, minibar.
Price Double 17,500-19,000Pts. **Meals** Breakfast 1,300Pts, served 8:00-10:30. **Restaurant**
Service 1:30PM-4:30PM, 8:30PM-11:30PM (8:30PM-12:00AM in summer); mealtime specials 3,700Pts.
Credit cards All major. **Pets** Dogs not allowed. **Facilities** Swimming pool, parking.
Nearby Cártama - Alora and Convento de Nuestra Señora Flores - Tropical gardens of the Hacienda
de la Concepción - El Chorro and the Garganta del Chorro - Club Campo de Málaga golf course (18-
Hole). **Open** All year.

Situated on the Gibralfaro hill, the parador enjoys an uninterrupted view over the town and commercial port. The hotel has just a few comfortable and air-conditioned rooms, which is a considerable advantage in this part of Spain. Each room has its own terrace while the restaurant also has one from which one can see the Malagueta quarter and the bullring. On a summer evening it is fun to linger at the bar and have a drink while watching the lighted ships pass by. Guests can enjoy the attractive swimming pool on the roof as well as pleasant walks in the gardens of the ancient fortress close to the hotel.

How to get there (Map 25): 1km from the center of Málaga.

Molino de Santillan

29730 Rincón de la Victoria (Málaga)
Ctra. de Macharaviaya, km 3
Tel. 95-211 57 80-81 - Fax 95-211 57 82
Sr Carlos Marchini

Rooms 14 with telephone, bath, satellite TV, minibar. **Price** Double 6,950-8,250Pts, extra bed +4,000Pts. **Meals** Breakfast 1,300Pts, served 8:00-11:00; half board 10,950Pts, full board 13,950Pts. **Restaurant** Service 1:00PM-4:00PM, 8:00PM-12:00AM; mealtime specials 3,000Pts. Specialties: fish and shellfish. **Credit cards** All major. **Pets** Dogs not allowed. **Facilities** Swimming pool, parking. **Nearby** Ojén - Coín - Rio Real los Monteros golf course (18-Hole), Nueva Andalucia golf course (18-Hole). **Closed** Jan 10 - Feb 10.

A few kilometers from Málaga, but well-protected from tourist bustle and urban sprawl, the fishing village of Rincón de la Victoria gives you an excellent idea of what this region once was. The hotel is located on a hill overlooking the countryside that extends all the way to the sea. Built around a small central garden, the house is in Andalusian *cortijo* style. The dining room offers delicious regional cooking where seafood is featured in a very congenial atmosphere around a fireplace in the center of the room. The rooms are decorated in rustic style and are thoroughly comfortable. The garden too is very pleasant, and the swimming pool below with its view of sea on the horizon is a delight, an ideal spot for an afternoon aperitif. The pleasant gray-sand beaches of Rincón have a family clientele, another reason for stopping off - at a reasonable price - on the Costa del Sol.

How to get there (Map 25): 17km east of Málaga.

La Fonda

29639 Benalmádena Pueblo (Málaga)
C/. Santo Domingo, 7
Tel. 95-256 82 73 - Fax 95-256 82 73
Sr José Antonio Garcia

Category ★★★ Rooms 28 with air-conditioning, telephone, bath, WC, TV, minibar. **Price** Single 6,325-9,900Pts, double 9,000-13,860Pts, triple 9,900-16,060Pts, apart. (1-2 pers.) 7,150-15,125Pts, apart. (3-5 pers.) 9,900-19,800Pts; extra bed +1,000Pts. **Meals** Breakfast included. **Restaurant** Service 1:00PM-3:00PM, closed Sat, Sun and National Holidays; mealtime specials and also à la carte. Regional and international cooking. **Credit cards** All major. **Pets** Dogs not allowed. **Facilities** Heated swimming pool in winter, parking. **Nearby** Marbella - Málaga - Cártama - Alora and Convento de Nuestra Señora Flores - Tropical gardens of the Hacienda de la Concepción - El Chorro and the Garganta del Chorro - Club Campo de Málaga golf course (18-Hole). **Open** All year.

Impossible to resist its charm! This hotel is located a few paces from the ravishing little square of Benalmádena where it is delightful to linger among the orange trees. Despite its proximity to the tourist-magnet coast only 4km away, the village has been preserved by some miracle. Built out of earlier houses, one is surprised to find no less than three different patios, one of them boasting a swimming pool. The purest Andalusian style, with the white of the walls set off by prettily arranged green plants and flowers, is highly attractive, while the superb view of the sea further emphasizes the architecture of the hotel. The most pleasant bedrooms are those enjoying this view.

How to get there *(Map 25): 20km south of Málaga, on the highway Málaga-Cádiz, exit Benalmádena.*

Hotel Mijas

29650 Mijas (Málaga)
Urbanizacion Tamisa, 2
Tel. 95-248 58 00 - Fax 95-248 58 25
Sr Martinez

Category ★★★★ **Rooms** 94 and 3 suites with air-conditioning, telephone, bath, WC, satellite TV. **Price** Single 8,750-13,000Pts, double 10,750-15,000Pts, suite 21,000-29,500Pts. **Meals** Breakfast 1,500Pts, served 7:30-10:30; half board +4,600Pts, full board +7,700Pts. (per pers.). **Restaurant** With air-conditioning. Service 1:00PM-3:30PM, 8:00PM-10:30PM; mealtime specials 3,000Pts, also à la carte. **Credit cards** All major. **Pets** Dogs not allowed. **Facilities** Swimming pool, tennis, sauna (1,500Pts), parking. **Nearby** Costa del Sol - Málaga - Benalmádena - Marbella - Club Campo de Málaga and Mijas golf course (18-Hole). **Open** All year.

If you are afraid of the crowds on the over-visited Costa del Sol but adore its sunshine and tanning all year round, you must make a trip up to the village of Mijas. Here on the small hills between Málaga and Marbella, among the pines and palm trees with a view that cannot be taken away, is located the Mijas Hotel with a typically Andalusian character and a certain English spirit. The public rooms are sober but very comfortable, while the terraces promise delicious breakfasts in the shade of the olive trees and are the ideal setting for summer dinners. The Mijas offers comfortable bedrooms but the suites are the most comfortable even though only three have the best views. Two beautiful swimming pools, a tennis court and a health center add to the attractions of this hotel.

How to get there *(Map 25): 30km southwest of Málaga via N340 towards Cádiz; at Fuengirola take small road for Mijas.*

Refugio de Juanar

Juanar 29610 Ojén (Málaga)
Tel. 95-288 10 00 - Fax 95-288 10 01
Sr Gomez Avila

Category ★★★ **Rooms** 25 with telephone, bath, WC, satellite TV, minibar. **Price** Single 8,600-9,800Pts, double 10,100-11,500Pts, 4 pers. 16,300-17,500Pts, suite 13,200-19,500Pts, suite Alpha or Bravo and apart. 6 pers. 25,000-28,000Pts, extra bed +3,200Pts. **Meals** Breakfast 975Pts, served 8:30-11:00; half board +3,300-3,800Pts, full board +6,500Pts. (per pers.). **Restaurant** Service 1:00PM-4:00PM, 8:00PM-10:30PM; mealtime specials 3,300Pts, also à la carte. Specialties: game. **Credit cards** All major. **Pets** Dogs not allowed. **Facilities** Swimming pool, tennis, parking. **Nearby** Marbella (18km) - Coín - Alozaina - Ronda. **Open** All year.

Aparador in other times, this hotel has now been taken over by its employees. Starting from Ojén, take a small mountain road rising to 780 meters above sea level to the Sierra de Ronda, a major center for hunting the *capra hispanica* as well as smaller game: partridges, rabbits, etc. Hidden in this superb countryside is this former property of the Marquis de Tarios, a favorite hunting ground of King Alfonso XIII. Set among pines and oaks, this is a comfortable mountain hotel where, in a pleasing rustic decor, an ambiance of warmth reigns, and where a good cuisine based on game is available. For the bedrooms, our favorite is no. 3 in which General de Gaulle completed the writing of his memoirs! This is an excellent hotel for an extended stay as it has a swimming pool, tennis courts and offers numerous woodland trails for hiking. The anisette distilleries of Ojén provide easy choices for holiday souvenirs.

How to get there *(Maps 24 and 25): 65km southwest of Málaga via N340 to Marbella, then continue via C337; 10km after Ojén.*

El Castillo de Monda

29110 Monda (Málaga)
Tel. 95-245 71 42 - Fax 95-245 73 36

Category ★★★ **Rooms** 26 with air-conditioning, telephone, bath, satellite TV; elevator. **Price** Single 12,500Pts, double 15,000-28,000Pts, suite 70,000Pts. **Meals** Breakfast 1,500Pts, served 8:30-11:00. **Restaurant** Service 1:00PM-4:00PM, 8:00PM-10:30PM; mealtime specials 3,000Pts, also à la carte. **Credit cards** Amex, Visa, Eurocard, MasterCard. **Pets** Dogs not allowed. **Facilities** Swimming pool, parking. **Nearby** Marbella (15km) - Coín - Alozaina - Ronda - Nueva Andalucia golf course (18-Hole). **Open** All year.

Monda is a pristine white village some fifteen kilometers outside Marbella and well out of range of its jet-tour summer visitors. You can't miss the Castillo which overlooks the village from a rocky peak whose gray stone contrasts with the blazing whiteness of the houses. This luxury address is run by an English couple who successfully wed two cultures, one Spanish, the other British. The architecture and decoration veer away from Moorish influences in favor of Anglo-Saxon comfort. All here is new, explaining the lack of patina. The top floor offers all guests a high-angle view through the often narrow openings of the castle walls. Rooms are spacious, functional, comfortable and well-furnished with attractive bathrooms, while the deluxe accommodations even offer jacuzzis. Rooms 701 and 702 have terraces, and the most luxurious are in the tower, comfortably away from the main building and situated on the cliff making them even more impressive. The terraced garden, the swimming pool with its splendid view and the fine food are equally to be commended. The atmosphere is elegant and somewhat formal.

How to get there *(Maps 24 and 25): 65km southwest of Málaga via N340 to Marbella, Ojén and Monda.*

Marbella Club Hotel

29600 Marbella (Málaga)
Bulevar Principe Alfonso Von Hohenlohe
Tel. 95-282 22 11 - Fax 95-282 98 84 - Sr Javier Rosenberg
E-mail: hotel@marbellaclub.com - Web: www.marbellaclub.com

Category ★★★★ **Rooms** 130 with air-conditioning, telephone, bath, WC, satellite TV, safe, minibar. **Price** Single 27,000-48,000Pts, double 34,500-58,000Pts, junior-suite 48,000-80,000Pts, suite 72,000-125,000Pts, bungalows 2-3 bedrooms 135,000-245,000Pts. **Meals** Breakfast (buffet) 3,000Pts, served 8:30-11:00; half board +10,000Pts, full board +14,000Pts (per pers.). **Restaurant** Service from 1:30PM and 8:30PM; mealtime specials 7,800Pts, also à la carte. Mediterranean cooking. **Credit cards** All major. **Pets** Dogs not allowed. **Facilities** Heated swimming pool, swimming pool, beach, tennis, sauna, parking. **Nearby** Ojén - Coín - Rio Real los Monteros golf course (18-Hole), Nueva Andalucia golf course (18-Hole). **Open** All year.

In a magnificent and faultlessly maintained garden, the Marbella Club Hotel's bungalows assure complete privacy and unmatched comfort. The impeccable decor matches the image of the place, luxurious and refined. Bathrooms in marble, coordinated printed fabrics - nothing is left to chance. Those Hollywood stars coming here to find relaxation in line with their standing will not be disappointed. Besides the fully-equipped beach and the beautiful swimming pools, all the services you could wish for are assured and guarantee a "de luxe" and charming stay.

How to get there *(Map 25): 56km southwest of Málaga via N340.*

Puente Romano

29600 Marbella (Málaga)
Tel. 95-282 09 00 - Fax 95-277 57 66
Sr Peter Roth
E-mail: hotel@puenteromano.com - Web: www.puenteromano.com

Category ★★★★★ **GL Rooms** 226 with air-conditioning, telephone, bath, WC, satellite TV, safe, minibar. **Price** Single 26,500-43,000Pts, double 29,600-55,000Pts, suite 35,000-300,000Pts. **Meals** Breakfast (buffet) 2,900Pts, served 8:00-11:00; half board +10,400Pts, full board +15,000Pts. **Restaurant** Service 1:00PM-4:00PM, 8:00PM-12:00AM; à la carte 7,500Pts. International cooking. **Credit cards** All major. **Pets** Small dogs allowed in the room and in the garden. **Facilities** Swimming pools, tennis, fitness center, sauna, parking. **Nearby** Ojén - Coín - Rio Real los Monteros golf course (18-Hole), Nueva Andalucia golf course (18-Hole). **Open** All year.

A "grand luxe" hotel, the Puente Romano sports its five stars with serenity and without ostentation. With its elegant Andalusian architecture (unfortunately beside a busy national road), the hotel is made up of small bungalows in an admirable garden of exquisite freshness. The contemporary decor is luxurious but in good taste and the super-abundance of equipment of all sorts - 3 swimming pools, a gym, 3 restaurants, a private beach - and the quality of service will satisfy even the most demanding. Situated in the "Milla d'Oro", the nicest district between Marbella and Puerto Banus, the hotel is a true oasis in an extremely built-up region.

How to get there (Maps 24 and 25): 56km southwest of Málaga via N340.

Hotel San Gabriel

29400 Ronda (Málaga)
Calle José M. Holgado, 19
Tel. 952-19 03 92 - Fax 952-19 01 17 - Familia Arnal Pérez
E-mail: sangabriel@ronda.net - Web: www.ronda.net/usuar/hotelsgabriel

Rooms 16 with air-conditioning, telephone, bath, satellite TV, minibar. **Price** Single 8,000-9,000Pts, double 10,000-11,000Pts, suite 12,000-13,000Pts. **Meals** Breakfast 600Pts, served 8:00-11:00. **Restaurant** See p. 304. **Credit cards** All major. **Pets** Dogs not allowed. **Nearby** Setenil - Alozaina - Serriana de Ronda to San Pedro de Alcántara - Grazalema - Ronda road in Ubrique - Feria de Ronda (May 20-22). **Open** All year.

The San Gabriel is just the address that has been lacking in Ronda, an indispensable stop-over for any visitor to Andalucia. The hotel is a private home converted to receive guests and provide the intimate and refined atmosphere of a friend's home while at the same time guaranteeing the independence and service of a Hotel of Charm. Very nicely located in the city's historic center, this noble and traditional Andalusian dwelling has a majestic door complete with coat-of-arms plus a flowered wrought iron balcony while remaining well off the beaten tourist track. The lounge with its genuine family furniture plus a pleasant little bar where breakfast may be ordered are on the ground floor. The best rooms are upstairs, especially Rooms 9 and 10 which offer Hispanic decoration including furniture in solid dark wood and rich brown-red motifs. The family that welcomes you is invariably attentive to your comfort in keeping with their motto informing you that here is *su casa en Ronda*. The *dueño* might propose a visit to the small underground salon and regale you with stories of the artists and intellectuals such as Orson Welles who have stayed there and contributed to the fame of Ronda.

How to get there *(Map 24): 96km north of Algeciras. After the Puente Nuevo (in the direction of La Cuidad), take the second street on the right.*

Hotel la Fuente de la Higuera

Partido de los Frontones 29400 Ronda (Málaga)
Calle José M. Holgado, 19
Tel. 952-11 43 55 - Mobile 610 84 77 31 - Fax 952-11 43 56
E-mail: lafuente@ncs.es - Web: andalucia.com/lafuente/

Rooms 10 with air-conditioning, telephone, bath, satellite TV, minibar. **Price** Double 12,000-15,000Pts, junior-suite and apart. 15,500-19,500Pts, suite 18,000-23,000Pts, double-suite 24,000-29,000Pts. **Meals** Breakfast included, served 8:00-11:00. **Restaurant** See p. 304. **Credit cards** All major. **Pets** Dogs not allowed. **Nearby** Setenil - Alozaina - Serriana de Ronda to San Pedro de Alcántara - Grazalema - Ronda road in Ubrique - Feria de Ronda (May 20-22). **Open** All year.

Here is the other hotel of charm where you may currently escape the unrelenting - and yearlong - assault laid to the village of Ronda. Situated in a valley, this hotel was formerly a mill devoted to turning out olive oil although few traces remain apart from very comfortable interior space. This scarcely matters as the complete restructuring of the buildings surrounded by ten hectares of olive trees has produced a small country hotel, both modern and refined. The interior architecture has favored white and luminous walls over old stone. The antique furniture in the patio whose columns support the gallery evoke the region's traditions. The rooms are spacious and elegant with handsome furniture and subtle colors. The bathrooms are particularly attractive, and certain rooms have fireplaces assuring complete comfort whatever the season. Whether you choose to have breakfast under the gallery or to lounge under the swimming pool's acacia or in the library, the atmosphere is invariably one of peace and quiet. This is an address very likely to tempt you into prolonging your stay in the beautiful Sierra de Ronda.

How to get there *(Map 24): 6km northwest of Ronda towards Arriate.*

Molino del Santo

29370 Benaoján (Málaga)
Tel. 952-16 71 51 - Fax 952-16 73 27
Anoy Chapell - Paolina Elkin
E-mail: molino@logiscontrol.es

Rooms 14 and 1 suite (n°15) with telephone, bath or shower. **Price** Double standard 5,460-6,825Pts, double superior 6,275-7,585Pts, suite 7,455-8,875Pts; extra bed +2,500Pts. **Meals** Breakfast (buffet) included, served 8:00-10:30; half board (obligatory from Apr to Sept) 9,030-13,465Pts. **Restaurant** Service 1:30PM-4:30PM, 8:30PM-11:30PM; mealtime specials and also à la carte. **Credit cards** All major. **Pets** Dogs not allowed. **Facilities** Swimming pool. **Nearby** Ronda - Setenil - Alozaina - Serriana de Ronda to San Pedro de Alcántara - Grazalema - Ronda road in Ubrique - Feria de Ronda (May 20-22). **Closed** Nov 14 - Feb 12.

As it leaves Ronda, the road winds between mountains and olive groves until it reaches Benaoján, a truly magical route. The village is nestled at the bottom of a small valley. The Molino is a collection of small buildings, all glistening white, centered around a garden and a swimming pool. The decoration is of a refreshing simplicity featuring pastel shades and flowery fabrics. Most rooms have terraces - Rooms 10 through 14 - and while unattached, they offer little in the way of intimate living; the largest is no. 15. The English owners pay particular attention to the food served here. This is a place filling all the requirements of relaxation and set in splendid natural surroundings with numerous walking tours to very attractive places nearby. The prices are equally attractive.

How to get there (Map 25): 9km south of Ronda.

La Posada del Torcal

29230 Villanueva de la Concepción (Málaga)
Tel. 95-203 11 77 - Fax 95-203 10 06 - Sra Karen Ducker
E-mail: laposada@mercuryin.es - Web: www.andalucia.com/posada-torcal

Rooms 9 and 1 suite with air-conditioning, telephone, bath, WC, satellite TV, minibar. **Price** Double 12,000-45,000Pts. **Meals** Breakfast 1,800Pts, served 9:00-11:30. **Restaurant** Service 8:00PM-9:30PM; mealtime specials 4,500Pts. **Credit cards** All major. **Pets** Dogs not allowed. **Facilities** Swimming pool, tennis, gymnasium, sauna, mountain bikes, parking. **Nearby** Antequera - Cueva de Menga and Cueva de Viera - Cueva del Romeral - El Torcal. **Open** Feb 14 - Nov 14.

Antequera, the gorgeous back country north of Málaga, is where you will find a wealth of Andalusian art along with the Sierra del Torcal, offering exceptional landscapes of eroded red rock. It is on a butte surrounded by a fertile plain that Karen Ducker has created her charming posada surrounded by four hectares of almond trees. This location offers a gorgeous view of the magnificent panorama. The entrance to the *cortil* with its traditional well offers complete respect to local tradition, but once inside the Posada, traces of the past give way to contemporary renovation. This scarcely matters because the spirit of the days gone by is invariably present, particularly in the rooms. Each is decorated differently with wrought-iron beds, antique furniture, attractive artisanal objects, along with a handsome reproduction by Greg Ducker of a painting by one of Spain's masters. Each, naturally, has a superb view. The lounge offers comfortable alcoves, and fires are lit in all the fireplaces as soon as the weather turns cold. The summer, of course, allows the guests to take advantage of the natural surroundings and the garden lying between the hill and the swimming pool. Here is yet another face of Andalucia.

How to get there *(Map 25): 60km northwest of Malága towards Antequera via N331, exit 148 Casabermeja, then towards Villanueva.*

Hotel Alfonso XIII

41004 Sevilla
San Fernando, 2
Tel. 95-422 28 50 - Fax 95-421 60 33
Sra Jeannine Perié

Category ★★★★★ **Rooms** 146 with air-conditioning, telephone, bath, WC, satellite TV, minibar; elevator. **Price** Single 42,500-59,000Pts, double 55,500-75,500Pts, triple 65,500-87,000Pts, suite 109,000-122,000Pts. **Meals** Breakfast 3,000Pts, served 7:00-11:00; half board +7,200Pts (per pers.). **Restaurant** Service 1:00PM-3:30PM, 8:30PM-11:30PM; mealtime specials 4,500Pts. Regional and international cooking. **Credit cards** All major. **Pets** Dogs not allowed. **Facilities** Swimming pool (Mar - Oct), parking, garage (2,250Pts). **Nearby** Cantillana - Carmona - Alcalá de Guadaira - Sanlúcar la Mayor - Convento de San Isidoro del Campo in Santiponce and ruins of the Roman colony of Itálica - Romero de Rocio of Huelva - Semana Santa (Holy Week in Mar) and the April Fair (2 weeks after Holy Week); Golf e Hipodromo del Club Pineda golf course (9-Hole). **Open** All year.

The Alfonso XIII was built to receive leading visitors to the Hispano-American Exhibition in 1929, and since then it has continued as a luxury hotel linked to the very history of Sevilla. The work of the architect Espinau-Munoz who insisted that the hotel should truly represent the city, it was designed as a major Hispano-Moorish palace. The building is set around a large central patio surrounded by a glazed gallery, with arches deployed above white marble columns. Gardens planted with tropical vegetation surround the four facades of the palace. Sumptuous lounges follow each other in succession; while the bedrooms are perfect, we would have preferred if they gave onto the garden.

How to get there (Map 24): Alongside the cathedral.

Hotel Tryp Colon

41001 Sevilla
Canalejas, 1
Tel. 95-422 29 00 - Fax 95-422 09 38

Category ★★★★★ **Rooms** 218 with air-conditioning, telephone, bath, WC, satellite TV, minibar; elevator; rooms for disabled persons. **Price** Double 23,150-42,000Pts. **Meals** Breakfast 1,650Pts, served 7:00-11:00; half board +5,700Pts, full board +7,840Pts (per pers.). **Restaurant** Service 2:00PM-3:30PM, 9:00PM-11:30PM; mealtime specials 4,100Pts, also à la carte. Regional and international cooking. **Credit cards** All major. **Pets** Dogs not allowed. **Facilities** Fitness room, sauna, parking, garage (2,200Pts). **Nearby** Cantillana - Carmona - Alcalá de Guadaira - Sanlúcar la Mayor - Convento de San Isidoro del Campo in Santiponce and ruins of the Roman colony of Itálica - El Rocio of Huelva - Semana Santa (Holy Week in Mar) and the April Fair (2 weeks after Holy Week) - Golf e Hipodromo del Club Pineda golf course (9-Hole). **Open** All year.

The Tryp Colon was built on the edge of Sevilla's historic center for the Exposition of 1929 and its architecture is an authentic reflection of the style of the period. Its imposing facade gives way to a majestic circular reception area and large salon with a lovely Art-Deco stained-glass ceiling. It is truly luxurious hotel and offers all the comfort and service that one may expect in a hotel of this category.

How to get there *(Map 24): Near the Museo of Bellas Artes.*

Hotel Los Seises

41004 Sevilla
Segovias, 6
Tel. 95-422 94 95 - Fax 95-422 43 34 - Sr Reinoso
E-mail: seises@jet.es - Web: www.sol.com/hotel-los-seises

Category ★★★★ **Rooms** 43 with air-conditioning, telephone, bath, WC, satellite TV, safe, minibar; elevator. **Price** Single 15,000-22,000Pts, double 18,000-27,000Pts. **Meals** Breakfast 2,000Pts, served 8:00-10:30. **Restaurant** Service 1:30PM-3:30PM, 9:00PM-11:00PM; à la carte. **Credit cards** All major. **Pets** Dogs not allowed. **Facilities** Swimming pool, parking. **Nearby** Cantillana - Carmona - Alcalá de Guadaira - Sanlúcar la Mayor - Convento de San Isidoro del Campo in Santiponce and ruins of the Roman colony of Itálica - Romero de Rocio of Huelva - Semana Santa (Holy Week in Mar) and the April Fair (2 weeks after Holy Week); Golf e Hipodromo del Club Pineda golf course, (9-Hole). **Open** All year.

L os Seises is a "de luxe" hotel of very unique design in the heart of Sevilla. During the conversion of a 16th-century palace into a hotel, numerous ancient remnants were found and conserved in this neo-Art-Deco style with its very pure lines. Thus one comes across a Roman mosaic, an Arab well and 16th-century marble columns, among other discoveries. The bedrooms are very elegant with their beds harmonizing with the light-colored walls and terracotta tiled floors. Without useless knick-knacks, one easily feels at home, while certain rooms can be surprising–such as no. 219, traversed by an ancient stone arch that creates an astonishing contrast. The last surprise is the hotel roof which has been transformed into a large terrace with a view of the roofs of the town; it also has a swimming pool, an inestimable attraction in Sevilla. At weekends, the hotel offers very interesting rates.

How to get there *(Map 24): Near to the Giralda.*

Hotel Casa Imperial

41003 Sevilla
C/. Imperial, 29
Tel. 95-450 03 00 - Fax 95-450 03 30 - Sr Jochen Knie
Web: www.casaimperial.es

Category ★★★★★ Junior suites 24 and 14 suites with air-conditioning, kitchenette, telephone, bath, WC, satellite TV, minibar. **Price** Junior suite single 21,963-28,618Pts (S. Santa and Feria 6 days min. 46,089Pts); Junior suite double 24,126-30,781Pts (S. Santa and Feria 6 days min. 48,252Pts); Suite double 30,781-36,605Pts (S. Santa and Feria 6 days min. 59,067Pts); Suite triple 39,933 -47,420 Pts, 73,210 Pts. **Meals** Breakfast (buffet) included, served 8:00-11:30. **Restaurant** See pp. 304-305. **Credit cards** All major. **Pets** Dogs not allowed. **Nearby** Cantillana - Carmona - Alcalá de Guadaira - Sanlúcar la Mayor - Convento de San Isidoro del Campo in Santiponce and ruins of the Roman colony of Itálica - Romero de Rocio of Huelva - Semana Santa (Holy Week in Mar) and the April Fair (2 weeks after Holy Week); Golf e Hipodromo del Club Pineda golf course, (9-Hole). **Open** All year.

Located in the center of the city in a network of small Sevillian streets, the Casa Imperial offers a surprising decor for anyone dreaming of a surprising Andalusian decor. Here you find all the beauty and soul of an old house, the kind few tourists have the opportunity of seeing as most have remained private homes. Close to the famous Casa Pilatos, this *palacio*, formerly owned by Alfonso Villafranca and now the Casa Imperial, housed the administration. The house is built around three patios, a guarantee of cool breeze and sunlight. A maze of galleries and staircases leads to the rooms. Each one offers superb comfort while being different from the others: alcove beds, marble floors, *azulejos*, personalized bathrooms plus a terrace on the roof of some of them. The Moorish-style architecture is complex, allowing for the presence of different intimate lounges which add to the charms of the hotel's patios, columns, arcades and ponds. A magic atmosphere that comes with a high price tag.

How to get there *(Map 24): Near the Plaza Pilatos.*

Taberna del Alabardero

41001 Sevilla
Zaragozas, 20
Tel. 95-456 06 37 - Fax 95-456 36 66
M. Luis Lazama

Category ★★★★ **Rooms** 7 with air-conditioning, telephone, bath, WC, satellite TV, safe, minibar; elevator. **Price** Single 16,500Pts, double 19,800Pts. **Meals** Breakfast included, served 8:00-10:30. **Restaurant** Service 1:00PM-4:00PM, 9:00PM-12:00AM; à la carte 4,100-7,000Pts. Basque and Andalusian cooking. **Credit cards** All major. **Pets** Dogs not allowed. **Facilities** Garage (1,900Pts). **Nearby** Cantillana - Carmona - Alcalá de Guadaira - Sanlúcar la Mayor - Convento de San Isidoro del Campo in Santiponce and ruins of the Roman colony of Itálica - Romero de Rocio of Huelva - Semana Santa (Holy Week in Mar) and the April Fair (2 weeks after Holy Week); Golf e Hipodromo del Club Pineda golf course (9-Hole). **Closed** Aug.

R ight in the heart of the Andalusian capital, close to the famous Real Maestranza bullring and the Santa Cruz quarter, here is found the Taberna del Alabadero. This 19th-century house formerly belonged to the Spanish poet José Antoine Cavestany before becoming a well-known restaurant famed for its Basque-Andalusian cuisine. To add perfection to all this, a few bedrooms have been opened, all luxurious, very refined and very comfortable. Some look onto the typical Sevillian narrow streets, others onto the patio. As so often, everything radiates out from the large hallway on the ground floor, filled with the splashing sounds from the refreshing fountain and lit by a large glazed roof. This is the heart of the house and it is here that one can have a meal or a drink at the bar. A beautiful address.

How to get there (Map 24): In the Arenal district.

Hotel San Gil

41002 Sevilla
C/. Parras, 28
Tel. 95-490 68 11 - Fax 95-490 69 39
E-mail: hsangil@arrakis.es

Category ★★★ **Rooms** 39 with air-conditioning, telephone, bath, WC, TV, minibar. **Price** Single 12,500-15,000Pts, double-duplex 14,700-18,100Pts, suite (4 pers.) 21,300-25,400Pts. **Meals** Breakfast included, served 7:30-11:00. **Restaurant** See pp. 304-305. **Credit cards** All major. **Pets** Dogs not allowed. **Facilities** Swimming pool. **Nearby** Cantillana - Carmona - Alcalá de Guadaira - Sanlúcar la Mayor - Convento de San Isidoro del Campo in Santiponce and ruins of the Roman colony of Itálica - Romero de Rocio of Huelva - Semana Santa (Holy Week in Mar) and the April Fair (2 weeks after Holy Week); Golf e Hipodromo del Club Pineda golf course (9-Hole). **Open** All year.

The Hotel San Gil has only recently opened in the center of Sevilla in an old building with a loggia and balconies in wrought iron, and framed by two more recent wings that respect the traditional architecture. The entry, reception and elevator areas are abundantly decorated with a patchwork of colored ceramics in the Moorish style, and the lounges are in this older part of the building. The bedrooms are in the windowed building surrounding the interior garden with its inevitable fountain. Most are in duplex-style or apartments with well-equipped kitchens for a longer stay. One finds pastel colors with a mix of modern and older-style furniture, along with well-appointed bathrooms, and all ensure full comfort. The swimming pool on the roof is also a major attraction for those visiting southern Spain in the summer. This is definitely "algo mas que un hotel" ("more than just a hotel"), as the brochure tells us.

How to get there *(Map 24): Near the Arco de Macapena.*

Hotel Ciudad de Sevilla

41013 Sevilla
Avenida Manuel Siurot, 25
Tel. 95-423 05 05 - Fax 95-423 85 39

Category ★★★★ Rooms 94 with air-conditioning, telephone, bath, WC, satellite TV, pay-TV, video games, minibar, safe; elevator. **Price** Double 15,700-35,000Pts, duplex 40,000-55,000Pts. **Meals** Breakfast 1,600Pts, served 7:00-11:00. **Restaurant** Service 1:30PM-3:30PM, 8:30PM-11:30PM; à la carte 4,500-5,000Pts. Basque and Andalusian cooking. **Credit cards** All major. **Pets** Dogs not allowed. **Facilities** Swimming pool, garage (1,600Pts). **Nearby** Cantillana - Carmona - Alcalá de Guadaira - Sanlúcar la Mayor - Convento de San Isidoro del Campo in Santiponce and ruins of the Roman colony of Itálica - El Rocio of Huelva - Semana Santa (Holy Week in Mar) and the April Fair (2 weeks after Holy Week) - Golf e Hipodromo del Club Pineda golf course (9-Hole). **Open** All year.

This hotel, built for the Exposition of 1927, is in a comfortable residential district, close to the Plaza de España ruins of the Roman colony of Itálica - El Rocio de Huelva - Holy Week and the April Fair; Golf e Hipodromo del Club Pineda golf course. It features columns and coats of arms along with works in varnished terracotta and even an exquisite little bell tower at the far end of the building. The interior is truly contemporary, even if the patio is surrounded with ungainly gangways leading to the rooms which are spacious and furnished with attractive modern furniture and stunning modern paintings reminiscent of the finest works of Tapiés. Our first choice would be the duplex with its own living room. From the roof, you look down on the swimming pool and the luxurious greenery on the Avenida de la Palmera.

How to get there (Map 24): Near the María Luisa Park.

Patios de la Cartuja

41002 Sevilla
Lumbrera, 8-10
Tel. 95-490 02 00- Fax 95-490 20 56
Sra Myriam Ortiz

Apartments 34 with air-conditioning, kitchen, 1 bedroom, 1 lounge, telephone, bath, WC, satellite TV, safe. **Price** Single 7,700-8,800Pts (S. Santa and Feria 16,500Pts), double 9,700-11,000Pts (S. Santa and Feria 21,000Pts); extra bed for children under 4 +2,500Pts. **Meals** Breakfast 700Pts, served 8:00-11:00. **Restaurant** See pp. 304-305. **Credit cards** All major. **Pets** Dogs not allowed. **Facilities** Garage (1,200Pts). **Nearby** Cantillana - Carmona - Alcalá de Guadaira - Sanlúcar la Mayor - Convento de San Isidoro del Campo in Santiponce and ruins of the Roman colony of Itálica - El Rocio of Huelva - Semana Santa (Holy Week in Mar) and the April Fair (2 weeks after Holy Week) - Golf e Hipodromo del Club Pineda golf course (9-Hole). **Open** All year

Two residential hotels, under the joint name of Patios de Sevilla, have opened here in the center of Sevilla with an excellent quality/price ratio. The apartments are for two people and include a well-equipped kitchen, a bedroom, a bathroom and a lounge with a fold-up bed making it possible to accommodate three or even four. Both hotels are virtually identical in their furnishings but we prefer the Patio de la Cartuja for its charm as it is a long building with balconies decked with hundreds of small geranium pots surrounding a superb patio. The apartments are in a somewhat standardized Sevillian style but the atmosphere is a very comfortable one and the service very efficient. This is an especially good choice for a stay in Sevilla at the best possible price as lodging in this city is particularly expensive.

How to get there *(Map 24): Via the Plaza Duque de la Victoria and Calle Jésus del Grand Poder.*

Patios de Alameda

41002 Sevilla
Alameda de Hércules, 56
Tel. 95-490 49 99- Fax 95-490 02 26
Sra Myriam Ortiz

Apartments 22 with air-conditioning, kitchen, 1 bedroom, 1 lounge, telephone, bath, WC, satellite TV, safe. **Price** Single 7,700-8,800Pts (S. Santa and Feria 16,500Pts), double 9,700-11,000Pts (S. Santa and Feria 21,000Pts); extra bed for children under 4 +2,500Pts. **Meals** Breakfast 700Pts, served 8:00-11:00. **Restaurant** See pp. 304-305. **Credit cards** All major. **Pets** Dogs not allowed. **Facilities** Garage (1,200Pts). **Nearby** Cantillana - Carmona - Alcalá de Guadaira - Sanlúcar la Mayor - Convento of San Isidoro del Campo in Santiponce and ruins d'Itálica - El Rocio de Huelva - Semana Santa (Holy Week in Mar) and the April Fair (2 weeks after Holy Week) - Golf e Hipodromo del Club Pineda (9-Hole). **Open** All year.

Under the same management and with the same concept is the Patio de Alameda, located on a large square frequented by people of the neighborhood because of the numerous small bars and restaurants nearby. Here again are apartments with well-equipped kitchens that can accommodate up to four people, even if this causes slightly crowded conditions. The cleaning is done daily and the reception desk is open 24 hours. We expect the Patio de Alameda to attract an increasing number of faithful clients. The higher prices indicated are those applied during Holy Week and the April Feria.

How to get there *(Map 24): Via the Plaza Duque de la Victoria and Calle Jésus del Grand Poder.*

Hotel Doña Maria

41004 Sevilla
Don Remondo, 19
Tel. 95-422 49 90 - Fax 95-421 95 46
Sr Rodriguez Andrade

Category ★★★★ **Rooms** 61 with air-conditioning, telephone, bath, WC, TV, safe, 20 with minibar; elevator. **Price** Single 11,000-19,000Pts (S. Santa and Feria 21,000Pts), double 15,000-28,600Pts (S. Santa and Feria 29,000Pts), triple 26,100-36,400Pts (S. Santa and Feria 40,000Pts). **Meals** Breakfast (buffet) 1,500Pts, served 8:00-11:00. **Restaurant** See pp. 304-305. **Credit cards** All major. **Pets** Dogs not allowed. **Facilities** Swimming pool on the roof, parking. **Nearby** Cantillana - Carmona - Alcalá de Guadaira - Sanlúcar la Mayor - Convento de San Isidoro del Campo in Santiponce and ruins of the Roman colony of Itálica - Romero de Rocio of Huelva - Semana Santa (Holy Week in Mar) and the April Fair (2 weeks after Holy Week) - Golf e Hipodromo del Club Pineda golf course (9-Hole). **Open** All year.

In the heart of the city, the Hotel Doña Maria is newly constructed. Nonetheless, the arcades of the interior architecture, the wrought iron work, the old furniture and the ravishing patio with its exuberant and exotic plants all give it a very Andalusian character. The bedrooms are all personalized and beautiful, but Room 310, all white with lace and a canopied bed, gets our top vote; it also has a balcony opening onto the square, the orange trees and the cathedral. However, the supreme luxury of this hotel is the swimming pool on the roof with the tower of the Giralda rising beside it just a few meters away. This is a major asset in the summer. A classic hotel in Sevilla which, although generally full, seems to be living on past laurels which may explain the lackadaisical attitude found at the reception desk.

How to get there *(Map 24): Next to the cathedral, facing the Giralda.*

Hotel Casas del Rey de Baeza

41004 Sevilla
Plaza Cristo de la Redención, 2
Tel. 95-456 14 96 - Fax 95-456 14 41 - José Alfonso Martinez
Web: www.ibernet.net/lascasas

Category ★★★★ **Rooms** 44 with air-conditioning, telephone, bath, satellite TV, minibar, safe; elevator.
Price Single 13,600-16,000Pts (S. Santa and Feria 25,600Pts), double 17,000-20,000Pts (S. Santa and
Feria 32,000Pts), double with lounge 19,500-23,000Pts (S. Santa and Feria 37,000Pts). **Meals** Breakfast
(buffet) 1,700Pts, served 7:30-11:30. **Restaurant** See pp. 304-305. **Credit cards** All major. **Pets** Dogs
not allowed. **Facilities** Swimming pool. **Nearby** Cantillana - Carmona - Alcalá de Guadaira - Sanlúcar
la Mayor - Convento de San Isidoro del Campo in Santiponce and ruins of the Roman colony of Itálica -
Romero de Rocio of Huelva - Semana Santa (Holy Week in Mar) and the April Fair (2 weeks after Holy
Week); Golf e Hipodromo del Club Pineda golf course (9-Hole). **Open** All year.

After Las Casas de la Judería, this new hotel rates highest among those
recently opened here in Sevilla. Built around a small square and very
centrally located in a charming neighborhood that sees relatively few tourists, it
is a traditional house with a white exterior, yellow trim and blue woodwork. The
bar is adjacent to the reception area and runs the length of a patio with banana
trees. The decoration is contemporary with a slate floor, columns made of natural
stone and resolutely up-to-date furniture, all signs of true refinement. Access to
the rooms is through the galleries that go around two patios. Its charm is ever
present in the ceilings and the deep blue railings, the wealth of potted plants, the
floors made with small pebbles and the attractive wicker baskets overflowing
with oranges. The rooms, while principally concerned with comfort and technical
proficiency, enjoy the same care, particularly the very elegant bathrooms. We
prefer those having a lounge and those with a view of the square. The outstanding
attribute of this fine address is its rooftop pool overlooking a sea of ochre tiles.

How to get there (*Map 24*): *In the historic center of the city.*

55

Hotel Casas de los Mercaderes

41004 Sevilla
Calle Alvarez Quintero, 9-13
Tel. 95-422 58 58 - Fax 95-422 98 84
Web: www.ibernet.net/lascasas

Category ★★★ **Rooms** 47 with air-conditioning, telephone, bath, satellite TV, minibar; elevator. **Prix** Single 10,000-12,000Pts (S. Santa and Feria 19,500Pts), double 14,500-17,500Pts (S. Santa and Feria 28,500Pts); extra bed +3,000-6,000Pts. **Meals** Breakfast (buffet) 1,500Pts, served 7:30-11:30. **Restaurant** See pp. 304-305. **Credit cards** All major. **Pets** Dogs not allowed. **Nearby** Cantillana - Carmona - Alcalá de Guadaira - Sanlúcar la Mayor - Convento de San Isidoro del Campo in Santiponce and ruins of the Roman colony of Itálica - Romero de Rocio of Huelva - Semana Santa (Holy Week in Mar) and the April Fair (2 weeks after Holy Week) - Golf e Hipodromo del Club Pineda golf course (9-Hole). **Open** All year.

Belonging to the Casas family, here is another good address in Sevilla, nicely located amid the shopping arteries of the city and close to the *Ayuntamiento* - the City Hall. The building makes extensive use of red brick and has a luxurious interior. The lobby is immense and very elegant with a marble floor, wicker furniture and large Persian rugs. Beyond the reception area is a covered patio with a superb colonnade plus arches painted in white and burgundy. The rooms are more classic in appearance, decorated in distinctly "international hotel" style. Still, the fabrics are well-chosen and the thick carpets create a warm and subtle atmosphere. Your choice, naturally, should be among those on the street, avoiding those on the patio.

How to get there *(Map 24): In the historic center of the city near the Ayuntamiento.*

Hotel Casas de la Judería

41004 Sevilla
Callejon de dos Hermanas, 7
Tel. 95-441 51 50 - Fax 95-442 21 70

Category ★★★ **Apartments** 57 with air-conditioning, telephone, kitchen, bath, WC, minibar. **Price** Single 10,500-14,400Pts (S. Santa and Feria 21,000-24,000Pts), double 15,000-21,000Pts (S. Santa and Feria 30,000-34,000Pts), suite 25,000-29,000Pts (S. Santa and Feria 45,000Pts). **Meals** Breakfast (buffet) 1,200Pts, served 7:30-11:30. **Restaurant** See pp. 304-305. **Credit cards** All major. **Pets** Dogs not allowed. **Facilities** Garage (500-1,000Pts). **Nearby** Cantillana - Carmona - Alcalá de Guadaira - Sanlúcar la Mayor - Convento de San Isidoro del Campo in Santiponce and ruins of the Roman colony of Itálica - Romero de Rocio of Huelva - Semana Santa (Holy Week in Mar) and the April Fair (2 weeks after Holy Week) - Golf e Hipodromo del Club Pineda golf course (9-Hole). **Open** All year.

In the real heart of historic Sevilla, Las Casas de la Judería is a very old private hotel transformed into suites of one, two or three rooms. Long stays are possible here as most suites have a kitchen. The architecture of the place is really exceptional, with numerous flowered patios made pleasant by fountains and offering peace and quiet in the shade of the arcades. The quality refurbishing of this house does not stop at the exterior and a real effort has been made to decorate the rooms (all different) with old furniture or quality reproductions. Finally, you can go up on the terraces with their view over the city roofs. The personnel are friendly and this is a stopping place of real charm.

How to get there (Map 24): In the historic center of the town.

La Rábida

41001 Sevilla
Castelar, 24
Tel. 95-422 09 60 - Fax 95-422 43 75

Category ★★ **Rooms** 100 with air-conditioning, telephone, bath or shower, WC, satellite TV; elevator. **Price** Single 6,100Pts, double 9,300Pts. **Meals** Breakfast 600Pts, served 8:00-10:30. **Restaurant** Service 1:00PM-3:00PM, 8:00PM-10:00PM; mealtime specials 1,950Pts. **Credit cards** All major. **Pets** Dogs not allowed. **Nearby** Cantillana - Carmona - Alcalá de Guadaira - Sanlúcar la Mayor - Convento de San Isidoro del Campo in Santiponce and ruins of the Roman colony of Itálica - Romero de Rocio of Huelva - Semana Santa (Holy Week in Mar) and the April Fair (2 weeks after Holy Week) - Golf e Hipodromo del Club Pineda golf course (9-Hole). **Open** All year.

Even though it is in the historic center of Sevilla and close to the cathedral, La Rábida is a comfortable hotel; the reception is pleasant, the rooms are well-furnished, and the service is efficient. Apart from the historical and artistic interest of the city itself, the capital of Andalusia, Sevilla organizes each year two major events, Holy Week and "La Feria", which attract a large number of tourists from around the world. This is why it is so difficult to find lodgings and we can only recommend that reservations be made as early as possible.

How to get there (Map 24): In the city center.

Hotel Residencia Sevilla

41003 Sevilla
Calle Daóiz, 5
Tel. 95-438 41 61 - Fax 95-490 21 60
M. José Arenas

Category ★★ **Rooms** 38 with air-conditioning, telephone, bath or shower, WC; elevator. **Price** Single 4,500-7,500Pts, double 6,500-10,500Pts. **Meals** No breakfast. **Restaurant** See pp. 304-305. **Credit cards** Amex, Visa, Eurocard, MasterCard. **Pets** Dogs allowed. **Facilities** Parking (1,300Pts). **Nearby** Cantillana - Carmona - Alcalá de Guadaira - Sanlúcar la Mayor - Convento de San Isidoro del Campo in Santiponce and ruins of the Roman colony of Itálica - Romero de Rocio of Huelva - Semana Santa (Holy Week in Mar) and the April Fair (2 weeks after Holy Week) - Golf e Hipodromo del Club Pineda golf course (9-Hole). **Open** All year.

This is a small and unpretentious hotel, a very precious stop-off in Sevilla. The hotel is on a charming and very quiet square scented by the orange trees lining it. The hotel offers a pretty flowered patio and simple but comfortable rooms, plus a handy central location. No breakfast is served but the attractive bar opposite fills the bill very nicely.

How to get there (Map 24): In the city center via Sierpes Street.

Hotel Oromana

41500 Alcalá de Guadaira (Sevilla)
Avenida de Portugal
Tel. 95-568 64 00 - Fax 95-568 64 00

Category ★★★ **Rooms** 30 with air-conditioning, telephone, bath, WC, TV; elevator; wheelchair access. **Price** Single 7,700-15,000Pts, double 10,200-15,000Pts. **Meals** Breakfast included, served 8:00-11:00. **Restaurant** Service 1:30PM-3:30PM, 8:00PM-11:00PM; à la carte 2,000-3,000Pts. Specialties: Croquelos de Ave - Arroz caldoso con Gambas. **Credit cards** All major. **Pets** Dogs not allowed. **Facilities** Swimming pool, parking. **Nearby** Gandul - Sevilla - Carmona - Sanlúcar la Mayor - Golf e Hipodromo del Club Pineda golf course (9-Hole). **Open** All year.

After a long period of exclusively feminine management, the Hotel Oromana has changed in all respects. Located fourteen kilometers outside of Sevilla, this hotel is well-suited to those looking for peace and quiet along with cool, fresh evening air. The hotel is in a wooded park not far from the Guadaira River which is lined by old Arab mills; a authentic example of Andalusian architecture, it is immediately inviting. Inside, its intimate decor gives an air of a family home, and all the rooms offer comfort and view of countryside. The restaurant currently serves good local dishes which, in addition to the ease of parking, will probably make you prize this hotel.

How to get there *(Map 24): 14km southeast of Sevilla via N334; in the pine woods of Oromana.*

Hotel Hacienda San Ygnacio

41950 Castilleja de la Cuesta (Sevilla)
Calle Real, 190
Tel. 95-416 40 80 - Fax 95-416 14 37
E-mail: sygnacio@arrakis.es - Web: www.arrakis.es/~sygnacio/index.htm

Category ★★★★ **Rooms** 16 with air-conditioning, telephone, bath, WC, satellite TV, minibar. **Price** Single 7,000-14,000Pts, double 10,000-19,000Pts, suite 45,000-65,000Pts. **Meals** Breakfast 1,100Pts, served 8:00-10:00. **Restaurant** Almazara, service 2:00PM-3:30PM, 9:00PM-11:00PM; closed Sun evening and Mon; à la carte 2,500-3,000Pts. **Credit cards** All major. **Pets** Dogs not allowed. **Facilities** Swimming pool, parking. **Nearby** Gandul - Sevilla - Carmona - Sanlúcar la Mayor - Golf e Hipodromo del Club Pineda golf course (9-Hole). **Open** All year.

Only 6 kilometers from Sevilla, this is a good bet for those bold enough to visit southern Spain in summertime. They will find peace and quiet here and can pass the hottest hours of the day beside the swimming pool before setting off on an excursion. The hotel is a former "hacienda" that has retained its architecture intact - a variety of buildings with a mixture of roofs, chimneys, terraces, bell-towers, all enclosing a large central courtyard planted with four superb palm trees. The large dining room of the "Almazara", in the former mill of the "hacienda" gives straight onto this beautiful patio. There are not many rooms and they are sober, decorated with wrought iron beds and rustic furniture, but all are spacious and comfortable. The swimming pool is in a corner of the garden, surrounded by palm and orange trees.

How to get there (Map 24): 6km northwest of Sevilla via A49, towards Huelva, exit 3.

Cortijo El Esparragal

41860 Gerena (Sevilla)
C/. de Merida, km 795
Tel. 95-578 27 02 - Fax 95-578 27 83 - Sr Enrique Soto

Rooms 12 and 6 suites with air-conditioning, telephone, bath, WC, satellite TV. **Price** Single 13,000-20,000Pts, double 16,000-20,000Pts, suite 18,000-23,000Pts; extra bed +5000Pts. **Meals** Breakfast included, served 7:30-11:30. **Restaurant** Service 1:30PM-3:00PM, 8:30PM-10:00PM; mealtime specials 3,000Pts. **Credit cards** All major. **Pets** Dogs not allowed. **Facilities** Swimming pool, parking. **Nearby** Sevilla - Cantillana - Carmona - Alcalá de Guadaira - Sanlúcar la Mayor - Convento de San Isidoro del Campo in Santiponce and ruins of the Roman colony of Itálica. **Open** All year.

The Cortijo is one of the properties belonging to important land owners and have been transformed into hotels of luxury and charm. El Esparragal is a genuine oasis with a lawn garden with trees and flowers. The building, formerly a convent of the Order of the Jeronimos, is magnificent with a beautiful white facade featuring ornamental pediments and pinnacle turrets, all covered in bougainvillae. Beyond the reception area is a patio with plentiful greenery, an excellent place for breakfast or a drink. The rooms are for the most part spacious with very high ceilings and thick walls. The dark wooden furniture is 19th century, giving the convent-style architecture a note of noble austerity. The decoration and furnishings provide a very livable quality. While all the rooms are attractive, our preference is for those on the second floor overlooking the garden. The 3,000 hectares of this property offer numerous walking tours, but in the summer, the good life is at poolside under the palm trees.

How to get there *(Map 24): 21km north of Sevilla on SE 30 towards Merida until km 795 where you turn left for Gerena. The hotel is a kilometer and a half from this turn-off, before entering Gerena.*

62

El Morrito ^{TR}

41860 Gerena (Sevilla)
C/. Gerena-El Garrobo, km 5,500 - Francisco De Jodar
Tel. 908-75 93 68 - 95-46 36 198 - Mobile 610 56 30 27 - Fax 95-578 28 24

Rooms 8 with bath. **Price** Double 12,800Pts. **Meals** Breakfast included, served 7:30-10:45. **Evening meals** By reservation. **Credit cards** Visa, Eurocard, MasterCard. **Pets** Dogs not allowed. **Facilities** Swimming pool, parking. **Nearby** Sevilla - Cantillana - Carmona - Alcalá de Guadaira - Sanlúcar la Mayor - Convento de San Isidoro del Campo in Santiponce and ruins of the Roman colony of Itálica. **Open** All year.

From Gerena, one takes a lovely route passing through groves of cork trees, then a dirt road leading to El Morrito. Were it not for the large swimming pool featuring waterfalls visible at the entrance to the property, the impression of suddenly being in the 19th century is inescapable. Beyond the large gate is a huge coach house with a collection of old carriages and stalls just opposite them for the horses belonging to the owner. And beyond this paved courtyard is another in clay with palm trees and bougainvillae leading up to the house. The interior is astonishing, alive with memories and souvenirs of preceding generations. Its ownership by the same family, which included the Archbishop of Pamplona, accounts for the familial respect so prominent in the decoration; this may be seen in the numerous religious paintings and the naming of the rooms after saints: Omnium Santorum, Santa Rosalia, Santa Isabel, all very attractive with blue and white bedspreads plainly evoking Heaven. Among them, Santa Clara is the most enjoyable. Praise is also due the dining room, watched over by a large portrait of the *abuela* - grandmother - steadfastly surveying her furniture and family possessions. The patio, the garden and the swimming pool all make for a very pleasant stay close to Sevilla and lets one feel the ambiance of a certain highly religious bourgeoisie that once existed in Spain.

How to get there *(Map 24): 21km from Sevilla on the "El Garrobo" route. After 5.5km, turn right on the small road that is discreetly indicated.*

Cortijo Torre de la Reina

41209 Torre de la Reina (Sevilla)
C/. Paseo de la Alameda
Tel. 95-578 01 36 - Fax 95-578 01 22 - Sra Paz Medina

Rooms 6 and 6 suites with air-conditioning, telephone, bath, WC, satellite TV, minibar. **Price** Single 13,000-17,000Pts, double 15,000-19,000Pts, suite 19,000-24,000Pts. **Meals** Breakfast 1,200Pts, served 8:00-10:30; half board +4,200Pts, full board +7,000Pts (per pers.). **Restaurant** Service 1:30PM-3:00PM, 8:30PM-10:00PM; mealtime specials 3,200Pts. **Credit cards** All major. **Pets** Small dogs allowed on request. **Facilities** Swimming pool, parking. **Nearby** Sevilla - Cantillana - Carmona - Alcalá de Guadaira - Sanlúcar la Mayor - Convento de San Isidoro del Campo in Santiponce and ruins of the Roman colony of Itálica - Romero de Rocio of Huelva - Semana Santa (Holy Week in Mar) and the April Fair (2 weeks after Holy Week); Golf e Hipodromo del Club Pineda golf course (9-Hole), Real Club golf course. **Open** All year.

A scant fifteen kilometers from Sevilla, this superb and historic property was occupied successively during the 13th and 14th centuries by King Fernando III during the conquest of Sevilla, and later by Queen Doña Maria de Molina. Its conservation and restoration have earned it the classification of a National Monument. Today, it receives essentially wealthy guests. Its gorgeous garden surrounds a series of buildings connected by arcades and patios, all bearing the marks of both Arab and Andalousian architecture. The interior is intimate and luxurious, creating an atmosphere reminiscent of a private home, one having changed very little over the years; there are rugs, furniture and old paintings as well as books and photographs, all seeming part of a carefully-kept personal collection. The rooms are very comfortable, matching the high standard of their decoration. It should be noted, however, that noisy events in the reception room may disturb other guests.

How to get there *(Map 24): 12km north Sevilla via SE30 towards Merida. Junction for La Algaba and Torre de la Reina.*

Trasierra

41370 Cazalla de la Sierra (Sevilla)
Tel. 954-88 43 24 - Fax 954-88 33 05
Sra Charlotte Scott

Rooms 6 with bath, lounge. **Price** Double 15,000Pts (per pers.). **Meals** Breakfast included, served at any time. **Evening meals** By reservation. Service 1:00PM-4:00PM, 8:30PM-10:00PM; mealtime specials 4,000Pts. Regional cooking. **Credit cards** Visa, Eurocard, MasterCard. **Pets** Dogs not allowed. **Facilities** Swimming pool, tennis, riding, painting lessons, parking. **Nearby** Sevilla - Córdoba. **Open** All year on request.

Residential hotels are not very common in Spain and the rare examples we have found are always homes opened by foreigners in love with this country. This is the case with Charlotte and Nick Scott who have restored a large olive oil mill and its surrounding buildings in the Sierra Morena, about one hundred kilometers from Sevilla. This was a sizeable job and needed all the passion of the owners and skills of the local workers to restore the spirit of the property. The bedrooms are vast and sober, decorated with travel souvenirs or traditional articles from the neighboring village which are also sold in the hotel's small boutique. The wild environment of the Sierra Morena is superb and your very welcoming hosts will be your best guides.

***How to get there** (Map 18): 100km north of Sevilla.*

La Cartuja de Cazalla

41370 Cazalla de la Sierra (Sevilla)
A-455, km 3
Tel. 95-488 45 16 - Fax 95-488 47 07
E-mail: cartujsv@teleline.es - Web: www.skill.es/cartuja

Rooms 12 with bath. **Price** Single 8,000Pts, double 12,000Pts, double with lounge 16,000Pts.
Restaurant Mealtime specials 3,500Pts. **Credit cards** Visa, Eurocard, MasterCard. **Pets** Dogs
allowed. **Facilities** Swimming pool, riding (3,000Pts/hour), parking. **Nearby** Constantina - Sevilla
- Natural Park. **Open** All year.

Cazalla de la Sierra is known not only for its Stone Age relics and the restoration of a statue of Marcus Aurelius but also for its outstanding anisette and eau de vie. Here, you can visit several lovely churches in *mudéjar* style and the romantic ruins of the old charter house. Carmen Ladrón de Guevara bought them all with an eye to restoring them. So far, work on several buildings has been completed and some offer rooms and small apartments, others have large exhibition halls for artists who come here seeking the calm necessary for their work. Let's wish her the best of luck on her courageous undertaking as the village is a particularly friendly one.

How to get there *(Map 24): 85km north of Sevilla, C431 to Cantillana, Pedroso and Cazalla.*

Casa de Carmona

41410 Carmona (Sevilla)
Plaza de lasso
Tel. 95-419 10 00 - Fax 95-419 01 89 - Sr Michel Miller

Category ★★★★★ **Rooms** 30 with air-conditioning, telephone, bath, WC, satellite TV, safe, minibar; elevator. **Price** Double 25,000Pts, special double 29,000Pts. **Meals** Breakfast 1,500Pts, served 8:30-11:00; half board +4,000Pts, full board +8,000Pts (per pers.). **Restaurant** Service 12:30PM-4:00PM, 8:30PM-12:00AM; mealtime specials 4,000Pts, also à la carte. Regional and international cooking. **Credit cards** All major. **Pets** Dogs allowed. **Facilities** Swimming pool, fitness club, sauna, parking. **Nearby** Church of Santa Maria, Roman Necropolis (Elephant Vault, Servilia Tomb...), in Carmona - Fuentes de Andalucia - Sevilla - Córdoba - Granada - Golf course in Sevilla. **Open** All year.

Just a few kilometers from Sevilla, the ancient Andalusian city of Carmona shelters one of the most luxurious hotels of charm in Spain. Opened in 1991, the Casa de Carmona is a former palace furnished with a luxury of refinements. The public rooms are remarkable: the admirable patio with its flowery pot plants gives a tone to the entrance, and two lounge-conference rooms decorated with portraits of aristocrats and ancient finery all give you the impression of being received by some Spanish grandee. The small swimming pool is ravishing and allows you to freshen up in the shade of the marble columns. All the rooms are different and each has its own personality thanks to a subtle mix of old furniture and coordinated pastel shades and fabrics. We recommend no. 6 for its admirable ceiling of Andalusian woodwork, but also Rooms 14 and 18 for their views over the town. With the new management, the maintenance of the hotel should be better.

How to get there (Map 24): 33km east of Sevilla via N4, towards Córdoba.

Hotel Cortijo Aguila Real

41210 Guillena (Sevilla)
Tel. 95-578 50 06 - Fax 95-578 43 30 - Sra Martinez
E-mail: hotel@aguilareal.com - Web: www.aguilareal.com

Category ★★★★ **Rooms** 11 and 3 suites with air-conditioning, telephone, bath, WC, satellite TV. **Price** Double 16,500-19,000Pts, junior suite 25,000-27,000Pts. **Meals** Breakfast (buffet) 1,500Pts, served 8:00-11:00; half board +4,500Pts, full board +7,000Pts (per pers.). **Restaurant** Service 1:15PM-4:00PM, 8:00PM-11:30PM; mealtime specials 3,500Pts, also à la carte. Specialties: game. **Credit cards** All major. **Pets** Dogs not allowed. **Facilities** Swimming pool, parking. **Nearby** Sevilla - Satiponce - Itálica - Alcalá del Rio - Cantillana - Carmona. **Open** All year.

At some twenty kilometers from Seville, you arrive at Cortijo Aguila Real via a road lined with wheat fields, sunflowers and arid land. Little by little, much like an oasis in the desert, the Cortijo appears on the summit of a distant hill. It was formerly a farm and the buildings surrounding the large courtyard have been arranged to give welcome independence to visitors. The rooms are spacious and have regional furniture; three have open fireplaces. All are perfectly comfortable and impeccably maintained. Meals may be had either in the dining room, on the terrace or in the shade of the pine trees beside the swimming pool which offers a splendid view of the plain with Sevilla in the distance. The menus allow you to choose anything that strikes your fancy; game along with fresh and natural produce are the basics here. The hotel organizes bullfighting demonstrations in the ring on the property as well as horse-back trips and tourists visits. Peace and quiet plus a warm welcome make this hotel an admirable address. There is a two-night minimum for reservations at the height of the season.

How to get there *(Map 24): 20km north of Sevilla via E803, to Merida; at Guillena (after the Itálica ruins, take the road to the right between two gas stations), then to Burguillos.*

Hacienda Benazuza

41800 Sanlúcar La Mayor (Sevilla)
Tel. 955-70 33 44 - Fax 955-70 34 10
E-mail: hbenazuza@arrakis.es - Web: www.hbenazuza.com

Category ★★★★ GL **Rooms** 44 suites with air-conditioning, telephone, bath, WC, satellite TV, safe, minibar. **Price** Single 31,000-47,000Pts, double 39,000-57,000Pts, suite 52,000-170,000Pts. **Meals** Breakfast 1,500-2,500Pts, served 7:00-12:00. **Restaurant** La Alqueira, service 1:00PM-4:00PM, 8:30PM-11:30PM; à la carte 8,500Pts, La Alberca (swimming pool), service 12:00PM-6:00PM; à la carte 6,000Pts. Specialties: Gazpacho de Bogavante perfumado a la albahaca - Ensalada de almejas casi crudas en vinegreta al aceite de oliva virgen - Hachi parmentier de gallo de Lendines con foie gras y trufa. **Credit cards** All major. **Pets** Dogs allowed. **Facilities** Swimming pool, tennis, paddle tennis, putting green, parking. **Nearby** Sevilla - Cantillana - Carmona - Alcalá de Guadaira. **Closed** Aug.

Hacienda Benazuza is a large hotel of charm in the Aljarafe (highlands) of Sevilla. Arabo-Andalusian in style, it is a collection of buildings assembled in the course of centuries. The surrounding wall reminds one of its Saracen origins in the 10th century, while the tower above the entry gate carries the coat of arms granted to the Counts of Benazuza in the 16th century. Careful work in the archives has given its original splendor back to the Hacienda. The walls have regained their ocre, red, yellow and orange colors, the lounges their *mudéjar* ceilings and terracotta floors and enameled tiles. The rooms and their bathrooms are superb even though one would have preferred that they retain their Hispano-Moorish style. In the restaurants one discovers both Mediterranean and Oriental flavors. The small Hacienda chapel plays an active part in Holy Week and the "Rocio de Sanlúcar La Mayor"; you will be well-placed to enjoy these events, some of the most important in Andalusian culture.

How to get there *(Map 24): 33km west of Sevilla via N431, towards Huelva.*

Parador La Concordia

44600 Alcañiz (Teruel)
Castillo de los Calatravos
Tel. 978-83 04 00 - Fax 978-83 03 66
Sr Cruz Sanchez

Category ★★★ **Rooms** 12 with air-conditioning, telephone, shower, WC, TV, minibar; elevator. **Price** Double 15,000-17,500Pts. **Meals** Breakfast 1,300Pts, served 8:30-11:00. **Restaurant** Service 1:30PM-4:00PM, 8:30PM-11:00PM; mealtime specials 3,500Pts, also à la carte. Specialties: Ternasco asado - Costilletas a la baturra - Dulces tipicos. **Credit cards** All major. **Pets** Dogs not allowed. **Nearby** Calaceite (Plaza Mayor) - Gretas - Valderrobres - Monastery of Rueda in Escatrón - Morella. **Open** Feb 2 - Dec 17.

At the summit of a hill dominating Alcañiz, the present chateau dates mainly from the 18th century and was converted into a parador in 1968. Today it is the ideal setting for a romantic stay and everything helps make this hotel such a charming place. The decor is sober but in good taste: white walls, Spanish furniture and polished floors. The rooms on the courtyard are rather small and a bit sober while those looking over the town and the River Guadalupe are much lighter. The bathrooms are spacious and attractive. The menu offers specialties of Aragonese cuisine, and certainly do not leave without trying the Almendrades (confectionery of almond paste), a specialty of Alcañiz.

***How to get there** (Map 15): 103km southeast of Zaragoza via N232.*

Torre del Visco

44587 Fuentespalda (Teruel)
Apartado 15
Tel. 978-76 90 15 - Fax 978-76 90 16 - Piers Dutton
Jemma Markham

Rooms 11 and 3 suites with bath, WC. **Price** Double with half bard for 2 pers. 26,000-32,000Pts; suite 40,000Pts. **Meals** Breakfast included, served at any time. **Restaurant** Only for residents by reservation. Service 1:30PM-4:00PM, 8:30PM-10:30PM – Mealtime specials of the day. **Credit cards** Visa, Eurocard, MasterCard. **Pets** Dogs not allowed. **Nearby** Alcañiz - Calaceite. **Closed** 2 weeks in Jan.

Lost in the countryside south of Alcañiz with the nearest town twelve kilometers away, Torre del Visco is a genuine godsend for those who want to enjoy nature in a refined atmosphere. Piers and Jemma have shown excellent taste and care in transforming these magnificent local stone buildings, some dating from the 15th through the 18th centuries, into a small deluxe hotel. Indeed, graffiti said to have been carved by sorcerers are still visible on some of the oldest walls. The ground-floor lounges are decorated in elegant pastel shades evoking a refreshing Anglo-Saxon atmosphere and yet avoiding the trap of "cottage style". The rooms are all very comfortable and livable thanks to their artful decoration. The suite, located in the tower, is quite simply extraordinary. The half-board plan is obligatory but one can hardly complain as the cooking is excellent and the setting enchanting. This is a very good address in the Sierra de Teruel, a region well worth visiting for its refreshing walking trips.

How to get there *(Map 15): 38km southeast of Alcañiz; 12km south of Valderrobres towards Fuentespalda via the forest route for 5km.*

Hotel Ciria

22440 Benasque (Huesca)
Avenida Los Tilos
Tel. 974-55 16 12 - Fax 974-55 16 86
Sr Jose Maria Ciria Plana

Category ★★★ **Rooms** 40 with telephone, bath, WC, satellite TV, 6 with minibar; elevator. **Price** Single 4,700-6,200Pts, double 7,500-10,500Pts, duplex with lounge 13,000-16,000Pts, suite with jacuzzi 18,500-21,500Pts. **Meals** Breakfast: 1,000Pts, served 8:30-10:30. **Restaurant** El Fogaril, service 1:00PM-4:00PM, 8:30PM-11:00PM; mealtime specials 2,000Pts, also à la carte. **Credit cards** Visa, Eurocard, MasterCard. **Pets** Small dogs allowed. **Nearby** The Pyrenees Route via C136 - Ordesa National Park. **Open** All year

The Aragon Pyrenees form a natural frontier between Spain and France, and on the Spanish side, the mountains are admirably suited for small ski resorts such as Benasque. Its charm lies especially in the beauty of its natural surroundings. The village, recognizing this, has built a number of small chalet-style buildings which in no way spoil its small streets where, starting in spring, they shed their white snowy mantle for luxurious greenery. On the street where the Hotel Ciria is located, the return of blossoms on the lime trees is a sure sign of the changing season. The restaurant, El Fogaril, is on the ground floor with slightly formal rustic decoration but is an excellent place to taste the specialties of Aragon and dishes prepared over a charcoal fire. The rooms overlook the street or the mountain. The Ciria family pay special attention to the decor which is at once comfortable and cozy. The result may lack patina but the warm and friendly atmosphere makes this address one that already enjoys an excellent reputation.

How to get there *(Map 7): North of Lerida and south of Bagnères-de-Luchon (France).*

Hotel Almud

22145 Sallent de Gallego (Huesca)
Espadilla, 11
Tel. 974-48 83 66 - Fax 974-48 83 66
Sr Mariano Martin de Cáceres - Sra Maria Jose Zandundo Ramirez

Rooms 11 with telephone, bath, satellite TV, minibar. **Price** Double 10,500-13,000Pts. **Meals** Breakfast included, served 8:00-10:30. No restaurant at the hotel but dinner by reservation; mealtime specials 1,500Pts. **Credit cards** All major. **Pets** Dogs not allowed. **Facilities** Garage (1,000Pts). **Nearby** The Pyrenees Route via C136 - Ordesa Park National. **Open** All year.

It has taken Maria José and Mariano two years to convert an 18th-century stable into what it is today. South of Lourdes and not far from the winter sports centers of Formical and Panticosa lies the village of Sallent in the small Tena Valley, nicely situated on the edge of a lake. The hotel is in the village center, an attractive stone building with a slate roof. The interior is truly that of a private home, its lounge offering Persian rugs, comfortable sofas, a collection of drawings and a fire in the fireplace assuring a warm and comfortable atmosphere. The eleven rooms each have personalized decoration including antique beds, old photos and family portraits. Your best choice would be one facing the mountain. The Hotel Almud is surely the Hotel of Charm in this region, receiving sports enthusiasts all year long, devotees of skiing, hiking and fishing in particular.

How to get there (Map 7): 52km northeast of Jaca, 78km from Pau (France).

Villa de Alquézar

22145 Alquézar (Huesca)
Pedro Arnal Cavero, 12
Tel. 974-31 84 16/908 03 02 07 - Fax 974-31 84 16
Sr Mariano Altemir

Category ★★ **Rooms** 20 with bath, TV. **Price** Single 3,500-4,000Pts, double 5,500-6,000Pts.
Meals Breakfast included, served 8:00-11:30. No restaurant. **Credit cards** Visa, Eurocard,
MasterCard. **Pets** Dogs not allowed. **Facilities** Parking. **Nearby** Alquézar: plaza mayor, castle,
Collegiate church (cloister) - Barbastro - Huesca. **Open** All year.

The Aragon region is a fascinating one, a place with villages where time seems to have stood still. Alquézar enjoys a truly exceptional location, perched on a rocky peak above a plateau surrounded by canyons. The network of tiny streets connected by small tunnels leads up to this former Moorish castle along with a church dating from the Middle Ages. Every morning herds of livestock can be seen heading for their grazing areas. There are few foreign visitors, but the region is well-known to cave explorers, fans of hang-gliding and off-road specialists, all of whom find the Sierra de Guara an adventurer's paradise. The hotel is in the village itself and its interiors are up-to-date with a sober rustic quality that never betrays the beauty of the outside. The areas shared by guests are spacious and in the breakfast room you can enjoy a marvelous selection of honey cakes and regional cheeses. The best rooms are those giving on to the street; Rooms 10, 11, 12 and 13 are on the top floor with a breathtaking view. A precious and authentic address allowing you to discover a truly magic village. There is no restaurant, but the charming Mesón del Vero is very close by.

How to get there *(Map 7): 45km east of Huesca.*

Posada del Almudí

50360 Daroca (Zaragoza)
C/. Granjera, 5, 7, 9
Tel. 976-80 06 06 - 976-80 12 96 - Fax 976-80 11 41
E-mail: posadadelalmudi@oem.es

Rooms 13 with air-conditioning, telephone, bath, WC, TV; elevator. **Price** Double 6,800-8,000Pts, duplex 16,000Pts. **Meals** Breakfast included, served 8:00-11:00. **Restaurant** Service 1:00PM-5:00PM, 9:00PM-11:00PM; mealtime specials 1,300Pts, also à la carte. Specialties: borrajas, cordero. **Credit cards** Visa, Eurocard, MasterCard. **Pets** Dogs not allowed. **Facilities** Parking. **Nearby** Gorges of Calmazara with its vulture colony - Hoz Barrage - Alhama de Aragon - Jaraba - Cetina - Ariza - Catalayud. **Open** All year.

Daroca is truly a unique place. Nestled in a valley and surrounded by two hills, this former Moslem fortress made up of houses in pink rock blending beautifully with its environment has been considered part of Humanity's Legacy since 1931. What remains are four kilometers of wall, twelve towers and two massive doors along with Roman and Gothic churches, a Renaissance fountain and palaces dating from the 15th through the 18th centuries. Part of one of these is now the Posada del Almudí where, in the summer, a guest can enjoy the cool temperature and the sobriety of the aging stone and rich dark wood of its patio. The rear of the house gives on a garden with a terrace ideal for breakfast. The rooms are elegant with yellow walls and blue trim, antique furniture and attractive fabrics uniting flowers and squares. The lounge is an equally enjoyable place where the fireplace blazes in winter. There is a bodega in the cellar for wine tasting as well as a good restaurant featuring regional specialties. The hotel and its surroundings make an excellent stop at the crossroads of routes leading anywhere in Spain.

How to get there *(Map 14): 85km southwest of Zaragosa via N330.*

Hotel Monasterio de Piedra

50210 Nuévalos (Zaragoza)
Tel. 976-84 90 11 - Fax 976-84 90 54
Sr Montaner
Web: www.zar.hnet.es/monastpiedra

Category ★★★ **Rooms** 61 with telephone, bath, WC, TV. **Price** Single 7,500Pts, double 9,000-12,000Pts, suite 13,500Pts, triple 14,000Pts. **Meals** Breakfast 550Pts, served 8:15-11.00; half board +3,300Pts, full board +5,500Pts (per pers., 2 days min.). **Restaurant** Service 1:00PM-5:00PM, 9:00PM-11:00PM; mealtime specials 2,750Pts, also à la carte. Specialties: Migas con huevo frito - Trucha del monasterio - Ternasco de Aragón. **Credit cards** All major. **Pets** Dogs allowed (except in restaurant). **Facilities** Swimming-pool, tennis, pisciculture center. **Nearby** Gorges of Calmazara with its vulture colony - Hoz Barrage - Daroca - Alhama de Aragon - Jaraba - Cetina - Ariza - Catalayud. **Open** All year.

Founded in the 12th century by Cistercian monks, this remarkably well-conserved monastery has a great beauty. This is an astonishing site and a real and fresh oasis, full of greenery and rising right out of the Meseta, a dry and rugged region surrounded by steep sierras. Here the genius of man has joined with the genius of nature. One should note the monumental staircase, illuminated by opaque alabaster windows to give a dream-like light. The rooms are simple in the former monks' cells with access via long and vaulted galleries. Some have terraces, others are located around the cloisters, yet others surround the entrance courtyard with its elm tree planted in 1681. Certainly do not leave the hotel without having visited the other parts of the monastery and having walked in the woods with the many lakes, waterfalls and caves.

How to get there *(Map 14): 30km southwest of Catalayud via C202 to Nuévalos, then follow the signs for Monasterio de Piedra.*

Parador Fernando de Aragón

50680 Sos del Rey Católico (Zaragoza)
Arquitecto Sainz de Vicuña, 1
Tel. 948-88 80 11 - Fax 948-88 81 00
Sr Rizos Garrido

Category ★★★ **Rooms** 65 with air-conditioning, telephone, bath, WC, TV, minibar; elevator. **Price** Double 12,500–15,000Pts. **Meals** Breakfast 1,300Pts, served 8:00–11:00. **Restaurant** Service 1:00PM–3:30PM, 8:30PM–10:30PM; mealtime specials 3,600Pts, also à la carte. Regional cooking. **Credit cards** All major. **Pets** Dogs not allowed. **Nearby** Uncastillo (Church of Santa Maria and the Casa Consistorial) - Longas road. **Closed** Jan 12 - Feb 22.

Situated in the historically classified village of Sos, the Parador Fernando de Aragón was built a few years ago by one of the best Spanish architects with respect for just one rule: the Aragonese style. Thus the craftsman's finish has been conserved and the stone already seems to have several centuries behind it. The rooms are very large with polished floor tiles and beds of copper. Those on the second floor have a gallery, while the rooms on the third have balconies. The bathrooms are successfully designed and not short of practical fittings. The dining room on the fourth floor, with its massive pillars, overlooks the valley and the restaurant is one of the best in the region.

How to get there *(Map 6): 63km southeast of Pamplona via N240 towards Jaca, then C127.*

Gran Hotel

50001 Zaragoza
Calle Joaquin Costa, 5
Tel. 976-22 19 01 - Fax 976-23 67 13
Sra G. Elizaga

Category ★★★★ **Rooms** 140 with air-conditioning, telephone, bath, WC, satellite TV, minibar; elevator. **Price** Double 17,000Pts, junior-suite 20,700Pts. **Meals** Breakfast 1,600Pts, served 7:00-11:00. **Restaurant** Service 1:00PM-3:30PM, 8:00PM-11:00PM; mealtime specials 3,500Pts, also à la carte. Seasonal cuisine. **Credit cards** All major. **Pets** Small dogs allowed. **Facilities** Parking (1,700Pts). **Nearby** Basilica de Nuestra Señora del Pilar in La Seo, Palacio de la Aljafería in Zaragoza - Churches in Utebo, Alagon, San Mateo de Gállego, Zuera - Cartuja Aula Dei - Alfajarín - Pina. **Open** All year.

Opened in 1929 by King Alfonso XIII and recently restored, this hotel has known how to keep its class, delightful atmosphere and refinement, in a town where any establishment of character is sadly rare. The rather luxurious ambiance is not at all starchy. The large round lounge with its glazed roof is a good example of the elegant decor. The bedrooms are spacious and very comfortable, and decorated with taste, each with its own functional and very neat bathroom. You can, for example, take the suite in which King Juan Carlos lived when a student at the Zaragoza military academy. A good welcome, an excellent quality-price ratio, and private parking are further reasons for choosing this hotel located right in the town center.

How to get there *(Map 15): Near the Plaza del Aragón.*

Hotel La Casona de Amandi

Amandi
33311 Villaviciosa (Asturias)
Tel. 98-589 01 30 - Fax 98-589 01 29
Sr R. Fernandez

Category ★★★ **Rooms** 9 with telephone, bath, WC, TV. **Price** Double 10,900-12,500-13,900Pts.
Meals Breakfast 850Pts. No Restaurant. **Credit cards** Visa, Eurocard, MasterCard. **Pets** Dogs not
allowed. **Facilities** Parking. **Nearby** In Amandi: Church of San Juan; Fiesta de la Virgen del Protal
(Sept 5 - 11) - Oviedo - Tazones - Romanesque church of Priesca - Villabona - Monastery San
Salvador of Valdedios. **Closed** Jan.

Very well situated between sea and mountains, the little village of Amandi
is a real refuge of tranquility at the foot of the first peaks of the Asturias,
and yet only 15 kilometers from the beaches. The "Casa" is a marvellous little
house from the 19th century that has kept all the atmosphere of a private home,
surrounded by a vast very green and flowery garden. The beautiful rustic
wooden planking has been retained, as have the thick slats of wood in the very
large bedrooms, all personalized with antique furniture. In the very well
equipped bathrooms, the original ceramics have been restored. Various small
lounges allow one to read, rest or have breakfast - provided one does not prefer
the winter garden arranged on the first floor. In the fine weather one can then
appreciate the large garden planted with magnolias and other handsome trees.
All the comforts and good taste are to be found here, ensuring a most enjoyable
stay.

How to get there (Map 3): 30km east of Gijón, towards Villaviciosa.

La Casona de Pío

33150 Cudillero (Asturias)
Riofrío, 3
Tel. 98-559 15 12 - Fax 98-559 15 19

Category ★★ **Rooms** 11 with telephone, bath, WC, TV. **Price** Double 7,000-10,000Pts. **Meals** Breakfast 800Pts, served 8:30AM-12:00PM. **Restaurant** Service 1:30PM-3:30PM, 8:30PM-11:30PM; à la carte. Specialties: Almejas a la marinera - Pixín amariscado - Merluza del "pincho" de Cudillero rellena de marisco - Fideos con bogavante. **Credit cards** Visa, Eurocard, MasterCard. **Pets** Dogs not allowed. **Nearby** El Pito - Beaches of Concha de Artedo - San Martín de Luiña and Soto de Luiña. **Closed** Jan 15 - 31.

The small village of Cudillero is nestled by a creek at the foot of two green hills. The houses are tightly clustered around the square where the town hall, the church and the port are located. In an old and elegant residence which has been very carefully restored you find one of the most charming small hotels on the Asturian coast. The rooms have attractive regional furniture and are extremely comfortable; there is even hydro-massage in the bathtubs. The delightful dining room is a fine setting in which to enjoy meals (of somewhat uneven quality) that include traditional dishes of fish and seafood from the Cantabrian Sea. The welcome you receive here is incredibly friendly, and the management offers everything from light lunches prepared to your order to the organization of excursions in the region. The Casona de Pío is truly a tiny patch of Asturian paradise.

How to get there *(Map 3): 61km northwest of Oviedo, 54km west of Gijón.*

Los Capios

Las Isla 33320 Colunga (Asturias)
Tel. 98-585 20 98 - 98-585 20 14 - Fax 98-585 20 97

Category ★★★ **Rooms** 10 with telephone, bath, WC, TV; wheelchair access. **Price** Double 12,000-15,000Pts, suite 15,000-18,000Pts. **Meals** Breakfast 850Pts, served 9:00AM-12:00PM. No restaurant. **Credit cards** Visa, Eurocard, MasterCard. **Pets** Dogs not allowed. **Facilities** Swimming pool. **Nearby** Lastres - Ribadesella - Colunga (jurásico parque) - Caravla - Cueva de la Morla **Open** All year.

Here on the border of Galicia lies a truly privileged village, facing the Pico Pienzu, the highest peak of the Sierra del Sueve. Only five minutes from local beaches, it is a hunting preserve where stags and eagles may be seen. The hotel, dating from the Thirties, is surrounded by a lovely garden with palm and apple trees. The large lounge, decorated with hunting themes, is both rustic and elegant with a fireplace in one corner, plus a vast terrace from which both the Pienzu and the sea may be seen. It is at this level that you will find the most attractive rooms, particularly the one overlooking the large and sunny country-style gallery with a fine view of the Sea of Cantabria. Those on the ground floor are more simple, decorated in solid colors. A good address will always prove itself by the breakfast it serves and here you will find delicious crêpes, light pastries and home-made cakes. There are numerous restaurants, both in the small fishing ports or in the back country.

How to get there *(Map 3): 43km east of Gijón to Lastres, then Colunga; 3km from Colunga via N632.*

Palacio de Vallados

33330 Lastres (Asturias)
Pedro Villarta
Tel. 98-585 04 44 - Fax 98-585 05 17 - M. Ernesto Seijas
E-mail: vallados@netcom.es - Web: www.netcom.es/vallados

Category ★★★ **Rooms** 28 with telephone, bath, WC, satellite TV, minibar; elevator. **Price** Single 5,800-8,000Pts, double 7,250-11,000Pts. **Meals** Breakfast 600Pts, served 8:00-11:00, half board +2,600Pts, full board +4,600Pts. **Restaurants** Service 1:00PM-4:00PM, 8:30PM-11:30PM; mealtime specials 2,600Pts. Regional cooking. **Credit cards** All major. **Pets** Dogs not allowed. **Facilities** Garage, parking. **Nearby** Ribadesella - Colunga - Caravia - Cueva de la Moria. **Closed** Feb.

In this charming village where all the white houses with their red tile roofs seem to straddle the port, the Palacio de Vallados assumes the character of a "grand hotel." It is a residence once belonging to nobles and well up on a hill which means most of its rooms have a view of the sea. The subtly-lighted interior is of a lovely pink, although the decor is perhaps a little too functional despite the quality of the comfort of its rooms. The view, however, is nothing less than picture-perfect.

How to get there (Map 3): 46km east of Gijón.

Hotel La Arquera

La Arquera
33500 Llanes (Asturias)
Tel. 98-540 24 24 - Fax 98-540 01 75

Category ★★★ **Rooms** 12 with telephone, bath, WC, TV, minibar, kitchenette. **Price** Double 8,000-12,000Pts, triple 10,000-14,000Pts, 4 pers. 11,000-17,000Pts. **Meals** Breakfast 900Pts. No restaurant. **Credit cards** Visa, Eurocard, MasterCard. **Pets** Dogs not allowed. **Facilities** Garage, parking. **Nearby** Vidiago - Cave of Pindal in Pimiango - Beaches of Celorio and Nueva. **Open** All year.

At the foot of the Sierra de Cuera, Llanes is an attractive little port with a very picturesque Old Town. Numerous beaches such as the "Playa de Toro" and "Playa del Sablon" have made its tourist reputation. The Spanish also come here to celebrate the local feasts, giving the "Llaniscos" every occasion to remember all their traditions in a colorful manner. The hotel occupies a country house typical of this region and has retained its granary. 2 kilometers from the village, the hotel is well-protected by its little garden. The lounges have a wonderful view onto the mountains, while the bedrooms are large and well-equipped for long stays, since as well as the traditional comforts, they also have small kitchens with stoves and refrigerators. Some rooms can accommodate up to four people. Besides the pleasures of the beach, do not miss those of the small village of Celorio and in Nueva, the "Playa del Mar"—the region is rich in prehistoric sites that are all of interest.

How to get there *(Map 4): 96km from Santander and 2km south of Llanes.*

La Posada de Babel

La Pereda 33509 Llanes (Asturias)
Tél. 98-540 25 25 - Fax 98-540 26 22

Category ★★★ **Rooms** 11 with air-conditioning, telephone, bath, WC, TV. **Price** Double 9,500-12,000Pts, suite 14,000-16,000Pts. **Meals** Breakfast 900Pts. **Restaurant** Closed Tues and Feb; à la carte 3,400-4,500Pts. Regional cooking. **Credit cards** Amex, Visa, Eurocard, MasterCard. **Pets** Dogs allowed. **Facilities** Bikes, practice golf, parking. **Nearby** Vidiago - Cave of Pindal in Pimiango - Beaches of Celorio and Nueva - Picos de Europa. **Open** All year.

In this beautiful region of the Asturias, La Posada de Babel offers a quality retreat for those appreciating the serenity of an all calming nature, but also with the possibility no farther than 3 kilometers away of plunging into the more lively activities of the beaches. The hotel enjoys a superb site looking over fields and woods, surrounded by a park of more than 1 hectare, planted with magnolias, apple trees and camelias. The house is a beautiful modern construction in the spirit of Le Corbusier. The ground floor houses the lounge, library and dining room, and via a large glazed gallery, directly communes with nature. The more traditional interior has kept a very warm ambiance: classical furniture in good taste, beautiful canvasses and lithographs on the walls and an open fire in season. The same cozy atmosphere is in the bedrooms, and five of them have terraces. Our preference is for no. 8, a tiny little house on two floors in the garden, but always with the same charming decoration, both simple but carefully chosen. An attractive and modern building houses two rooms and a suite. The restaurant is excellent and with offerings from the daily market, it lets you discover the specialties of the region. The hotel has bikes available and can also organize horse riding or 4x4 outings. The welcome is flawless at this excellent address.

How to get there (Map 4): 96km from Santander and 4km south of Llanes.

El Habana

La Pereda 33500 Llanes (Asturias)
El Pedroso
Tel. 98-540 25 26 - Fax 98-540 20 75 - Maria Eugenia Caumel
E-mail: elhabana@losintel.net

Rooms 11 with air-conditioning, telephone, bath, TV. **Price** Double 10,000-11,500Pts, suite 15,000-18,000Pts. **Meals** Breakfast 700Pts. **Restaurant** Mealtime specials 1,800Pts, also à la carte. **Credit cards** Visa, Eurocard, MasterCard. **Pets** Dogs allowed. **Facilities** Swimming pool, parking. **Nearby** Vidiago - Cave of Pindal in Pimiango - Beaches of Celorio and Nueva - Picos de Europa **Open** All year.

A few steps from the nearby address already noted, a visitor is still deeper into the green Asturian countryside. El Habana lies at the misty foot of the first mountain summit of Los Picos de Europa. It is in this grandiose setting that Maria Caumel has created her hotel. It is a recently-built house constructed in truly traditional style, yellow and white and surrounded by a large lawn. The lounges and dining room take up the entire ground floor which give on the garden and the swimming pool. The decor features numerous works of African art, and a huge trunk recalls the owners' adventurous past. Upstairs, the rooms are pretty and those giving on the mountain are very spacious with large bay windows offering sunlight and a view of the countryside. The suites, situated on the corners, are particularly remarkable for their decor which brings out the best in Spanish design. The house is a fine starting point for short walks among the cows and the enormous pig who acts as the hotel's mascot. An attractive and bucolic address situated only a short distance from local beaches.

How to get there (Map 4): 96km from Santander and 4km from Llanes.

El Molino de Tresgrandas

33500 Tresgrandas - Llanes (Asturias)
Tel. 98-541 11 91- Fax 98-541 11 91
Luis Sanz Hippolito - Carmen Garcia Fernandes
E-mail: molino@mail.ddnet.es - Web: www.ddnet.es/molinotresgrandes

Rooms 8 with telephone, bath, TV. **Price** Double 7,500-9,500Pts. **Meals** Breakfast 850Pts, served 9:00-11:00; half board +2,750Pts (per pers.). **Restaurant** Mealtime specials 2,600Pts, also à la carte. **Credit cards** Visa, Eurocard, MasterCard. **Pets** Dogs not allowed. **Facilities** Parking. **Nearby** Vidiago - Cave of Pindal in Pimiango - Beaches of Celorio and Nueva - Picos de Europa. **Open** All year.

Time has stopped in Tresgrandas, a delightful Asturian hamlet that Nature has totally submerged. In fact, once outside the village you are obliged to go cross-country to finally arrive at El Molino, there to be greeted by a large sheep dog, a prominent native of the region. As its name indicates, El Molino is an old mill that Carmen and Luis have turned into a rural hotel. A small river has long flowed past the millwheel and today, another survivor of an earlier time is a glass flagstone in the floor of the paneled living room through which you can see the water flow down the millrun. The dining room is entirely in wood and decorated with intriguing rural objects. The rooms are located in both buildings; they are small and done in country style with large rustic commodes and brightly colored bedspreads. Here is peace and calm but silence is somewhat relative due to the Microcosmos discotheque very audibly nearby.

How to get there *(Map 4): 80km from Santander and east of Llanes.*

La Casona de Villanueva

33590 Villanueva de Colombres - Ribadedeva (Asturias)
Tel. 98-541 25 90 - Fax 98-541 25 14
Sra Nuria Juez - Sr Angel Gascón
E-mail: casonavillanueva@abonados.cplus.es

Category ★★ **Rooms** 8 with telephone, bath. **Price** Single 6,500-7,500Pts, double 8,000-9,500Pts, suite 13,000-15,000Pts. **Meals** Breakfast 900Pts, served 8:00-11:00. No restaurant but snacks available on request; mealtime specials 2,500Pts. **Credit cards** All major **Pets** Dogs not allowed. **Facilities** Parking. **Nearby** LLanes - Vidiago - Cave of Pindal in Pimiango - Beaches of Franca - Picos de Europa. **Open** All year.

Villanueva is yet another of those marvelous Asturian villages ideally situated between mountain and sea, between the Sea of Cantabria and the Picos de Europa Park. This 18th-century *casona* - Asturian farm - houses a small and discreet hotel with a charm that is the reflection of its owner, Nuria Juez. It has been carefully and respectfully restored and decorated with numerous personal objects giving the house an intimate and lived-in atmosphere. The most touching and attractive is the *habitacion de la abuela* as Nuria has furnished this charming and spacious corner room with furniture her grandmother received as wedding gifts. In addition, there is an old piano and superb bathroom furnishings. The dining room is in the garden where you can enjoy dinners you may order in advance. This pleasant garden is also a good place to have a quiet drink, and the welcome you receive here is everything you could wish for.

How to get there *(Map 4): 80km from Santander and 23km southeast of Llanes.*

Hotel Casona d'Álevia

33579 Álevia (Asturias)
Peñamellera Baja
Tel. 98-41 41 76 - Fax 98-41 44 26 - Sra Mari-Lupe González
E-mail: alevia@nauta.es

Category ★★★ **Rooms** 9 with telephone, bath, satellite TV. **Price** Double 8,600-10,800Pts, special double 12,000-14,500Pts. **Meals** Breakfast 750Pts, served 8:30-11:30. No restaurant but snacks available on request; mealtime specials 2,500Pts. **Credit cards** Visa, Eurocard, MasterCard. **Pets** Dogs not allowed. **Facilities** Parking. **Nearby** LLanes - Potres - Santillana del Mar - Vidiago - Cave of Pindal in Pimiango - Cave of Loja in Panes - Beaches of Franca - Picos de Europa. **Open** All year.

Upward and onward, this time from the valley of the rivers Cares and Deva to the gateway to the celebrated Picos mountains. Set in a magnificent environment, the village has managed to keep all its old houses intact. The Casona d'Álevia is one of them, surrounded by chestnut trees and with splendid stone construction visible everywhere. The house's atmosphere is mountain-and-rustic with a large living room and a low ceiling where the stone and wood retain the delightful scent of the logs in the vast fireplace. Each of the large rooms is different; Rooms 8 and 9 are duplexes, nestled under the roof and offering even more space. Here, the guest is received with a dish of hazelnuts as a sign of welcome, just another example of the spirit of a place at once simple and friendly.

How to get there *(Map 4): 80km from Santander and 23km southeast of Llanes.*

Hotel de la Reconquista

33004 Oviedo (Asturias)
Calle Gil de Jaz, 16
Tel. 98-524 11 00 - Fax 98-524 11 66 - Sr Ramón Felip
E-mail: reconquista@hoteldelareconquista.com
Web: www.hoteldelareconquista.com

Category ★★★★★ **Rooms** 142 with air-conditioning, telephone, bath, WC, TV, minibar; elevator.
Price Single 23,950Pts, double 29,950Pts, suite 50,000-85,000Pts; extra bed +9,250Pts. **Meals**
Breakfast 2,100Pts, served 6:30-11:00; half board +7,950Pts, full board +11,700Pts (per pers.).
Restaurant Service 1:30PM-4:00PM, 9:00PM-11:30PM; mealtime specials 5,850Pts, also à la carte.
Specialties: Fabada. **Credit cards** All major. **Pets** Dogs not allowed. **Facilities** Sauna (1,200Pts),
garage. **Nearby** Cathedral of Oviedo - Church of Santa Maria del Naranco - San Claudio; Club
Deportivo la Bargariza golf course (9-Hole). **Open** All year.

This former hospice-hospital was built in the 18th century by the renowned
architect P. A. Menendez. The building has only two floors but is
dominated by a huge Spanish coat of arms in the center, a remarkable example
of baroque sculpture. Having traversed the porch, you find yourself in a vast
rectangular lounge lit by a glazed roof. A mezzanine runs all around and is
supported by a double stone colonnade. The hotel offers exceptional facilities:
a gym, a sauna, conference rooms and also a concert hall set out in the very
beautiful chapel, with an octagonal plan and two tiers of superposed seating.
The bedrooms and service are those of a real palace.

How to get there *(Map 3): In the town center near the San Francisco Park.*

Hotel Casa del Busto

33120 Pravia (Asturias)
C/ Rey Don Silo, 1
Tel. 98-582 27 71 - Fax 98-582 27 72 - Sr Mencos
E-mail: casadelbusto@estanciases.es

Category ★★★ **Rooms** 27 with telephone, bath or shower, WC, TV. **Price** Single 5,000-7,000Pts, double 7,500-9,500Pts. **Meals** Breakfast 500-750Pts, served 9:00-11:00. **Restaurant** Service 1:30PM-3:30PM, 9:00PM-11:00PM; mealtime specials 1,200Pts, also à la carte. Specialties: Fabes - Arroz con leche. **Credit cards** Amex, Visa, Eurocard, MasterCard. **Pets** Dogs allowed. **Nearby** Beaches of Aguilar, Santa and María del Mar - Cudillero - El Pito - Cabo de Vidio - Catedral of Oviedo. **Open** All year.

Only a few kilometers inland from the charming village of Cudillero and the beautiful Concha de Artado beach is an old caserón dating from the 16th century that has been converted into a hotel. The sobriety of its exterior is particularly noteworthy. Inside, its furniture and regional fabrics harmonize nicely with the rustic architecture. In the large outdoor patio with its traditional overhead glass-enclosed gallery, you can enjoy a coffee, a drink or a snack as well as a view of the mountainous surroundings. There is an interior patio with a pleasant decor of stone columns and an intimate restaurant. The rooms are in attractive provincial style and very comfortable. This is a very well placed hotel in the triangle formed by Ovido, Gijón and Aviles.

How to get there *(Map 3): 55km from Oviedo on the Oviedo-Pravia highway. Take the Barco-Pravia exit; Asturias-Pravia airport.*

Hotel Marina

33056 Ribadesella (Asturias)
Tel. 98-586 00 50 - Fax 98-586 01 57
Sra Anesada Lidu

Category ★★ **Rooms** 46 with telephone, bath, WC, satellite TV; elevator. **Price** Double 7,000-9,000Pts. **Meals** Breakfast 600Pts, served 7:00-11:00. **Restaurant** Service 12:30PM-3:00PM-8:30PM-11:30PM; mealtime specials 2,250Pts. Regional cooking. **Credit cards** All major. **Pets** Dogs not allowed. **Nearby** Ribadesella: the Old Town, cave of Tito Bustillo; fiesta (Jun 29 and 1st Sat of Aug) - Cueva de la Moria - San Estebán de Leces - Carvia - Colunga - Lastres. **Closed** Nov - Feb.

Ribadesella is one of the seaside resorts on the Asturian coast known for the kayak run stretching from Arriondas to the port which spectators can watch from the small train that runs parallel to the river. This small fishing port does not have the charm of nearby Llanes or San Vicente, but it has a lovely setting at the mouth of the Sella River. This historical town has some attractive 17th- and 18th-century palaces which are totally unlike the Hotel Marina which is noteworthy for the use of the color green in its architecture which is not unlike that of Vienna or Prague. The interior seems a bit dated with lamps from the 50s and sofas from the 70s, all contributing to an amusing and faintly kitsch ambiance. We recommend the rooms offering balconies with view. This hotel can nicely break up the trip from Santander to Gijon.

How to get there *(Map 3): 67km east of Gijón.*

Posada del Valle

33549 Collía (Asturias)
Tel. 98-584 11 57 - Fax 98-584 15 59 - Nacho and Joan Burch
E-mail: hotel@posadadelvalle.com - Web: www.posadadelvalle.com

Category ★★ **Rooms** 8 with bath, WC, TV. **Price** Single 6,000-7,200Pts, double 7,000-9,000Pts.
Meals Breakfast 750Pts, served 8:00-11:30. No restaurant but poss. dinner by reservation before
6:00PM; mealtime specials 1,900Pts, also à la carte. **Credit cards** All major. **Pets** Dogs not allowed.
Nearby Ribadesella: Old Town, cave of Tito Bustillo, beaches; fiesta (Jun 29 and 1st Sat of Aug) -
Cueva de la Moria - San Estebán de Leces - Carvia - Colunga - Lastres. **Closed** Oct 16 - Mar 14.

The road from the Ribadesella coast to Collía hugs the side of the mountain
and the countryside changes subtly. The Posada de Valle is a small country
hotel with a classic reception desk and traditional hotel service. The brand-new
lounge is on the ground floor and while the atmosphere tends to be somewhat
impersonal, the taste is flawless. The dining room is set up to take maximum
advantage of the hotel's location with a view of the mountains and the sheep
grazing in the fields. All is both simple and attractive with green table linen
and multi-colored Scottish-style chairs. The rooms are not to be outdone; they
are in beige with natural stone appearing occasionally and with wooden beams
and floors, light cast-iron beds and bedspreads of refined print or square
patterns. It is, of course, a good idea to choose one of those giving on the
valley. The welcome you receive from Joan and Nacho is irresistible and this
friendly English couple will help you share their passion and enthusiasm for
this magnificent region.

How to get there *(Map 3): 81km east of Gijón and 14km south of Ribadesella*
via N634 to Arriondas, towards Collía.

La Rectoral

33775 Taramundi-La Villa (Asturias)
Tel. 98-564 67 67 - Fax 98-564 67 77
Sr Barrenechea

Category ★★★★ **Rooms** 18 with air-conditioning, telephone, bath, WC, TV, minibar. **Price** Single 11,000-13,000Pts, double 13,000-16,000Pts, extra bed +3,000Pts. **Meals** Breakfast 975Pts; half board 16,500Pts (per pers.). **Restaurant** Service 1:00PM-3:00PM, 9:00PM-10:00PM; mealtime specials 3,000Pts. **Credit cards** All major. **Pets** Dogs not allowed. **Facilities** Sauna, gymnasium, parking. **Nearby** Mazo de Teixois - Tapia de Casariego - Castropol - Figueras. **Open** All year.

This is one of the most charming of Spanish inns, in the heart of deepest Spain in a tiny village on the frontier between the Asturias and Galicia - and so the local reputation is based not on its cutlery alone! This former 18th-century presbytery has been transformed into a comfortable hotel. The barn has become the lounge, and next to it a bar (where the bartender will let you taste the local liqueurs), and then the dining room. The bedrooms have been decorated in the traditional style of the Asturias, and are welcoming, opening onto a small private terrace with a superb view over the gentle green hills. Everything here is simple, very authentic and top quality. A good halting place for discovering a different Spain.

How to get there *(Map 2): 65km northeast of Lugo, via N640 to Puentanuevo; then take the small road on the right.*

Palacete Peñalba

42100 Figueras del Mar (Asturias)
El Cotarelo
Tel. 98-563 61 25 - Fax 98-563 62 47

Category ★★★ Rooms 12 with telephone, bath, WC, TV. **Price** Single 8,000-9,000Pts, double 10,500-12,000Pts, suite 14,500-16,000Pts. **Meals** Breakfast 800Pts, served at any time. **Restaurant** Peñalba (Tel. 98-563 61 66), av. Trenor-Puerto, service 1:00PM-3:00PM, 8:00PM-10:00PM; à la carte 4,500-5,800Pts. Regional cooking and fish. **Credit cards** Amex, Visa, Eurocard, MasterCard. **Pets** Small dogs allowed. **Facilities** Parking. **Nearby** Beaches - Valley of Masma via N634 from Barreiros (Lourenza, Lindin). **Open** All year.

Built in 1912 by a disciple of Gaudí, the Palacete Peñalba is about to be classified a historic monument. Converted into a hotel five years ago, it has a rather faded charm, an impression given by the colors and furnishings although the sheets and towels, while spotless, are often very well worn. The bedrooms will delight any lover of big spaces, while Rooms 12, 14 and 15 have large terraces. In the suites, the bathrooms are set in a veranda. Very peaceful, the house is surrounded by a garden planted with various species of pine trees, along with a superb palm tree. The welcome guests receive here is beyond reproach. There is no restaurant in the hotel but in the little port of Figueras, just 200 meters away, the same proprietor also owns a restaurant whose renown has spread beyond the frontier of the Asturias and even of Spain, due in large part to the excellent fish dishes. It should be noted, however, that the prices are high and the service does not match the surroundings.

How to get there *(Map 2): 150km northeast of Oviedo, on the coast and 3km from Ribadeo.*

Hotel Asturias

33201 Gijón (Asturias)
Plaza Mayor, 11
Tel. 98-535 06 00/01/02 - Fax 98-534 68 72
Sr Juan Luis Alfonso

Category ★★ **Rooms** 65 with telephone, bath, WC, TV. **Price** Single 5,800-7,500Pts, double 9,000-10,500Pts. **Meals** Breakfast 550Pts, served 7:30-11:00; half board 8,600-10,500Pts, full board +11,400-13,650Pts (per pers.). **Restaurant** Service 12:30PM-3:00PM, 8:30PM-11:30PM; mealtime specials 1,500Pts. Regional cooking. **Credit cards** All major. **Pets** Dogs not allowed. **Nearby** Castiello golf course (18-Hole). **Open** All year.

The Hotel Asturias is the only hotel on the Plaza Mayor in the heart of this city on the Cantabrian coast. It is very close to the attractive port and the large and well-maintained San Lorenzo Beach. The entrance way with its elliptical glass roof suggests a 19th-century bodega rather than a hotel. The lobby is spacious with ample facilities for quiet conversations. The comfortable and classically decorated rooms are upstairs, the best among them giving on the square, but you should bear in mind, especially in the summer, that the cafés, the bars and the fishermen's restaurants in the port stay open all night.

How to get there (Map 3): 29km northeast of Oviedo.

Casal del Castro

39520 Comillas (Cantabria)
San Jerónimo
Tel. 942-72 23 91 - Fax 942-72 00 61
Sr Angel Gonzalez Mirones

Category ★★★ **Rooms** 43 with telephone, bath, WC, satellite TV; elevator. **Price** Single 5,500-8,500Pts, double 7,000-12,500Pts, suite 14,000-20,500Pts. **Meals** Breakfast included, served 9:00-11:00. **Restaurant** Service 1:00PM-4:00PM, 8:00PM-11:00PM; mealtime specials 2,200Pts, also à la carte. Specialties: fish. **Credit cards** Visa, Eurocard, MasterCard. **Pets** Dogs not allowed. **Facilities** Parking. **Nearby** Santillana del Mar (Collegiate) - cave of Altamira. **Open** All year.

Comillas is a very charming seaside resort, once the royal residence of King Alphonso XII. What remains from the date of his reign are the palace and, in the garden, a pavilion he commissioned Gaudí to design. Today, that is where you will find a fine, elegant restaurant called *El Caprichio de Gaudí*. The hotel itself occupies part of the casona, a noble residence dating from the 17th century and typical of the region. The ground-floor lounges still reflect some of the magnificence of that period. The best rooms are in this older part and some of them have a view of the village. A more recent addition, extending from the old white building, has far less charm although it lacks nothing in terms of comfort. The restaurant features a great deal of fish dishes and offers a very pleasant terrace. And should you choose to try something a little different, we recommend the very pleasant *El Molino*, a restaurant in Puente Arce on the road to Santander.

How to get there *(Map 4): 49km west of Santander.*

Hotel del Oso

39539 Cosgaya (Cantabria)
Tel. 942-73 30 18 - Fax 942-73 30 36
Sra Ana Rivas

Categories ★★ and ★★★ **Rooms** 34 and 16 with telephone, bath, WC, satellite TV; elevator. **Price** Single 5,900-7,000Pts - 6,000-7,200Pts, double 7,500-8,200Pts - 8,000-9,100Pts. **Meals** Breakfast 900Pts, served 9:00-11:00. **Restaurant** Service 1:00PM-4:00PM, 9:00PM-11:00PM; mealtime specials 3,500-4,000Pts, also à la carte. Regional cooking. **Credit cards** All major. **Pets** Dogs not allowed. **Facilities** Swimming pool, tennis, parking. **Nearby** Puerto de Pandetrave - Monastery of Santo Toribio de Liébana - Church of Santa Maria de Lebeña - Santa Maria de Piasca - Torre del Infantado (Potes) - Torre de Mogrovejo - Convento of San Raimundo - Funicular of Fuente Dé and the "balcon del cable". **Closed** Jan 1 - Feb 15.

Between Oviedo and Santander is a region dominated not only by the towering Picos de Europa with their wild landscape of gorges and mountain passes but also by lovely green valleys and rivers brimming with fish. The Hotel del Oso, which has been run by the same family over several generations, is undoubtedly the hotel the most professionally operated, offering guests the finest accommodation in the Liebana Valley, along with a swimming pool. It is a truly attractive place in the mountains where two old houses face each other across the river, one with rooms slightly larger than the other, explaining the one-star difference in rating. The only ones to be avoided are those overlooking the parking lot. Here you find stunning flowers everywhere, and the restaurant offers a menu with numerous regional specialties. This a family hotel where outdoor tourism is very much the tradition.

How to get there *(Map 4): 140km west of Santander (to Gijón) at half-way road to Potes, Camaleño and Coscaya.*

El Rebeco

39588 Fuente Dé (Cantabria)
Tel. 942-73 66 01/02 - Fax 942-73 66 00
Sr Ottomar Casado Polantinos

Category ★★ **Rooms** 30 with telephone, bath, WC, satellite TV. **Price** Single 6,500Pts, double 8,800Pts, 4 pers. 12,800Pts. **Meals** Breakfast 600Pts, served 8:30-10:00. **Restaurants** Service 12:30PM-3:00PM, 8:00PM-11:00PM; mealtime specials 1,600Pts. Regional cooking. **Credit cards** All major. **Pets** Dogs not allowed. **Facilities** Parking. **Nearby** Monastery of Santo Toribio de Liébana - Church of Santa Maria de Lebeña - Santa Maria de Piasca - Torre del Infantado (Potes) - Torre de Mogrovejo - Convento of San Raimundo - Funicular of Fuente Dé and the "balcon del cable" - Natural Park of Covadonga - Excursions in the Picos de Europa. **Open** All year.

You leave the Cantabrian coast, the sea and the heat to travel inland on N621 for some seventy kilometers and reach a height of over 1,500 meters. The vegetation changes rapidly along this magnificent highway leading to the towering Picos de Europa. The Hotel Rebeco is in the center of a kind of amphitheater surrounded by mountains rising to 2,600 meters and resembling a lunar landscape. It is a small chalet built of stone and wood with warm and simple decoration based on bright colors, mostly reds, livening up the dark heavy wood of the furniture. You shouldn't miss the view of the Picos and better still, ask for a room with a small terrace. The restaurant offers local specialties plus a year-long panoramic vista. There is a lift and you will have an excellent opportunity for hiking and visiting the wild animal preserve.

How to get there (Map 4): 140km west of Santander (to Gijón) at half-way road to Potes, Camaleño and Fuente Dé.

La Casona de Treviño

Treviño 39587 Camaleño (Cantabria)
Tel. 942-73 30 26
Sra Maria Ester Velez

Rooms 4 with bath. **Price** Double 5,000-6,000Pts. **Meals** Breakfast 500Pts, served 8:00-10:00; half board 4,700Pts (per pers.). **Evening meals** Mealtime specials 1,200Pts. **Credit cards** Not accepted. **Pets** Dogs not allowed. **Facilities** Parking. **Nearby** Monastery of Santo Toribio de Liébana - Church of Santa Maria de Lebeña - Santa Maria de Piasca - Torre del Infantado (Potes) - Torre de Mogrovejo - Convento of San Raimundo - Natural Park of Covadonga - Excursions in the Picos de Europa. **Open** All year.

The back country behind the coast is a particularly pretty mountainous region, crisscrossed by valleys where environmental tourism has increasingly developed. When you leave the road from Camaleño, you travel through two kilometers of extraordinary countryside where flowered plains follow pine forests at the foot of the majestic Picos de Europa. It is here in these delightful surroundings that you will find the Casona de Treviño at the end of a long rose-lined alley, an 18th-century farm house that has been very well preserved. The parquet floors are particularly interesting with a patina that grows ever more attractive. There is the same rustic authenticity in the four furnished rooms with their large, solid-wood beds and luxurious eiderdowns. In the morning, you can open the windows for a splendid view of the mountain or the valley. Here is a simple hotel but one which offers a genuine change of scene.

How to get there *(Map 5): 140km west of Santander (to Gijón) at half-board road to Potes, Camaleño and Treviño.*

Hotel San Roman de Escalante

39795 Escalante (Cantabria)
Carretera de Escalante a Castillo, Km 2
Tel. 94-267 77 45 - Fax 94-267 76 43 - Sr Melis
E-mail: sanromanescalante@mundivia.es

Category ★★★★ **Rooms** 16 with air-conditioning, telephone, bath, WC, TV, minibar. **Price** Double 13,000-25,000Pts. **Meals** Breakfast 1,250Pts, served 8:00-10:30; half board +5,200Pts, full board +8,250Pts (per pers.). **Restaurant** Service 1:30PM-4:00PM, 9:00PM-11:30PM; à la carte. Specialties: Almejas en salsa verde con setas - Mero con manteca de cacao i vanilla con verduritas - Filetto de pato en costra de sesamo i crujiente de Iberíco - Helado de vinagre de Modena. **Credit cards** All major. **Pets** Dogs allowed. **Facilities** Parking, parking. **Nearby** In Santoña: Church of Santa Maria and Monastery of Montehano - Noja - Romanesque church of Bareyo - Beaches of Isla and Ajo. **Closed** Dec 18 - Jan 18.

Escalante is a few kilometers away from the important fishing port of Santoña whose fortress has defended the deep bay cutting into the land since the 17th-century. The hotel owes its name to the hermitage dating from Roman times on the property. The house is a former noble residence whose fine walls rise out of a garden shaded by trees, and in which sculptures by contemporary artists are on display. Here one actually lives surrounded by works of art, both old and modern, as the hotel also has an art gallery and boutique selling antiques. The stables have been converted into a very good gastronomic restaurant which contributes to the hotel's reputation. Comfort is in the rooms which are large with their little lounge areas. This is an excellent address from which to discover - in luxury - the Cantabrian coastland.

How to get there (Map 4): 42km east of Santander

La Tahona de Besnes

33578 Alles (Cantabria)
Tel. 98-541 57 49 - Fax 98-541 57 49

Rooms 25 (13 with telephone) with bath, WC, TV. **Price** Single 5,440-7,040Pts, double 6,800-8,800Pts, 4 pers. 11,000-15,000Pts. **Meals** Breakfast 750Pts, served 8:30-11:30; half board +2,600Pts, full board +4,200Pts. **Restaurant** Service 1:00PM-4:00PM, 8:00PM-11:00PM; mealtime specials 1,850Pts. Regional cooking. **Credit cards** Visa, Eurocard, MasterCard. **Pets** Dogs not allowed. **Facilities** Parking. **Nearby** Hermida - Cares Gorges by Poncebos road. **Open** All year.

Between Oviedo and Santander stretches the mountain chain of the "Picos de Europa" (the Peaks of Europe), that offers magnificent attractions to all nature lovers: trails, gorges and rivers filled with salmon and trout. This site has favored rural tourism such as one finds it at Alles. Access to the little village is through of a forest with many winding little streams. Several former farm buildings shelter the rooms, and the decor is very rustic, very sober and very authentic – but all the comforts of a traditional hotel are present although you should note that the bathrooms only have small hip-baths. All is calm and you may rediscover the scents of the countryside - and with the cock's crow for alarm clock! A young and enthusiastic team runs the house and they suggest all kinds of activities: bike rental, canoe outings through the gorges of the Cares and the Deva, 4x4 excursions, horse riding - and more. If you add the sea, some thirty kilometers away, to the program, you have everything for a perfect holiday.

How to get there *(Map 4): 89km west of Santander to Panes and Alles. Then, take the road to Cangas de Onis for 10.5km.*

Hotel Don Pablo

33594 Pechón (Cantabria)
Tel. 942-71 95 00 - Fax 942-71 95 00
Sr Pablo Gomez

Category ★★ **Rooms** 31 and 4 suites with bath. **Price** Double 6,900-9,800Pts. **Meals** Breakfast included, served 8:30AM-12:30PM. No restaurant. **Credit cards** Visa, Eurocard, MasterCard. **Pets** Dogs allowed. **Nearby** Hermida - Cares Gorges by Poncebos road. **Open** All year.

Pechón is a frontier village situated between Asturia and Cantabria. You leave the main highway running along the coast and continue beside the eucalyptus-lined river that flows to the sea. Magdalena and Pablo Gomez have made a hotel of this recently-built house facing the sea. Already delighted by the beautiful view, you pass through an attractive loggia to reach the lounge and find a very personal style of decoration, albeit somewhat overdone. At first glance, it is surprising to find Louis XV pieces here but in the end, a certain charm persists. The rooms are pleasant and sober, particularly those with a view, especially Rooms 301 and 303.

How to get there *(Map 4): 65km west of Santander towards Llanes.*

Hotel Hosteria de Quijas

39590 Quijas (Cantabria)
Carret. N 634
Tel. 942-82 08 33 - Fax 942-83 80 50
Sr Castañeda

Category ★★★ **Rooms** 14 and 5 suites with telephone, bath, jacuzzi, WC, satellite TV, minibar. **Price** Single 6,800Pts, double 8,500Pts, suite 17,000Pts. **Meals** Breakfast 750Pts, served 7:00-11:00. **Restaurant** Service 1:30PM-3:30PM, 8:30PM-11:00PM; à la carte. Specialties: Ensalada templada de mollejas de pato y habitas - Calabacines rellenos de bacalaó tres salsas. **Credit cards** All major. **Pets** Dogs not allowed. **Facilities** Swimming pool, parking. **Nearby** Santander - Santillana del Mar - Picos de Europa; Pedreña golf course (18-Hole). **Closed** Dec 20 - Jan 4.

Are peace and quiet your top priorities? Then lose no time getting to the Hotel Hosteria de Quijas. This former 18th-century palace is set in a magnificent garden with centuries-old trees and superb magnolias. The bedrooms are refined and furnished with pieces from the 17th and 18th centuries. Choose the ones facing the garden, quieter than those that face the street. Small lounges are scattered through the hotel. Bare stonework and caisson ceilings all contribute to its charm. The dining room is pleasant with wooden beams and pillars. A variety of trips can be planned starting from the hotel.

How to get there (Map 4): *25km southwest of Santander to Torrelavega, towards Oviedo, Puente San Miguel and Quijas (N634).*

Posada Torre de Quijas TR

39590 Quijas (Cantabria)
B° Vinueva, 76
Tel. 942-82 06 45 - Fax 942-83 82 55 - Pilar Lozano

Rooms 20 with telephone, bath, satellite TV, minibar. **Price** Double in the casona 7,500-8,900Pts, double in the annex 7,500-9,600Pts, suite 12,000-15,000Pts. **Meals** Breakfast 600Pts, served 7:00-11:00. No restaurant. **Credit cards** Visa, Eurocard, MasterCard. **Pets** Dogs not allowed. **Nearby** Santander - Santillana del Mar - Picos de Europa; Pedreña golf course (18-Hole). **Closed** Dec 20 - Jan 4.

This *posada* is an attractive residence built very much in the tradition of the region. The ground floor is truly out of the ordinary where a wide hallway of polished stone slabs and decorated with works by local artisans leads to a superb living room with wooden beams. The comfortable white sofas confer genuine elegance and put the guest immediately at ease and the temperatures are refreshingly cool in summer, the fireplace offering welcome warmth in winter. There are ten rooms in the main building, each with the name and picture of a flower on its door. It is wise to choose one giving on the lawn. We particularly like Limonero that features a wooden vaulted ceiling and very pretty lace curtains. Peral and Mimosa are large rooms with wooden floors and balconies while Gladiolo is on the top floor with a sloping ceiling. Some of them have mezzanines designed for children. The remaining five are in an annex with somewhat less charm although still very comfortable. Pilar welcomes you with exemplary warmth and you will enjoy chatting with this charming hostess. There is a small covered patio where Carmen weaves and designs clothing that she will be very happy to sell you. As for restaurants, we recommend the Hosteria de Quijas.

How to get there (Map 4): *25km southwest of Santander to Torrelavega towards Oviedo, Puente San Miguel and Quijas on N634.*

Hotel Real

39005 Santander (Cantabria)
El Sardinero - Paseo Pérez Galdós, 28
Tel. 942-27 25 50 - Fax 942-27 45 73
Sr Peter Lezius

Category ★★★★★ **Rooms** 123 with air-conditioning, telephone, bath, WC, satellite TV, minibar; elevator. **Price** Single 18,550-31,200Pts, double 23,200-39,000Pts, suite 49,000-95,000Pts, Real suite 85,000-135,000Pts. **Meals** Breakfast 1,700Pts, served 8:00-11:00; half board + 5,450Pts, full board +7,360Pts (per Pers.). **Restaurant** Service 1:30PM-3:30PM, 9:00PM-11:30PM; mealtime specials 3,600Pts, also à la carte. Regional and international cooking. **Credit cards** All major. **Pets** Dogs not allowed. **Facilities** Parking. **Nearby** Palacio de Eseldo in Pámanes - Prehistorics caves of Puente Viesgo; Pedreña golf course (18-Hole). **Open** All year.

This hotel, a race course and a casino were built in Santander when the royal family had its summer quarters in this town, and every effort was made to give satisfy all the requirements of such visitors. No details were spared and the hotel was given a privileged site overlooking the Bay of Santander and the Magdalena Beach. Since then it has been transformed and renovated, but has retained all the magnificence and luxury of an old and rather dated hotel "de luxe". All the bedrooms open onto terraces or balconies. The atmosphere here is one of calm and the furniture is classical in style. One "plus" is the dining room with its veranda and stone arcades and carefully selected furnishings. Next door are cozy lounges. All this makes the Real a luxurious way station in Cantabria.

How to get there (Map 4): 3.5km northeast of Santander (El Sardinero).

Hotel Central

39004 Santander (Cantabria)
General Mola, 5
Tel. 942-22 24 00 - Fax 942-36 38 29

Category ★★★ **Rooms** 41 with air-conditioning, telephone, bath, satellite TV, minibar; elevator. **Price** Single 7,400-10,350Pts, double 11,000-16,200Pts. **Restaurant** See p. 306. **Credit cards** All major. **Pets** Dogs not allowed. **Nearby** Palacio de Eseldo in Pámanes - Prehistorics caves of Puente Viesgo; Pedreña golf course (18-Hole). **Open** All year.

This address is a precious one for anyone wishing to stay in the center of the charming city of Santander, noted for its warm climate and the music and dance festivals held in the summer. The hotel is in a very attractive building, constructed in the late 19th century and recognizable by its sky-blue facade and its windows and pediments trimmed with white, a color nicely integrated inside the hotel, especially in the rooms where various fabrics abound. All of these are comfortable, but the only ones to avoid are those giving on the interior courtyard which miss out on the sunlight from the street. There are several rooms on the upper two floors with balconies overlooking the sea. This is a fine and useful address in a city that has remarkably few.

How to get there *(Map 4): In the city center behind the Paseo de Pereda opposite the Pereda gardens.*

Parador Gil Blas

39330 Santillana del Mar (Cantabria)
Plaza Ramón Pelayo, 11
Tel. 942-81 80 00 - Fax 942-81 83 91

Category ★★★ **Rooms** 54 with telephone, bath, WC, TV, minibar; elevator. **Price** Double 15,000-17,500Pts. **Meals** Breakfast 1,300Pts, served 8:00-11:00. **Restaurant** Service 1:00PM-4:00PM, 8:30PM-10:30PM; mealtime specials 3,500Pts, also à la carte. Specialties: Cocido - Merluza - Lubina - Salmón - Ternera al queso. **Credit cards** All major. **Pets** Dogs not allowed. **Facilities** Sauna, garage, parking. **Nearby** Colegiata de Santillana del Mar - Altamira Caves - Comillas - Picos de Europa - Beaches of Cobreces and Suances. **Open** All year.

Situated on the village square, the hotel occupies the very old and imposing home of the Barreda-Bracho family. The interior architecture is typical of the region: simple wooden columns give structure to most rooms, while the floors are shingled or of polished large parquet chips. On each floor there is a large lounge next to the corridor leading to the rooms which are very attractive: beds with columns in the Spanish style and everywhere a very beautiful choice of furniture, various objects and pictures. However, a special mention must be made of no. 222 with its panoramic terrace overlooking the village roofs and countryside. You will thus appreciate the calm in this region where the caves of Altamira attract a large number of visitors.

How to get there (Map 4): 31km southwest of Santander via N634, then C6316.

Hotel Altamira

39330 Santillana del Mar (Cantabria)
Calle Canton, 1
Tel. 942-81 80 25 - Fax 942-84 01 36
Sr Oceja Bujan

Category ★★★ **Rooms** 32 with telephone, shower, WC, satellite TV. **Price** Single 6,500-7,000Pts, double 7,500-11,500Pts; extra bed 1,700-3,000Pts. **Meals** Breakfast 670Pts, served 8:00-11:00. **Restaurant** With air-conditioning, service 1:15PM-4:00PM, 8:00PM-10:45PM; mealtime specials 1,750Pts, also à la carte. Specialties: Cocido montañes - Ensalada cantabra de salmon y almejas - Solomillo al vino tinto de rioja. **Credit cards** All major. **Pets** Dogs not allowed. **Facilities** Parking (100m). **Nearby** Colegiata de Santillana del Mar - Altamira Caves - Comillas - Picos de Europa - Beaches of Cobreces and Suances. **Open** All year.

The Hotel Altamira now occupies one of the aristocratic houses of Santillana, a medieval town classified as a historic monument that has conserved a beautiful collection of residences and palaces; the shields and arms of the knights and hidalgos who lived in them still appear on many them. This palace of the Valdevesco, rebuilt at the start of the 19th century, is a simple hotel but in excellent taste. The decor is sober and rustic in the lounges and two restaurants, with one of them serving only regional specialties. Beside the staircases and on the half-landings, there are small corners for reading, TV rooms and other amenities. The bedrooms offer good comfort but those on the upper floor are smaller and only have showers. In addition you'll find a delightful terrace, a nice place to enjoy a drink.

How to get there (Map 4): 31km southwest of Santander via N634, then C6316.

Hotel Los Infantes

39330 Santillana del Mar (Cantabria)
Avenida le Dorat, 1
Tel. 942-81 81 00 - Fax 942-84 01 03
Sra G. Mesones

Category ★★★ **Rooms** 28 with telephone, bath, WC, TV. **Price** Single 7,000-13,000Pts, double 9,000-15,000Pts. **Meals** Breakfast 700Pts, served 8:00-10:00; half board 7,200-10,200Pts, full board 9,200-12,200Pts (per pers.). **Restaurant** Service 1:00PM-4:00PM, 8:00PM-11:00PM; mealtime specials 2,000Pts, also à la carte. Specialties: Cocido montañes - Quesada en lechefritas - Solomillo al queso. **Credit cards** All major. **Pets** Dogs allowed (except in restaurant). **Nearby** Colegiata de Santillana del Mar - Altamira Caves - Comillas - Picos de Europa - Beaches of Cobreces and Suances. **Open** All year.

The Hotel Los Infantes occupies the former residence of the Calderons and its facade still bears their coat-of-arms. As soon as you go inside, you sense the intimate atmosphere of a hotel where everything has been done to make a guest feel perfectly at home. The ground-floor reception desk offers a warm welcome and the dining room has been built around a fireplace. Upstairs is a splendid lounge with character that is also present in the rooms. Our favorites are those facing the front as they are more spacious and two have a small lounge. In addition to excellent regional cooking and a very cordial reception, there is a discotheque… but it is not know for keeping the guests awake.

How to get there *(Map 4): 31km southwest of Santander via N634, then C6316.*

Hotel Don Pablo

39710 Solares (Cantabria)
General Mola, 6
Tel. 942-52 21 20 - Fax 942-52 20 00
Sr Alfredo Brava

Category ★★ **Rooms** 27 with air-conditioning, telephone, bath, WC, Satellite TV. **Price** Single 7,700-9,900Pts, double 9,700-12,200Pts; extra bed 2,500Pts. **Meals** Breakfast 900Pts, served 8:00-11:00; half board +2,000Pts, full board +3,500Pts. **Restaurant** Service 1:00PM-4:00PM, 8:00PM-12:00AM; mealtime specials 2,500Pts, also à la carte. **Credit cards** Amex, Visa, Eurocard, MasterCard. **Pets** Dogs allowed except in restaurant. **Facilities** Parking. **Nearby** Santander - Palacio de Acevedo in Hoznayo - Palacio de L'Eseldo in Pámanes - Casa de Cantolla and Palacio de Rañada in Liérganes - Puento Viergos Caves. **Open** All year.

In the back country behind the Cantabrian coast, Solares is a thermal spa known for its mineral waters, but the village and hotel are really interesting only because they are some twenty kilometers away from the bustle of Santander. The building is an aristocratic house dating from the 16th century and has retained its superb coat of arms and beautiful chapel. All the rest has been converted in the traditional, even standard, manner: a rustic atmosphere with stylish furniture, beams and terracotta tiled flooring. Comfort is fully assured with one or two extra services such as an internal video channel and satellite TV. There are only a few rooms but no fewer than three restaurants, so it is understandable that the hotel hosts a lot of receptions. An agreeable stop-off rather than a place to stay at any length. If you choose to eat away from the hotel, Casa Enrique is an excellent place to enjoy the guiso de alubias.

How to get there *(Map 4): 16km east of Santander.*

Es Castell AB

Mallorca
Binibona 07314 Caimari
Tel. 971-87 51 54 - Fax 971-87 51 54
Sra Mía Amer

Rooms 7 with bath. **Price** Single 18,000Pts, double 24,000Pts. **Meals** Breakfast included; half board 21,500Pts (1 pers.), 31,000Pts (2 pers.). **Restaurant** By reservation, only for residents. **Credit cards** Visa, Eurocard, MasterCard. **Pets** Dogs not allowed. **Facilities** Swimming pool. **Nearby** Campanet caves - Ruins of Alaró castel - Palma: Cathedral, Majorque museum, Llonja on paseo de Sagrera, Bellver castle - Pollensa golf course. **Open** All year.

The finca Es Castell has been in the same family since the 11th century. It was recently renovated and its exterior has preserved its original appearance and you readily understand the owners' unwillingness to alter the magnificent stone work so much in harmony with the subtle nuances of its surroundings. The property's 750 hectares are covered with olive trees and pines. Rooms for guests are in the main house which has a large living room with a fireplace and sofas which create a truly friendly atmosphere. The dining room in Mediterranean style is more intimate and its fine food is made from products of the farm itself. The rooms are simple and decorated in Mallorcan style with terracotta floors, lime-treated walls and colorful fabrics. A charming hotel in a bucolic setting.

How to get there (Map 10): 40km northeast of Palma via N713 to Inca, Caimari and Biniboma.

Scott's

Mallorca
07350 Binissalem
Plaza Iglesia, 12
Tel. 971-87 01 00 - Fax 971-87 02 67 - Dr George Scott
E-mail: scotts@bitel.es - Web: www.scottshotel.net

Rooms 17 with air-conditioning, telephone, bath, WC. **Price** Single 15,000Pts, double 25,000-28,000Pts, suite 33,000Pts. **Meals** Breakfast included. **Restaurant** Snacks 3 days by week, service 8:00PM-10:00PM or see pp. 306-307. **Credit cards** All major. **Pets** Dogs not allowed. **Facilities** Covered swimming pool, jacuzzi. **Nearby** Palma: Cathedral, Majorque museum, Llonja on paseo de Sagrera, Bellver castle - Pollensa golf course. **Open** All year.

Luxurious, elegant and refined is Scott's, a terribly British oasis in the center of Mallorca. The owner is, naturally, English and carefully maintains the hotel's coziness. The rooms with their antique furniture and floral percales offer incomparable sleeping accommodation which can be modified to suit the guest's requirements. A number of lounges, a library and a terrace with pleasant vegetation allow you to get away from it all with a minimum of effort. Breakfasts are a treat with a large choice of fruit juice plus pastries, yogurt and eggs along with local cold cuts. Children over the age of 12 are admitted.

***How to get there** (Map 10): 18km northeast of Palma, Consell/Binissalem exit.*

Son Espases ^{AB}

Mallorca
07012 Ciutat
Camino Son Espaces, 7
Tel. 971-75 06 14 - Fax 971-75 06 14 - Sr Felio de Cabrera

Rooms 3 with shared bath and 1 suite with private bath. **Price** Double 14,500Pts, suite 18,500Pts.
Meals Breakfast included. **Restaurant** See pp. 306/307. **Credit cards** Not accepted. **Pets** Dogs
not allowed. **Facilities** Swimming pool. **Nearby** Palma:Cathedral, Majorque museum, Llonja on
paseo de Sagrera, Bellver castle. **Open** May - Sept.

On this superb property very close to Palma is an absolutely magnificent 18th-century house. It is, however, the vast garden overflowing with tropical vegetation that catches your eye. The ground floor is a series of rooms surrounding the courtyard. Large paintings adorn the walls and the lounges have remarkable antique furniture. Rooms for the guests are upstairs, and of them, the suite is the most comfortable as the others share one bathroom. The suite is very large with a fine view of both the courtyard and the garden. You also have access to a swimming pool surrounded by well-kept lawns.

How to get there (Map 10): Take the exit going north out of Palma.

La Residencia

Mallorca
07179 Deiá (Mallorca)
Finca Son Canals
Tel. 971-63 90 11 - Fax 971-63 93 70 - Sra Maria Aastrop

Category ★★★★ **Rooms** 64 with air-conditioning, telephone, bath, WC. **Price** Single 18,500-29,000Pts, double 24,400-59,500Pts, junior-suite 41,850-74,000Pts, suite n°67 104,000-117,000Pts, suite with private swimming pool (2 pers.) 106,000-126,000Pts, suite with private swimming pool (4 pers.) 167,000-186,000Pts; extra bed 9,000Pts. **Meals** Breakfast included, served 8:00-11:30. **Restaurant** El Olivo, service 12:30PM-3:00PM, 8:00PM-11:00PM; à la carte 4,400-7,150Pts - Son Fony, service 12:30PM-3:00PM, 8:00PM-11:00PM; à la carte 3,500-6,000Pts. **Credit cards** All major. **Pets** Dogs not allowed. **Facilities** Swimming pool, tennis, private beach, parking. **Nearby** Palma - Northroad (Miramar, San Marroig, Lluc Alcari, Cala) - Monastery Real Cartuja de Valdemossa - Palma; Son Vida golf course (18-Hole), Bendinat golf course (9-Hole), Son Termens golf course (9-Hole). **Open** All year.

A real love affair is possible with La Residencia hotel. Fifteen kilometers from Mallorca and far from the tourist traps lies a hidden village full of charm. La Residencia is 16th-century manor house converted into a hotel, today one of the most delightful in the whole of Spain with hectares of woodlands, terraces with flowers sprouting out of the old stonework, flowered balconies and a succession of patios around the hotel. With its swimming pool facing the mountains, La Residencia is a genuine oasis. The owner is a veteran collector of pictures which cover all the walls. The bedrooms are vast and well-furnished, all with great refinement. La Residencia is without doubt one of our favorite hotels for reconciling you and the Balearics, all too often stripped of all charm by the over flow of tourists.

How to get there (Map 10): *27km north of Palma, towards Valldemosa.*

Hotel Costa d'Or

Mallorca
Lluc Alcari 07179 Deiá (Mallorca)
Tel. 971-63 90 25 - Fax 971-63 93 47
E-mail: costador@arrakis.es
Web: www.arrakis.es/~costador/home.html

Rooms 42 with air-conditioning, telephone, bath or shower, WC, TV, safe. **Price** Single 5,300Pts, double 9,500-13,200Pts (with terrace and view on the sea). **Meals** Breakfast included, served 8:00-11:30; half board 5,650-7,500Pts (per pers.). **Restaurant** Service 12:30PM-3:00PM, 8:00PM-11:00PM; mealtime specials, also à la carte. **Credit cards** Visa, Eurocard, MasterCard. **Pets** Dogs not allowed. **Facilities** Swimming pool, tennis, minigolf, parking. **Nearby** Northroad (Miramar, San Marroig, Lluc Alcari, Cala) - Monastery Real Cartuja de Valdemossa - Palma - Bendinat golf course (9-Hole) - Son Vida golf course (18-Hole). **Closed** Oct 28 - Apr 1st.

You leave Palma on a winding mountain road and pass through a majestic countryside with pine forests and cliffs that fall away to the sea. The Costa d'Or has a magnificent location overlooking a small bay. The older buildings have been renovated and the result is a comfortable and thoroughly modern hotel. A number of the rooms have terraces overlooking the sea which were those we preferred. The decoration is, unfortunately, reminiscent of the 70s. The hotel offers a swimming pool and tennis courts, a good panoramic restaurant plus a setting that makes it well worth a detour to enjoy it.

How to get there (Map 10): 28km north of Palma, towards Valldemosa or Sóller.

Sa Plana

Mallorca
07192 Estellencs (Mallorca)
Eusebi Pascual
Tel. 971-61 86 66 - Fax 971- 61 85 86

Rooms 4 doubles and 1 for 4 pers. with bath. **Price** Double 10,000-13,000Pts. **Meals** Breakfast included, served 8:00-11:30. **Evening meals** By reservation, service 12:30PM-3:00PM, 8:00PM-11:00PM; mealtime specials 2,500Pts. **Credit Cards** Diners, Visa, Eurocard, MasterCard. **Pets** Dogs not allowed. **Facilities** Parking. **Nearby** Monastery Real Cartuja de Valldemossa - Palma - Son Vida golf course (18-Hole) - Bendinat golf course (9-Hole). **Open** All year.

Estellenes is one of the typical Mallorcan mountain villages that is not far from the sea. This charming guest house is located on the edge of the village and its calm, family-like atmosphere is ideal for spending a relaxing vacation. You soon find a favorite spot, either in the living room or in the garden. The soberly-decorated rooms enjoy old furniture and are most comfortable. After a day of swimming, bicycle riding, fishing in the small Estellencs creek or hiking in the Serra de Tramuntana (devotees of minimal exertion may prefer riding on a donkey), guests gather around a large table in the garden for dinner. Meals here offer produce direct from the vegetable garden, and you will thoroughly enjoy Sa Plana's simplicity, friendliness and fine natural surrounding, all allowing you to simply take it easy.

How to get there (Map 10): 25km northwest of Palma.

Sa Posada d'Aumallia ^{AB}

Mallorca
07200 Felanitx
Camino Son Prohens
Tel. 971-58 26 57 - Fax 971-58 32 69 - Familia Marti Gomilla

Rooms 14 with air-conditioning, bath, WC, TV, minibar. **Price** Single 14,250-17,625Pts, double 19,000-23,500Pts, 4 pers. 33,250-41,125Pts; extra bed 2,375Pts (2-12 years old), 4,750-5,875Pts. **Meals** Breakfast included; half board +3,200Pts (per pers.). **Restaurant** Service 12:30PM-3:00PM, 8:00PM-11:00PM; *Mallorquin* mealtime specials 3,400Pts. *Mallorquine* specialties with products from the property. **Credit cards** Amex, Visa, Eurocard, MasterCard. **Pets** Dogs not allowed. **Facilities** Swimming pool, tennis. **Nearby** Palma: Cathedral, Majorque museum, Llonja on paseo de Sagrera, Bellver castle. **Closed** Nov, Dec and Jan.

In a lovely country setting and far from seaside tourist madness, the Posada d'Aumilia offers lodging at once refined and romantic. Two wings have been added to this old farm house but the spirit of the original architecture has been scrupulously respected. The dining room, the bar and the living room, all on the ground floor, are vast and you find furniture from the 30s peacefully coexisting with imposing pieces in solid wood, clearly in Spanish style. The rooms are in much the same spirit with beds of dark wood with twisted columns, chests of drawers and chairs in 19th-century style. Some of them are at garden level, but the rooms on the third floor are bigger, more imaginative and enjoy a terrace looking out on the olive trees. The others, in the wings of the building, are rather more ordinary, but there's always the swimming pool and tennis courts.

How to get there *(Map 10): 60km east of Palma. In the center of Felanitz, go towards Prohens.*

Es Rafal Podent ^{AB}

Mallorca
07500 Manacor
Carretera Calas de Mallorca, km 6
Tel. 971-18 31 30 - Fax 971-18 31 30 - Sr Juan Parera

Rooms 5 (2-5 pers.) with kitchenette, lounge, telephone, bath or shower, WC, TV. **Price** Near the tour 8,900-14,500Pts, near the swimming pool 13,000-16,500Pts (per pers., by day). **Meals** Breakfast 900Pts. **Restaurant** Service 12:30PM-3:00PM, 8:00PM-11:00PM; mealtime specials, also à la carte. **Credit cards** Not accepted. **Pets** Dogs not allowed. **Facilities** Swimming pool. **Nearby** Palma: Cathedral, Majorque museum, Llonja on paseo de Sagrera, Bellver castle. **Open** All year.

This 15th-century farm house lies peacefully in the shade of some olive trees with its smaller buildings built around a large square tower. Each of them has an independent entrance as well as a different decor although all have impressive interior stone walls, ceilings with exposed beams, antique furniture and a private terrace. The most attractive of them is on the third floor overlooking the olive grove. The garden is very pleasant with trees and a superb swimming pool. If you choose, you can make arrangements to have meals prepared or take advantage of the fine produce grown on the farm and do your own cooking. This is an excellent place for a family vacation.

How to get there *(Map 10): 60km east of Palma to Manacor, then towards Calas de Mallorca for 7km.*

Palacio Ca Sa Galesa

Mallorca 07001 Palma de Mallorca
Carrer de Miramar, 8
Tel. 971-71 54 00 - Fax 971-72 15 79 - Sr Crespi
E-mail: reservas@palaciocasagalesa.com - Web: palaciocasagalesa.com

Category ★★★★★ **Rooms** and suites 12 with air-conditioning, telephone, bath, WC, satellite TV, safe, minibar; elevator. **Price** Single 22,500Pts, double 30,250Pts, junior-suite 34,000Pts, suite 38,000-41,200Pts; extra bed 9,000Pts. **Meals** Breakfast 2,400Pts served 8:30-11:00. **Restaurant** See pp. 306-307. **Credit cards** All major. **Pets** Dogs not allowed. **Facilities** Swimming pool, sauna, parking (1,500Pts). **Nearby** Palma: Cathedral, Majorque museum, Llonja on paseo de Sagrera, Bellver castle. **Closed** Jan 10 - 27.

Here, the cathedral is a close neighbor and that is one of the reasons we found this intimate and refined palace irresistible, plainly one of the best hotels in Palma. Once through the entrance way, you discover a stone staircase leading to different salons that take up the entire second floor. These are beautifully decorated with inspiration from a number of sources and they include impressive Spanish furniture, a mahogany dining room set that is very English in style as well as the owner's highly personal touch, an exact replica of the dining room in Monet's house in Giverny. This is a splendid setting for tea and a slice of nut cake some quiet afternoon. Relaxation is the order of the day as well on the small patio with a refreshing fountain. The rooms, each bearing the name of a composer, have received particular attention from the owner and are elegant and comfortable. The service and facilities are absolutely perfect as you have a roof garden with an excellent view of the cathedral and the Old Town, while in the basement there is a Roman-style swimming pool plus a fitness center with a sauna. This is quite simply a marvelous place to stay.

How to get there (Map 10): Near the cathedral.

Hotel San Lorenzo

Mallorca
07012 Palma de Mallorca
C./ San Lorenzo, 14
Tel. 971-72 82 00 - Fax 971-71 19 01 - Sr Schmid
E-mail: sanlorenzo@fehm.es - Web: www.fehm.es/pmi/sanlorenzo

Category ★★★★ **Rooms** 6 with air-conditioning, telephone, bath, WC, satellite TV, minibar, safe.
Price Single 14,500-30,000Pts, double 17,000-32,500Pts. **Meals** Breakfast 1,000-1,400Pts, served
8:00-11:00. **Restaurant** See pp.306-307. **Credit cards** All major. **Pets** Dogs allowed on request.
Facilities Swimming pool. **Nearby** In Palma: Cathedral, Majorque museum, Llonja on paseo de
Sagrera, Bellver castle. **Open** All year.

W e immediately fell in love with the San Lorenzo, much as we did with
the preceding hotel and the one that follows. The three of them truly are
the most charming in Palma. You push open the ornate iron gate on this street
in the Old Town and discover a paradise of good taste and refinement. On the
ground floor is the bar, not unlike a Paris bistro with a zinc counter, bar stools
and naval maps, a perfect place for breakfast. One floor up is a terrace with a
swimming pool whose design is inspired by the lay-out of the Palma of
historical times. Beyond it are the rooms, comfortable, elegant, spacious and
bright with attractive regional ceramics in the bath rooms. Two of the rooms
have large terraces overlooking the roofs of the city. Whatever your budget,
you are sure to have a delightful stay in Palma.

How to get there *(Map 10): In the Old Town.*

Hotel Born

Mallorca
07012 Palma de Mallorca
C/. Sant Jaume, 3
Tel. 971-71 29 42 - Fax 971-71 86 18
E-mail: hborn@bitel.es

Category ★★ **Rooms** 26 and 3 suites with telephone, bath, WC, TV. **Price** Single 7,000-13,500Pts, double 10,000-15,000Pts, suite 18,000Pts. **Meals** Breakfast included. **Restaurant** See pp. 306-307. **Credit cards** Visa, Eurocard, MasterCard. **Pets** Dogs not allowed. **Nearby** In Palma: Cathedral, Majorque museum, Llonja on paseo de Sagrera, Bellver castle. **Open** All year.

The Hotel Born, located in the historical center of the city, is, for its category, one of our favorite hotels in Palma. Formerly a 16th-century residence having belonged to the Marquis Ferandell, it has conserved its grandiose architecture. Its spectacular entrance way opens onto a patio with three tall palm trees and impressive marble columns holding up large stone arches. A wide staircase leads to a lounge which serves the five most attractive rooms, some of which still have original frescoes on their ceilings. The decor is subtle with antique furniture and soft colors. It is advisable to take a room giving on the patio as those on the street are not all that far from the houses facing them. You should not miss the pleasure of having your breakfast on the marvelously cool patio. A delightful hotel in the very heart of the city.

How to get there *(Map 10): In the center of town near the Plazza Rei Joan Carlesi.*

Arabella Golf Hotel

Mallorca
Son Vida 07013 Palma de Mallorca
Carrer de la Vinagrella
Tel. 971-79 99 99 - Fax 971-79 99 97

Category ★★★★★ **Rooms** 59 and 24 suites with air-conditioning, telephone, bath, WC, satellite TV, safe, minibar; elevator. **Price** Double 23,750-66,250Pts. **Meals** Breakfast included, served 7:30-11:00. **Restaurant** Le plat d'Or (dinner), à la carte 3,500-5,000Pts. Le Foravila, near the swimming pool. **Credit cards** All major. **Pets** Dogs not allowed. **Facilities** Covered swimming pool, tennis, Arabelle beauty & Holistic, Sauna, 18-Hole golf, parking, garage. **Nearby** Palma: Cathedral, Majorque museum, Llonja on paseo de Sagrera, Bellver castle. **Open** All year.

The Arabella, now affiliated with the Sheraton chain, is six kilometers from Palma and overlooks the city. It is one of many hotels built near the Son Vida golf course. Surrounded by luxurious tropical vegetation, the new buildings maintain a distinctly Spanish style. The immense reception area has a marble floor, leather sofas and a multi-lingual staff as befits an international luxury hotel. The rooms are of different sizes, all providing the same sense of comfort. The hotel's proximity to the golf course explains the presence here of numerous golfers but there are other facilities that allow you to combine sports with the usual tourist pleasures.

How to get there *(Map 10): Near the cathedral.*

Son Brondo ^{AB}

Mallorca
07170 Palma a Valldemossa
Crta. Palma a Valldemossa, km 14,3 and 15,2
Tel. 971-61 61 90 - Fax 971-61 61 90   Sra Rossello

Rooms 3 with terrace and 3 suites with telephone, bath, WC, TV, minibar. **Price** Double 22,000Pts, suite 25,000Pts; extra bed 5,000Pts. **Meals** Breakfast 1,500Pts. **Evening meals** *Mallorcan* specialties. **Credit cards** Visa, Eurocard, MasterCard. **Pets** Dogs not allowed. **Facilities** Swimming pool, solarium. **Nearby** Palma: Cathedral, Majorque museum, Llonja on paseo de Sagrera, Bellver castle. **Open** All year.

Nicely located between the sea and the mountain, this is among the most beautiful settings on the entire island with the green of the pine trees harmonizing perfectly with the yellow of the hills. The road leads upward through the countryside and you soon find yourself at this noble and rustic house. The courtyard is surrounded by large earthenware jars, each overflowing with flowers. A staircase goes off it leading to vast lounge. The rooms for guests are on the fourth floor, well-furnished with regional furniture and *Mallorcan* fabrics, offering all the comfort of a hotel. The garden is only a few meters away with its swimming pool and solarium; even the sea is not far. A few kilometers from the famous charter house, Son Brondo enjoys surroundings that are ideal for casual country strolls.

***How to get there** (Map 10): 14km north of Palma.*

Finca Ses Rotetes [AB]

Mallorca
07509 Manacor
Carretera Porto Cristo - Porto Colom, km 13,9
Tel. 971-18 32 56 - Fax 971-18 32 56
Sr José-F. Moragues Villalonga

Rooms 2, 1 apartment (2 pers.), 1 house with 3 rooms (6 pers.), bath, WC, satellite TV. **Price** Double 11,800Pts, apart. (2 pers./day) 14,000Pts, apart. (4 pers./day) 25,000Pts, apart. (6 pers./day) 37,500Pts. **Meals** Breakfast 1,000Pts. **Evening meals** By reservation; mealtime specials 4,000Pts. **Credit cards** Not accepted. **Pets** Dogs not allowed. **Facilities** Swimming pool. **Nearby** Palma: Cathedral, Majorque museum, Llonja on paseo de Sagrera, Bellver castle. **Open** All year.

S es Rotetes is a typical Mallorcan finca built of pink limestone with green shutters on its two levels and surrounded by olive groves. The rooms on the third floor are rather small, but there are two apartments, decorated with regional fabrics which are more pleasant and private. The garden is set up for serving breakfast and meals throughout the day. There is a swimming pool and solarium at a lower level. A fine hotel offering at once the peace and quiet of its inland location while being close to beaches.

How to get there *(Map 10): 60km east of Palma towards Manacor, then Porto Cristo.*

Ca'n Coll AB

Mallorca
07100 Sóller
Cami de Ca'n Coll, 1
Tel. 971-63 32 44 - Fax 971-63 19 05 - Sra Emma Rodríguez
E-mail: can:coll@todoesp.es - Web: www.todoesp.es/can-coll

Rooms 5 and 3 suites with air-conditioning, bath, WC, satellite TV (in suite). **Price** Single 19,000Pts, double 22,000Pts, suite 33,000Pts; extra bed 6,000Pts. **Meals** Breakfast 1,500Pts; half board +3,745Pts. **Evening meals** Mealtime specials 4,000Pts. Mallorquine cooking. **Credit cards** Visa, Eurocard, MasterCard. **Pets** Dogs not allowed. **Facilities** Swimming pool, bicycle rentals, parking. **Nearby** Beaches in Puerto de Sóller - Palma: Cathedral, Majorque museum, Llonja on paseo de Sagrera, Bellver castle. **Open** All year.

Ca'n Coll is one of the best hotels on this island with a splendid location, impeccable service plus the ever-so-friendly welcome you receive here. A large red leather sofa stands in the center of a vast lounge giving onto the garden and has attractive modern furniture as well as fine paintings. The same things are found in the well-kept rooms, while the suites are absolutely sumptuous, one of which, the exception to the rule, is furnished with authentic antiques and has a terrace overlooking the valley. Summertime is a time to stretch out beside the pool, stroll among the orange and lemon trees and dine under the garden's palm trees. A real find if you choose "rural tourism."

How to get there *(Map 10): 30km north of Palma*

Finca Ca N'ai

Mallorca
07100 Sóller
Camí Son Sales, 50
Tel. 971-63 24 94 - Fax 971-63 18 99 - Sr Domingo Morell-Marti

Rooms 11 with air-conditioning, telephone, bath or shower, minibar. **Price** Double 32,414Pts. **Meals** Breakfast included; half board +3,900Pts (per pers.). **Restaurant** Closed Mon; mealtime specials 3,700Pts, also à la carte. **Credit cards** All major. **Pets** Dogs not allowed. **Facilities** Swimming pool, jacuzzi, parking. **Nearby** Beaches in Puerto de Sóller - Palma: Cathedral, Majorque museum, Llonja on paseo de Sagrera, Bellver castle. **Closed** Nov 15 - Feb 1st.

The reputation of Ca N'ai has long been established among Mallorcans who have recognized it as a truly gastronomic restaurant. Visitors cannot help but fall in love with this authentic finca surrounded by colorful and fragrant orange trees. The house is truly exquisite with delightful and refined rooms, especially the one with a mezzanine and terrace overlooking the countryside. The garden has been skillfully designed to let you take full advantage of the magnificent panorama whether beside the fountain, under the palm trees or from poolside. The restaurant here uses only the finest produce available at the market. Fourteen generations have followed one another here as evidenced by the documents and family portraits that cover the walls of the house. An excellent hotel.

How to get there *(Map 10): 30km north of Palma.*

Ca S'Hereu AB

Mallorca
07550 Son Servera
Rue Elisa Servera
Tel. (Association Agroturismo Balear) 971 72 15 08 - Fax 971-71 73 17
Sr Ventura Rubí

House (6 pers.) with 8 bedrooms (3 with double bed, 5 with twin beds), telephone, 2 baths, WC, TV. **Price** 26,000Pts (per 6 pers./day). **Restaurant** See pp. 306-307. **Credit oards** Not accepted. **Pets** Dogs allowed. **Nearby** Palma: Cathedral, Majorque museum, Llonja on paseo de Sagrera, Bellver castle - Son Servera golf course (9-Hole). **Open** All year.

This vast residence in stone with a turret was one of the twelve houses that belonged to the island's nobility in the 16th century. It now belongs to one of the oldest families on Mallorca. It is in the northeastern part of the island on open country and very close to the sea. On the ground floor is a large stone kitchen, a long dining room covered by a brick arch plus a vast lounge with attractive wrought-iron furnishings. Upstairs are rooms decorated in regional style with engravings depicting the conquest of the island along with religious paintings. There is a pleasant garden and you can swim only a few kilometers away.

How to get there *(Map 10): 70km east of Palma towards Manacor, then Porto Cristo and Son Cervera.*

La Ventana

07800 Ibiza
Dalt Vila - Sa Carossa, 13
Tel. 971-39 08 57 - Fax 971-39 01 45
Sr Philip Moseby

Rooms 13 and 2 suites with air-conditioning, telephone, bath, satellite TV, minibar. **Price** Double 19,800-29,200Pts, suite 33,700-48,000Pts. **Meals** Breakfast 1,200Pts. **Restaurant** By reservation (tel.: 971-30 35 37). **Credit cards** Visa, Eurocard, MasterCard. **Pets** Dogs not allowed. **Nearby** Dalt Vila and the Cathedral of Ibiza - Church of Jesus - Beach of Talamanca - Roca Llisa golf course. **Open** All year.

This small hotel is a real treasure. It is located at the edge of the city's fortifications and in one of the houses surrounding the cathedral. Coming here is much like visiting a private home as you find family furniture and personal items in the reception area and the bar. Although slightly monastic, the rooms are truly adorable in their simplicity with blue walls, white bed linen and muslin mosquito netting; some look out on the trees of the square (noisy in summer but, don't forget, the nightly *fiesta* is a tradition in Ibiza), the others face the courtyard. The only ones with air-conditioning are the suites. They have beautifully arranged terraces with a view of the old city.

How to get there *(Map 9): In the Old Town - "Dalt Vila."*

La Torre del Canónigo

07800 Ibiza
Calle Mayor, 8
Tel. 971-30 38 84 - Fax 971-30 78 43
Sr Balcazar

Apartments 4 and 5 studios with telephone, bath with jacuzzi or shower, satellite TV. **Price** Studio 12,000-60,000Pts (2 pers./day), apartment 30,000-113,000Pts (4 pers./day). **Restaurant** See pp. 306-307. **Credit cards** All major. **Pets** Dogs not allowed. **Nearby** Dalt Vila and the Cathedral of Ibiza - Church of Jesus - Beach of Talamanca - Roca Llisa golf course (9-Hole). **Closed** Nov - Mar.

The Torre del Canónigo was built in the 16th century in pure Catalan Gothic style as a lookout to stand watch over the port, the chateau and the entire city. Splendidly renovated, its 980 square meters offer apartments on two floors. They are of different sizes and can, if required, be combined. They are all very pleasant and well organized, using attractive traditional materials with nicely embroidered benches and headboards. On the ground floor are the large lounges and the bar where you can have your breakfast. The atmosphere is much like that of a summer house. In addition, Apartment 6 has a small private swimming pool. The service is attentive and efficient. This is an ideal hotel for an extended stay provided you avoid the months of July and August - unless, of course, you are a dyed-in-the-wool Ibiza fancier.

How to get there (Map 9): In the Old Town.

El Corsario

07800 Ibiza
Poniente 5 Dalt Vila
Tel. 971-30 12 48 - Fax 971-39 19 53
E-mail: elcorsario@ctv

Rooms 14 with shower. **Price** Double 16,000-18,000Pts, special double 20,000-22,000Pts, little suite 26,000-28,000Pts, junior-suite 40,000Pts, luxous suite 60,000Pts. **Meals** Breakfast included. **Restaurant** Service from 8:00PM; mealtime specials-à la carte 12,000-15,000Pts. **Credit cards** Visa, Eurocard, MasterCard. **Pets** Dogs not allowed. **Nearby** Dalt Vila and the cathedral of Ibiza - Church of Jesus - Beach of Talamanca; Roca Llisa golf course. **Open** All year.

An agreeable small hotel hidden in the Old Town, El Corsario is one of the oldest hotels on Ibiza, and the simplicity of this old house is one of its major charms. The hotel is very well kept and the service particularly friendly; breakfast may be taken on the terrace, which abounds with pots of flowers, and from it you have one of the best views of Ibiza. The restaurant is currently open every evening. The menu changes regularly and offers a dozen specialties and prices are very modest compared to others on this island.

How to get there *(Map 9): By boat from Barcelona and Valencia: contact the Cia. Transmediterránea company (Tel. 971-72 67 40); in the Old Town (Dalt Vila).*

Les Terrasses

07800 Ibiza
Carret. de Santa Eulalia, km 1
Tel. 971-33 26 43 - Fax 971-33 11 61 - Sra Pialoux
E-mail: lesterrasses@interbook.net

Rooms 8 with heating or air-conditioning, telephone, bath, WC. **Price** Single 14,500-17,000Pts, double 18,000-22,000Pts, suite 24,500-30,000Pts. **Meals** Breakfast included. **Restaurant** Open Tues and Fri evening, (snacks every day for residents); mealtime specials 2,500Pts (lunch), 3,700Pts (dinner), also à la carte. Specialty: Fish. **Credit cards** Visa, Eurocard, MasterCard. **Pets** Dogs allowed. **Facilities** 2 swimming pools, tennis, parking. **Nearby** Dalt Vila and the cathedral of Ibiza - Beach of Talamanca; Roca Llisa golf course. **Open** All year.

L es Terrasses has nothing to with a hotel – one comes here as a friend! A confidential location, only a large indigo blue stone at 1km on the road from Santa Eulalia indicates the entrance. Françoise, your host, is French and has converted this old house in the Ibizan countryside with a lot of talent. The ocres and indigos, the white chalked walls set off with blue frames doors of the windows all give the exterior a truly authentic character. There is the same charm indoors where the antique furniture, carefully selected at the local flea markets, mingles with the family pieces. The bedrooms have this same simplicity and good taste. The cuisine is good: light and fresh at lunch-time, with more intricate dishes at dinner. You can be deliciously idle by the swimming pool or on the beautiful shaded terrace where a delightful time may be had despite its location on a touristy island. This is a very agreeable place to stay.

How to get there *(Map 9): On the road towards Santa Eulalia, a blue stone on the right indicates the way.*

Hotel Las Brisas de Ibiza

San José 07830 Ibiza
Apartado 83 - Porroig
Tel. 971 80 21 93 - Fax 971-80 23 28
Web: www.lasbrisas-ibiza.com

Category ★★★★ **Rooms** 9 with air-conditioning, telephone, bath, WC, satellite TV, minibar, safe.
Price Double 26,000-35,000Pts, suite 47,000-67,000Pts. **Meals** Breakfast included. **Snacks**
available for lunch on the swimming pool, à la carte. Specialties: fish and shellfish. **Credit cards** All
major. **Pets** Dogs allowed. **Facilities** Swimming pool, tennis, mountain bikes, parking. **Nearby** Dalt
Vila, cathedral of Ibiza - Church of Jesus - Playa Talamanca - Roca Llisa golf course **Closed** Oct 31
- Apr 1st.

Beautifully situated at the top of a cliff, this hotel on the Porroig peninsula
overlooks the Bay of Es Cubells. The interior decoration has a great deal
of colorful Mediterranean personality with strong Moroccan and Andalusian
influences. The rooms, in yellow and white, all have attractive exotic or
traditional furniture, lamps made from pottery along with brightly colored
wool rugs. Each has its own terrace with a view of the sea. The lounge's
architecture is remarkable with special attention paid to its decorative aspect
producing a somewhat baroque effect with well-upholstered armchairs and
large, colorful jars. Sunny colors are omnipresent around the patio which
offers numerous *sol y sombra* corners for the enjoyment of the guests. The
first-class swimming pool may well tempt you to step into the garden, but a
five-minute walk will take you to a small, unspoiled creek with lovely white
sand. For those hungry for night life which breaks loose in July and August,
the town of Ibiza is a quarter of an hour away by car.

How to get there *(Map 9): West of Ibiza.*

Hotel Pikes

07800 Ibiza
San Antonio de Portmany
Tel. 971-34 22 22 - Fax 971-34 23 12
Sr A. Pikes

Category ★★★★★ **Rooms** 24 with air-conditioning, telephone, bath, WC, TV, minibar. **Price** Standard double 22,000-30,000Pts, junior-suite 28,000-40,000Pts, suite 35,000-70,000Pts, apart. 55,000-85,000Pts, duplex 72,000-120,000Pts. **Meals** Breakfast 1,200Pts, served 8.30-12.00. **Restaurant** Service 1:00PM-3:30PM, 8:30PM-12:00AM; à la carte. International cooking. **Credit cards** All major. **Pets** Dogs allowed. **Facilities** Swimming pool. **Nearby** Dalt Vila and the cathedral of Ibiza - Beach of Talamanca; Roca Llisa golf course. **Closed** Feb.

To uncover a hotel hidden away between gardens and pine woods on Ibiza is something of a miracle! This is, however, the case with the Hotel Pikes, a residence that is 600 years old. With only twenty rooms all differently decorated but each in the typical style of the island, the Hotel Pikes offers all the advantages of a hotel "de luxe" along with the informal ambiance of a friend's home. While most rooms are of a "standard" model, there are a large number of suites as well, all with personalized decoration and located near the swimming pool with a very nice view. Not far from the nightlife, you can rest and recover during the afternoon beside the pool after a heavy night out! With a bit of luck, you may also spot Julio (Iglesias) or possibly Grace (Jones). All things considered, this is a tiny paradise.

How to get there (Map 9): 15km of Ibiza.

Hotel Hacienda-Na Xamena

07080 Ibiza
Apartado 423 - San Miguel
Tel. 971-33 45 00 - Fax 971-33 45 14

Category ★★★★★ **Rooms** 53 and 10 suites with air-conditioning, telephone, bath, WC, satellite TV, minibar, safe; elevator. **Price** Single 22,500-44,500Pts, double 28,400-52,600Pts, Junior suite 37,700-55,600Pts. **Meals** Breakfast (buffet) 2,600Pts, served 7:00-11:00; half board +9,000Pts. **Restaurant** Service 1:30PM-4:00PM, 8:30PM/9:00PM-11:00PM; mealtime specials 6,400Pts, also à la carte. Specialties: Fish and shellfish. **Credit cards** All major. **Pets** Dogs allowed only in bedroom. **Facilities** 3 swimming pools (1 with air-conditioning), hammam, sauna, tennis, mountain bikes, parking. **Nearby** Dalt Vila and the Cathedral of Ibiza - Church of Jesus - Beach of Talamanca - Roca Llisa golf course. **Closed** Oct 31 - end Apr.

The Hacienda is one of Ibiza's top hotels. It is splendidly located and its architect drew all his inspiration from the surrounding countryside. Its buildings look down 180 meters on a delightful inlet with gleaming rocks. The truly courageous go there to swim. The lounges look out on a large patio, and its luxurious vegetation assures a pleasant temperature even on the hottest days. The rooms are lovely and truly comfortable, and there are bathtubs offering hydro-massage in most of them. All enjoy the impressive and exceptional view for which the hotel is famous. The swimming pools are superb, one of which is even air-conditioned, and you can tour the countryside on foot or bicycle, or simply enjoy the peace and quiet, often a rare commodity in Ibiza. There are several fine restaurants. Renting a car will allow you to take even greater advantage of this attractive island.

How to get there *(Map 9): From the airport, go towards Ibiza. At the first traffic circle, take the road to Sta Eulalia-San Juan for 7km, then towards San Miguel in the direction of the port for 4km. The hotel is marked with an arrow on the left side of the road.*

Ca's Pla

07800 Ibiza
San Miguel de Balanzat - P. O. Box N° 777
Tel. 971-33 45 87 - Fax 971-33 46 04
Sr N. Sanchez de Fenaroli

Rooms 16 with air-conditioning, telephone, bath, WC, satellite TV. **Price** Double 16,000-22,000Pts, suite 18,000-32,000Pts. **Meals** Breakfast 900-1,200Pts. **Snacks** By reservation, at the swimming pool. **Credit cards** Visa, Eurocard, MasterCard. **Pets** Dogs not allowed. **Facilities** Swimming pool, tennis (800Pts), parking. **Nearby** Dalt Vila and the cathedral of Ibiza - Beach of Talamanca; Roca Llisa golf course. **Closed** Dec 1st - Mar 31.

In the northwest of the island and some twenty kilometers from Ibiza and close to the port of San Miguel, the owners of this large villa have opened 14 rooms for their guests. Here, you are in a holiday home, received as friends, which means that you will be living in a very personalized and very warm atmosphere: lots of souvenirs, books, bouquets of dried flowers and so on. All the public rooms open wide onto the garden alive with plants and flowers, while the shady terrace offers many small and restful corners, and hammocks and armchairs allow the guest to be comfortably idle. The rooms have all been decorated with a care for your, comfort and well-being. Here you may enjoy all the fragrances that go with a good vacation: sea and country air plus the smell of pine trees.

How to get there (Map 9): To the northwest of Ibiza, at 3km of San Miguel take the road for the port. At 14km take the road on your right.

Hotel Palacio de los Velada

05001 Ávila
Plaza de la Catedral
Tel. 920-25 51 00 - Fax 920-25 49 00
E-mail: palaciov@isid.es

Category ★★★★ **Rooms** 85 with telephone, bath, WC, satellite TV, minibar; elevator. **Price** Single 15,750Pts, double 18,500Pts, suite 40,000Pts. **Meals** Breakfast 1,300Pts, served 7:30-11:00. **Restaurant** Service 12:30PM-4:00PM, 8:00PM-12:00AM; mealtime specials 4,000Pts, also à la carte. Regional cooking. **Credit cards** All major. **Pets** Dogs not allowed. **Facilities** Garage. **Nearby** Ávila: Cathedral, Church of San Vicente and Monastery of Santo Tomás - Cebreros. **Open** All year.

The hotel is on a square overlooked by a superb cathedral-fortress with two Greco-Roman towers. It is in a former palace where kings and courtiers once gathered. The immense volume of the entrance is indicative of the hotel's majestic architecture as is the vast patio overlooked by three stories of sculpted arcades. There is now a bar there with areas reserved for contemporary art shows. The hotel has a fine restaurant, La Taberna del Tostado. As in most large hotels, the rooms are not equipped with lounges. The decoration is plain and unpretentious, but the "grand hotel" atmosphere makes this an excellent address from which to visit the city of Santa Teresa where its numerous civil and religious buildings have earned it the name of *la cuidad de cantos y santos*.

How to get there (Map 12): 97km southeast of Salamanca via N501 - 115km *northwest of Madrid via A6, exit at Villacastín, then N110.*

Parador Raimundo de Borgoña

05001 Ávila
Marqués de Canales de Chozas, 2
Tel. 920-21 13 40 - Fax 920-22 61 66
Sr de la Torre Alcala

Category ★★★★ **Rooms** 61 with air-conditioning, telephone, bath, WC, satellite TV, minibar; elevator. **Price** Double 13,500-17,500Pts. **Meals** Breakfast 1,300Pts, served 8:00-11:00. **Restaurant** Service 1:00PM-4:00PM, 8:30PM-11:00PM; mealtime specials 3,700Pts, also à la carte. Specialtles: Judias del barco - Pucheretes teresianos - Yemas de la Santa. **Credit cards** All major. **Pets** Dogs not allowed. **Facilities** Parking, garage. **Nearby** In Ávila: Cathedral, Church of San Vicente, Monastery of Santo Tómas - Cebreros - Las Navas del Marqués - Arevalo - Sierra de Gredos. **Open** All year.

This parador bears the name of the man who reconquered, repeopled and reconstructed Ávila, also giving it the fantastic walls which, like an immense crown, encircle the ancient "Town of the Knights". The hotel was built on the ruins of the Benavides palace and still conserves some of the original structure: one of its facades, backing onto the walls, forms one side of the square which you enter via one of the nine town gates, La Puerta del Carmen. Its ideal location along with complete renovation makes this hotel one of undeniable charm. The rooms are spacious and sunny with decoration both elegant and intimate and offer new and modern comfort. Our preference is for those overlooking the square. The patio is a pleasant place to have a drink all year long and the dining room, with its warm and distinctly regional atmosphere, features specialties of the cooking of Ávila. A city and a hotel not to be missed.

How to get there (Map 12): 97km southeast of Salamanca via N501: or 115km northwest of Madrid via A6, exit Villacastín, then N110.

Hostería de Bracamonte

05001 Ávila
C./ Bracamonte, 6
Tel. 920-25 12 80 - Fax 920-25 38 38
Sr Costa

Category ★★★ **Rooms** 25 and 2 suites with telephone, bath, WC, TV. **Price** Single 6,000Pts, double 8,000-12,000Pts, suite 19,000Pts. **Meals** Breakfast 500Pts, served 8:00-10:30. **Restaurant** Service 12:30PM-4:00PM, 8:00PM-12:00AM, closed Tues and Nov; à la carte. Regional cooking. **Credit cards** Visa, Eurocard, MasterCard. **Pets** Small dogs allowed (except in the restaurant). **Nearby** In Ávila: Cathedral, Church of San Vicente, Monastery of Santo Tómas - Cebreros. **Open** All year.

The Hostería de Bracamonte is in the heart of Ávila and only a few steps away from the Plaza de la Victoria. Particular care has been given to the decor: the entry hall rewards the guest with its plain stonework, discreet lighting, the magnificent tapestries on the walls and the bright tiles of the floor. Around are spread the different restaurant rooms which you enter under attractive vaulted ceilings. The bar is decorated with photos of personalities of Spanish life who have honored it with their presence and it is a very lively spot. A stone staircase leads to the rooms furnished in an elegant Castillian style which is also found in the more recently-opened rooms. The suites deserve special mention as all are truly delightful. In a town not famous for night life, you will find a very friendly ambiance both in the restaurant and bar, before dropping peacefully off to sleep sheltered by such beautiful walls.

How to get there *(Map 12): 97km southeast of Salamanca via N501: or 111km northwest of Madrid via A6, exit Villacastín, then N110.*

Parador de Gredos

05132 Novarredonda de Gredos (Ávila)
Carretera Barraco, km 43 - Bejar
Tel. 920-34 80 48 - Fax 920-34 82 05
Sr Miguel Angel Chica

Category ★★★ **Rooms** 77 with telephone, bath, WC, satellite TV, minibar. **Price** Double 111,500-13,500Pts. **Meals** Breakfast (buffet) 1,300Pts, served 8:00-10:30. **Restaurant** Service 1:30PM-3:30PM, 8:30PM-11:00PM; mealtime specials 3,500Pts, also à la carte. Castillian and international cooking. **Credit cards** All major. **Pets** Dogs not allowed. **Facilities** Tennis, riding, parking (1,500Pts). **Nearby** Sierra de Gredos - Puerto del Pico - Cuevas del Valle - Monbeltrán - Ávila. **Open** All year.

Not far from Madrid rises the large hill called the Sierra de Gredos, and in 1926 King Alfonso XIII ordered that the first parador in Spain should be built on it. Hereabouts the winter is particularly severe, which is why the architecture relies on massive stonework, so attractive and giving a real impression of grandeur, notably to the columns and terraces. Inside, and as if to counter the cold, the use of wood has been generous: it is everywhere and very restful as well. The rooms are vast as in every parador and furnished in Castillian style. From the hotel you can enjoy all the pleasures of both hunting and fishing, while Ávila is only 60 kilometers away and absolutely deserves a visit as it is one of the most mythical and most attractive towns of Spain.

How to get there *(Map 12): 116km west of Madrid and 68km from Ávila via N502. Turn off on N500 towards Barco de Ávila.*

El Milano Real

05634 Hoyos del Espino (Ávila)
Tel. 920-34 91 08 - Fax 920-34 91 56 - Sr Francisco Sanchez

Rooms 14 with telephone, bath, WC, satellite TV, minibar; elevator. **Price** Single 7,500Pts, double 8,500Pts, suite 11,500Pts; extra bed 2,500Pts. **Meals** Breakfast (buffet) 650 and 1,400Pts, served 8:00-10:30; half board and full board 7,850Pts, 10,100Pts (per pers.). **Restaurant** Service 1:30PM-3:30PM, 8:30PM-11:00PM, à la carte. Gastronomic cooking. **Credit cards** All major. **Pets** Dogs not allowed. **Facilities** Sauna (1,100Pts), parking. **Nearby** Sierra de Gredos - Puerto del Pico - Cuevas del Valle - Monbeltrán - Ávila. **Closed** 20 days in Nov and 1 week end Jan.

An excellent place to lose yourself in La Sierra de Gredos. This vast mountainous area separating the two Castilles offers extraordinary places where jagged peaks look down on forests, fields and plains. The village of Hoyos del Espino at 1,584 meters is a fine starting point for an excursion taking you to Gredos at the foot of the Almazor, rising nearly 1,500 meters above you. The hotel is situated above the small town, and don't let its recent construction and banal appearance mislead you: the interior is a genuine and pleasant surprise. The location is remarkable, allowing you to look out over the entire valley from the terrace. The spacious rooms are paneled in ochre with nicely coordinated fabrics with motifs of stripes and squares. The largest ones have lounges and terraces but all have a lovely view. In addition, you can look forward to a gastronomic treat, starting with breakfast of warm, golden *brioches* along with serrano ham and eggs; meals are delicious and refined, the wine cellar well-stocked and there is a large choice of teas and coffees. This region which offers hiking all year long is certainly worth a detour even if you don't stay over.

How to get there *(Map 12): 130km west of Madrid and 68km from Ávila via N502. Turn off on N500 towards Barco de Ávila.*

Hostal Sancho de Estrada

05130 Solosancho (Ávila)
Castillo de Villaviciosa
Tel. and fax 920-29 10 82
Sr Avelino Mayoral Hernandes

Category ★★ **Rooms** 12 with telephone, bath, WC, satellite TV, minibar. **Price** Single 6,450Pts, double 9,775Pts, suite 13,350Pts. **Meals** Breakfast 650Pts, served 8:00-10:30. **Restaurant** Service 1:30PM-3:30PM, 8:30PM-11:00PM; mealtime specials 2,500Pts, also à la carte. Regional cooking. **Credit cards** Diners, Visa, Eurocard, MasterCard. **Pets** Dogs not allowed. **Facilities** Parking. **Nearby** Sierra de Gredos - Puerto del Pico - Cuevas del Valle - Monbeltrán - Ávila. **Open** All year.

You head south from Ávila on N502, a long and seemingly interminable straight line through the fields, until you get to the Solosancho exit. Next you see the craggy rock formations surrounding the plateau, a superb sight. It is from these rocks that a castle was built; it now houses the hotel which, despite restoration, has kept its medieval charm. The ground floor offers stone columns with sculpted capitals surrounding the court yard where you find the restaurant with elegant tables and sparkling white table linen, all in a space designed to be both comfortable and intimate. The rooms are upstairs and again, the decoration is based on the presence of stone. The rustic furniture and terracotta floors blend in nicely with the architecture. This is also true of the rest of the hotel which is decorated with tapestries, suits of armor and furniture that is often sculpted. As for the solarium above the dungeon, it offers a breathtaking view. An interesting address nicely located between Salamanca and Ávila.

How to get there (Map 12): 23km south of Ávila on N502.

Landa Palace

09000 Burgos
km 236 Carret. Madrid Irun
Tel. 947-20 63 43 - Fax 947-26 46 76
Sr Revuelta

Category ★★★★★ **Rooms** 37 and 5 suites with air-conditioning, telephone, bath, WC, satellite TV, safe, minibar. **Price** Single 15,100-18,000Pts, double 22,000-25,000Pts, suite 28,000-33,000Pts. **Meals** Breakfast 1,800Pts, served 8:00-11:00. **Restaurant** Service 1:00PM-4:00PM, 9:00PM-11:30PM; mealtime specials 5,800Pts, also à la carte. **Credit cards** Visa, Eurocard, MasterCard. **Pets** Dogs not allowed. **Facilities** Swimming pool, garage. **Nearby** In Burgos: Cathedral - Monasterio de las Huelgas Reales (Royal Convent) - Cartuja de Miraflores (Gothic charterhouse) - Monasterio de San Salvador at Oña - Church of Santa Maria la Real de Sasomón - Monasterio de San Pedro de Cardeña. **Open** All year.

The owner of a restaurant in Madrid, Mr Landa bought an ancient 14th-century military tower some thirty years ago. He had it taken down and rebuilt stone by stone some twenty kilometers from its original site. Two wings were added and the hotel opened its doors in 1964. The Landa Palace is very beautiful, very luxurious, very refined and shelters some charming collections as well: a collection of carriages in the courtyard, of watch movements on the ground floor, of pressing irons, tools and weighing scales–among others. The service and fittings of the rooms are perfect, but if you really prefer the truly "grand luxe", go for the royal suite. For more silence, opt for those rooms overlooking the countryside and swimming pool. The pool is "Hollywoodian" and covered with a Gothic roof.

How to get there (Map 4): 3km south of Burgos via N1.

Mesón del Cid

09003 Burgos
Plaza Santa Maria, 8
Tel. 947-20 59 71 - Fax 947-26 94 60
Sr Lopez Alzaga

Rooms 49 and 6 suites with bath, shower, WC, TV. **Price** Single 12,800Pts, double 16,000Pts, suite 22,000Pts. **Meals** Breakfast 1,000Pts, served 7:00-11:30. **Restaurant** Service 1:00PM-4:00PM, 8:00PM-12:00AM; mealtime specials 3,000-4,500Pts. Specialties: Alubias rojas - Cordero Lechal asado - Postre del abuelo. **Credit cards** All major. **Pets** Dogs allowed. **Facilities** Garage (1,000Pts). **Nearby** In Burgos: Cathedral - Monasterio de las Huelgas Reales (Royal Convent) - Cartuja de Miraflores (Gothic charterhouse) - Monasterio de San Salvador at Oña - Church of Santa Maria la Real de Sasomón - Monasterio de San Pedro de Cardeña. **Open** All year.

This imposing building is directly in front of Burgos' superb cathedral on a small tiled square decorated with a pretty stone fountain and has been the property of the same family for several generations. They first opened a well-known restaurant in a 15th-century house, the former printing shop of a disciple of Gutenberg. Decorated in the style of the period, the restaurant serves a typically Castillian cuisine. In the newer hotel they have kept the most representative elements – woodwork and tiled floors – of its past. In fact, the rooms are more functional than elegant and lack originality. Some of them overlook the cathedral while others offer a view of the town roofs. The location is ideal for discovering the charms of Burgos, best known as the city where the purest form of Castillian is spoken.

How to get there *(Map 4): Facing the cathedral.*

Hotel Arlanza

09346 Covarrubias (Burgos)
Plaza Mayor, 11
Tel. 947-40 64 41 - Fax 947-40 63 59 - Sr and Sra Miguel
E-mail: arlanza@ctv.es - Web: www.ctv.es/users/arlanza

Category ★★★ **Rooms** 38 and 2 suites with telephone, bath or shower, WC; elevator. **Price** Single 5,300-5,800Pts, double 9,000-9,600Pts. **Meals** Breakfast 650Pts, served 8:00-10.30. **Restaurant** Service 1:00PM-4:00PM, 8:30PM-11:00PM, closed Sun night; mealtime specials 1,800Pts; also à la carte. Specialties: Sopa serrana - Cordero. **Credit cards** All major. **Pets** Dogs not allowed in the restaurant. **Nearby** Collegiata de Covarrubias - Church of Santa Maria in Quintanillas de la Viñas - Monastery Santo Domingo de Silos - Lerma - Burgos. **Closed** Dec 1st - Feb 28.

Simple and without pretensions, this hotel deserves its selection thanks to its superb location: it overlooks the square of Covarrubias, a charming Castillian village. The hotel is a former noble's home and has been restored in rustic style, the interior refurbished with a desire for sobriety. The rooms would merit a rather brighter decor and this is why we prefer those looking out from the facade as they are larger and enjoy the view of the square. No sophisticated cuisine is served but good house dishes are made from the produce of the area.

How to get there *(Map 4): 39km south of Burgos via N234, to Cuevas de San Clemente, then small road to Covarrubias.*

Hotel Tres Coronas de Silos

09610 Santo Domingo de Silos (Burgos)
Plaza Mayor, 6
Tel. 947-39 00 47 - Fax 947-39 00 65
Sr Martín

Category ★★★ **Rooms** 16 and 9 in the annex with telephone, bath, WC, TV. **Price** Single 8,000-8,500Pts, double 10,500-11,000Pts. **Meals** Breakfast 975Pts, served 8:30-11:00; half board +4,500Pts (per pers.). **Restaurant** Service 1:30PM-3:30PM, 8:30PM-11:30PM; à la carte 3,500-4,000Pts. Specialties: Morcillos - Jamón - Picadillo - Menestra de verduras naturales - Entremeses caseros. **Credit cards** All major. **Pets** Dogs allowed. **Nearby** Monastery Santo Domingo de Silos - Covarrubias - Salas de los Infantes - Caves of the Yecla. **Open** All year.

Santo Domingo de Silos is a very beautiful and very authentic Castillian village renowned for its convent dating from the year 1000; Gregorian chants may be heard daily in its cloister. Opposite the main square and the church, a large 18th-century house restored by the local craftsmen has become an intimate family hotel. A charming dining room with a large wood-burning stove allows you to sample the house's regional cuisine. At the top of an attractive wooden staircase, the delightful and cozy rooms match the Castillian style of the whole residence. The welcome is friendly and relaxed. If you cannot find the hotel, ask for the Casa Grande as it is known by the village people.

How to get there (Map 4): 58km south of Burgos via N234 to Hacinas, then take the small road to Santo Domingo.

Hospederia del Monasterio de Valvanera

26322 Anguiano (La Rioja)
Tel. 941-37 70 44 - Fax 941-37 70 44
Fraï Martín

Category ★★ **Rooms** 28 with shower, WC. **Price** Single 4,500Pts, double 6,500Pts; extra bed 1,000Pts. **Meals** Breakfast 700Pts, served 9:00-10:30; half board +2,000Pts, full board +3,000Pts (per pers.). **Restaurant** Service 1:30PM-3:00PM, 8:30PM-9:30PM; mealtime specials 1,500Pts. Regional cooking. **Credit cards** Not accepted. **Pets** Dogs not allowed. **Facilities** Parking. **Nearby** San Millán de la Cogolla - Santo Domingo de la Calzada. **Closed** Dec 22 - Jan 7.

At the peak of a very green mountain an immense red-stone monastery looks out each evening on a picture-postcard sunset. The hotel occupies the rear part of the monastery to which one has access via the gallery. The architecture has remained sumptuous, and the rooms are simple but very clean. If you want to fill your lungs with good clean air in an exceptional environment of beauty and peace, the Hospederia del Monasterio de Valvanera is well worth a detour, albeit by a very difficult road. However, if you are looking for comfortable, in deed comfy, rooms it is better to drive on for an air of great sobriety reigns here; after all, you are, in a monastery.

How to get there *(Map 5): 48km southwest of Logroño via N120 to Nájera, then C113.*

Parador Marco Fabio

26500 Calahorra (La Rioja)
Era Alta - Quintiliano
Tel. 941-13 03 58 - Fax 941-13 51 39

Category ★★★ **Rooms** 62 with telephone, bath, WC, satellite TV, minibar. **Price** Double 13,500-15,000Pts. **Meals** Breakfast 1,300Pts, served 8:00-10:30. **Restaurant** Service 1:00PM-3:30PM, 8:30PM-11:00PM; mealtime specials 3,500Pts, also à la carte. Specialties: Cordero. **Credit cards** All major. **Pets** Dogs not allowed. **Facilities** Parking. **Nearby** Arnedo. **Open** All year.

This is a classical parador whose facade has an austere aspect but is surrounded by a flowery terrace at the back of the building. As in all paradors, the rooms are large and great use has been made of wood which gives them a warmer character. The furniture is classical and the floor tiles polished. Even if you are just passing through, do not leave without visiting the town cathedral known as the "Cathedral of the Sacristy".

How to get there *(Map 5): 100km southwest of Pamplona via A15, then A68 towards Logroño, exit Calahorra.*

Motel de Pradorrey

24700 Astorga (León)
Tel. 987-61 57 29 - Fax 987-61 92 20

Category ★★★ **Rooms** 64 with telephone, bath, WC, satellite TV, minibar. **Price** Single 8,100Pts, double 11,300Pts, suite 12,300Pts. **Meals** Breakfast 875Pts, served 8:00AM-12:00PM. **Restaurant** With air-conditioning, service 1:00PM-4:00PM, 9:00PM-12:00AM; mealtime specials 2,100Pts, also à la carte. Specialties: Carnes rojas - Embutidos. **Credit cards** All major. **Pets** Dogs allowed (except in restaurant). **Facilities** Parking. **Nearby** In Astorga: the cathedral - Monastery Santa Maria de Carrizo - La Bañeza - Church of Luyego - Castrillo de los Polvazares. **Open** All year.

At an altitude of 950 meters, the Motel de Pradorrey is housed in a medieval edifice that still bears both on its facade and inside vestiges of the constructions of the Templars Order. The beauty of its stones and the wrought ironwork are remarkable but the interior is less attractive. Why sacrifice to comfort the charm one might have expected from admiring the hotel's exterior? This said, the hotel is in a part of León that is still preserved from tourism, and where one can drive through some of the most typical villages of Spain, including Castrillo de Los Polvazares. Three kilometers away, one can also visit the famous cathedral of Astorga. Please note, the hotel's restaurant has a good reputation.

How to get there *(Map 3): 52km west of León via N120, then N6 towards La Coruña.*

Parador Hostal San Marcos

24001 León
Plaza San Marcos, 7
Tel. 987-23 73 00 - Fax 987-23 34 58
Sr Alvarez Montoto

Category ★★★★★ **Rooms** 256 with telephone, bath, WC, satellite TV; elevator. **Price** Double 19,000-21,500Pts. **Meals** Breakfast (buffet) 1,400Pts, served 7:45-11:30. **Restaurant** With air-conditioning, service 1:30PM-3:30PM, 9:00PM-11:30PM; mealtime specials 3,800Pts, also à la carte. Specialties: Trout "Hostal" - Cecina. **Credit cards** All major. **Pets** Dogs not allowed. **Nearby** In León: Cathedral, Monastery San Marcos, Basilica San Isidoro - Monastery San Miguel de Escalada - Castle of Valencia of Don Juan - Caves of the Robla. **Open** All year.

No, this is not a museum entrance but it really is the hotel San Marcos! A historical monument, the former Santiaguista convent is the pride of the province of León. Its facade is a beautiful example of the "plateresque" style, so called because of its resemblance to silver plate work. Inside, the massive and grandiose architecture of the cloister that surrounds the garden is in contrast to the grace of the arches of the upper gallery where tables are set out. A very beautiful lounge occupies the large room where monks once gathered under its astonishing *mudéjar* ceiling. There is unmatched comfort in all rooms, but naturally one prefers those of the main building as the annex has much less charm. Impeccable service and great friendliness are still the qualities of this classy hotel.

How to get there (Map 3): In the town center.

Hotel Castillo de Monzón

34410 Monzón de Campos (Palencia)
Tel. 979-80 80 75 - Fax 979-80 83 03

Category ★★★ **Rooms** 9 and 1 suite with telephone, bath, WC, satellite TV, minibar, safe. **Price** Single 8,000-10,000Pts, double 13,000-16,000Pts, suite 28,600Pts. **Meals** Breakfast 800Pts, served 8:00-11:00. **Restaurant** Service 1:30PM-3:30PM, 8:30PM-11:30PM; à la carte. Specialties: Meat dishes, regional cooking. **Credit cards** All major. **Pets** Dogs not allowed. **Facilities** Parking. **Nearby** In Monzón: the church - Cathedral of Palencia - Ribas de Campos - Amusco - Piña de Campos - Tamara. **Open** All year.

The town of Monzón is a former royal residence and it has converted its historic castle into a hotel. The arrival at this fortress on its small hill is impressive enough, with a very imposing building and its high tower and window-less walls. The interior however is welcoming and even if the architecture has been restored, the most attractive elements, such as a Roman arch and some beautiful ceilings, have been preserved. Comfort is also here in the rooms with their canopied beds and heavy drapes, to remind you that you are staying in a true castle. In a rustic atmosphere, a fine restaurant offers good braised meats and an excellent menu of regional specialties. The hotel is isolated but in fact only eleven kilometers from Palencia which has conserved a magnificent Gothic cathedral from its past and is well worth a visit. This is a most pleasant stop-over.

How to get there (Map 4): 11km north of Palencia.

Hostería El Convento

34492 Santa Maria de Mave (Palencia)
Tel. 979-12 36 11 - Fax 979-12 54 92
Familia Moral

Category ★★ **Rooms** 25 and 2 suites with telephone, bath. **Price** Single 6,000Pts, double 10,500Pts, suite 12,000Pts. **Meals** Breakfast 600Pts, served 8:00AM-12:00PM. **Restaurant** Service 1:30PM-3:30PM, 8:30PM-10:30PM; mealtime specials 1,500Pts, also à la carte. **Credit cards** All major. **Pets** Dogs not allowed. **Facilities** Parking. **Nearby** Hunting and fishing - Aguilar de Campoó - Monastery de Santa Maria La Real. **Open** All year.

Between Santander and Palencia in a region rich in Roman ruins, this very beautiful medieval priory shelters a hotel run in the family style, and where the charming daughters of the house look after the reception. Attached to the building, a pretty church is still in use. Understandably the rooms respect the spirit of the house and have a rather monastic aspect. The furniture is restricted to the essential, the walls bare and the entry doors small, but the bathrooms contribute a more contemporary touch. A little more sophisticated, the suites have canopied beds. The main room of the restaurant, with its beams, stone walls and tiled floors, is attractively light with an intimate table arrangement. It is with great pleasure that you relax in the garden and let your eyes wander out over the rocky canyon of the Horadada and the surrounding limestone formations. Peace and well-being are to be found here.

How to get there *(Map 4): 116km south of Santander, towards Palencia via N611.*

NH Palacio de Castellanos

37008 Salamanca
San Pablo, 58-64
Tel. 923-26 18 18 - Fax 923-26 18 19

Category ★★★★ **Rooms** 62 with air-conditioning, telephone, bath, WC, satellite TV, minibar, safe; elevator. **Price** Single 14,500-19,000Pts, double 19,000Pts, suite 14,500-27,000Pts. **Meals** Breakfast 1,300Pts, served 7:30-11:00. **Restaurant** Service 1:30PM-3:30PM, 8:30PM-10:30PM; mealtime specials 2,000Pts, also à la carte. **Credit cards** All major. **Pets** Dogs not allowed. **Facilities** Garage (2,000Pts). **Nearby** Castillo de Buen Amor - Peñaranda de Bracamonte - Ciudad Rodrigo - Candelario - La Alberca. **Open** All year.

This recently opened hotel is in a very calm part of Salamanca's historic city center. Located on the charming Plaza de Concilio de Trento with its plane trees opposite the majestic Convento de los Dominicos, this converted palace of exquisite architectural simplicity has beautiful windows with eye-catching details. A small staircase leads to the entrance which is surrounded by a terrace running along the facade and offering bar service. The lobby in the glass-covered patio has sober and stylish ochre stone columns. The floors with slabs of stone and marble plus the classic modern furniture and blue-gray tones all contribute to the impression created by the architecture. All the rooms are large with attractive furniture created especially for the hotel which, allied with dark wooden floors and very comfortable bathrooms, create a truly warm atmosphere. The rooms on the front have a view of the convent. This is a lovely hotel, completely in harmony with the beauty of Salamanca.

How to get there *(Map 11): 205 km northwest of Madrid on A63 towards Ávila; 98km from Ávila via N501.*

Hotel Rector

37008 Salamanca
Paseo Rector Esperabé, 10
Tel. 923-21 84 82 - Fax 923-21 40 08 - Sr Ferrán
E-mail: hotelrector@teleline.es - Web: www.teleline.es/personal/hrector

Category ★★★★ **Rooms** 14 with air-conditioning, telephone, bath, WC, satellite TV, safe, minibar; elevator. **Price** Single 11,5000-13,500Pts, double 17,000Pts, suite 22,000Pts. **Meals** Breakfast 1,000Pts, served 8:00-11:00. **Restaurant** See p. 308. **Credit cards** All major. **Pets** Dogs not allowed. **Facilities** Garage (1,000Pts). **Nearby** Castillo de Buen Amor - Peñaranda de Bracamonte - Ciudad Rodrigo - Candelario - La Alberca. **Open** All year.

The hotel is in a beautiful house of golden stone from the Villamayor region, like most of the other buildings in the town of Salamanca. Famous for its university, this is one of the most attractive towns in Spain. With a great wealth of monuments, it retains admirable remains from both the Renaissance and baroque periods, among them the Plaza Mayor, to name only one of them. The hotel has been fully renovated but with great refinement. The reception lounges on the ground floor have been made very light and airy. The furniture and chairs in mahogany and covered with salmon-pink fabrics, and assorted drapes give the decor an air of gentleness. Blue has been chosen for the rooms, which are very comfortable indeed, with their attractive bathrooms all in white marble. The hotel's small capacity ensures a very attentive service, along with a very friendly welcome. This is a very good staging post in a town that really deserves a visit.

How to get there *(Map 11): 205km northwest of Madrid via A63, towards Ávila; at 98km from Ávila, via N501.*

Hotel Doña Teresa

37624 La Alberca (Salamanca)
Ctra. Mogarraz
Tel. 923-41 53 08 09 - Fax 923-41 53 08 09 - Sr Fernando Rodriguez
Web: hotelteresa@gpm.es

Category ★★★★ **Rooms** 45 with air-conditioning, telephone, bath, WC, TV, minibar. **Price** Single 10,000Pts, double 12,000-16,000Pts; extra bed 2,500Pts. **Meals** Breakfast 700-1,300Pts, served 8:00-10:30. **Restaurant** Service 1:00PM-4:00PM, 8:30PM-11:00PM; mealtime specials 2,200Pts, also à la carte. **Credit cards** All major. **Pets** Dogs not allowed **Facilities** Sauna (1,500Pts), gymnasium, hydromassage, parking. **Nearby** Villages of Peña de Francia, La Alberca, Mogarraz, Miranda del Castañar, S. Martín del Castañar - Ciudad Rodrigo. **Open** All year.

Leaving Salamanca on the road to Portugal, you discover a magic countryside, a prelude to the Alentejo with colors ranging from those of verdant cork tree groves to those of golden wheat fields. The villages of the Valle de Francia, well-protected by their isolation, have remained virtual fossils, survivors of medieval times. La Alberca was the first community in Spain to be classified a *monumento nacional*. The architecture here is unusual; numerous houses are half-timbered with the remainder of their exteriors made up of stone and red earth. The hotel, which has a large lobby with attractive stone arches, is on the bank of a river and overlooks the village. The rooms come in various sizes and shapes, but all have identical decoration: wooden floors, sturdy wooden beds with white bedding colorfully embroidered in the local artisanal style. The most interesting are upstairs, some with a large terrace and a view of the village while others offer a small garden. Walking trips are always pleasant as the region is well-known for its flora and fauna.

How to get there *(Map 11): 45km east of Ciudad Rodrigo via N620; 77km south of Salamanca via N630.*

Hotel Las Batuccas

37624 La Alberca (Salamanca)
Ctra. de Batuecas
Tel. 923-41 51 88- Fax 923-41 50 55
Sr Francisco José Hernandez

Rooms 30 and 4 suites (with air-conditioning) with telephone, bath, WC, satellite TV, minibar. **Price** Double 7,200-15,000Pts. **Meals** Breakfast 700Pts, served 8:00-10:30. **Restaurant** Service 1:00PM-4:00PM, 8:30PM-11:00PM; mealtime specials 1,800Pts, also à la carte. Specialties: cabrito cuchifritto, hornazos, limón serrano, vinos del Soto. **Credit cards** Visa, Eurocard, MasterCard. **Pets** Dogs not allowed. **Nearby** Villages of the Batecuas valley: Peña de Francia, La Alberca, Mogarraz, Miranda del Castañar, S. Martín del Castañar - Monastery of N.S. de la Peña de Francia - Cathedral of Ciudad Rodrigo. **Open** All year.

Two hotels are pretty much what this village needs as it receives many visitors, especially Spanish tourists. The Hotel Las Batuecas, while simple, offers wholly adequate service and comfort. In addition, it is well off the highway and has an attractive loggia overlooking the garden which is a welcome haven when the summer heat arrives. The restaurant has gained a fine reputation offering traditional dishes made with regional wines from the hotel's bodega. Meals are served in a vast and attractively appointed dining room with a friendly atmosphere. The prices are equally friendly.

How to get there *(Map 11): 45km east of Ciudad Rodrigo via N620; 77km south of Salamanca via N630.*

La Posada de San Martín

37659 San Martín del Castañar (Salamanca)
C/. Larga, 1
Tel. and Fax 923-43 70 36
Sr Teodoro Santa Maria

Rooms 13 with telephone, bath, TV. **Price** Double 4,500-6,500Pts. **Meals** Breakfast 500Pts, served 8:00-10:30; half board +1,500Pts. **Restaurant** Service 1:00PM-4:00PM, 8:30PM-11:00PM; mealtime specials 1,200Pts, also à la carte. Traditional cooking. **Credit cards** Diners, Visa, Eurocard, MasterCard. **Pets** Dogs not allowed. **Nearby** Villages of the Batecuas valley: Peña de Francia, La Alberca, Mogarraz, Miranda del Castañar, S. Martín del Castañar - Monastery of N.S. de la Peña de Francia - Cathedral of Ciudad Rodrigo. **Closed** 2 weeks in Jan.

As you travel in this region so typical of Castille, you will find that the village of San Martín is clearly the most authentic *pueblo serrano* in the valley. Nestled in the lowlands, its small streets, its attractive houses with family crests and its aging *plaza de toros* are all spread out below the *castillo*, having mercifully escaped aggressive restoration. Here, you are still received by village elders who on summer days sit at the entrance to the Posada which is, in fact, a large house. On a sunken level of the ground floor where once animals were raised are the reception desk and dining room. Wooden beams and stone construction contribute to a rustic setting typical of this mountainous region. The rooms are relatively small but invariably very comfortable. The two largest have their own lounges. Ancestral traditions rate very high in this valley and are reflected in the dishes you can enjoy in the restaurant. A stop-over that cannot leave you indifferent to its charm.

How to get there *(Map 11): 45km east of Ciudad Rodrigo via N620; 77km south of Salamanca via N630.*

Hotel Infante Isabel

40001 Segovia
Plaza Mayor
Tel. 921-46 13 00 - Fax 921-46 22 17
Sr E. Cañada Cando

Category ★★★ **Rooms** 29 with air-conditioning, telephone, bath, WC, satellite TV, safe, minibar; elevator. **Price** Single 8,000Pts, double 12,700Pts. **Meals** Breakfast 925Pts, served 8:00-11:00. **Restaurant** See p. 308. **Credit cards** All major. **Pets** Dogs not allowed. **Facilities** Garage (1,000Pts). **Nearby** In Segovia: Roman aqueduct, the cathedral, churches of San Martín, San Millán and San Estebán (tower), Alcázar, Monastery de El Parral - Turégano - Pedraza de la Sierra - Castle Castilnovo - Sepúlveda - Royal Palace of La Granja - Palacio de Riofrio. **Open** All year.

A royal city, Segovia is one of the prettiest towns in Spain, and one comes here to visit its architectural treasures and also sample the gastronomic specialties (trout and above all its sucking pig roasted over a wood fire), which have made its reputation. The hotel is admirably situated opposite the cathedral, and it is a charming little hotel full of elegance and refinement. Everything is in good taste: modern comfort, classical decor and impeccable service. Breakfast is delicious and the welcome most attentive. The rooms are enchanting, bright and quiet, and most have a view of the cathedral. This is a very attractive address.

How to get there (Map 13): 87km northwest of Madrid.

Las Fuentes

40172 La Granja (Segovia)
C/. Padre Claret, 6
Tel. 921-47 10 24 - Fax 921-47 17 41 - Sr Juan Antonio Comeyn

Category ★★ **Rooms** 9 with telephone, bath, WC, TV. **Price** Double 12,500-13,500Pts. **Meals** Breakfast 950Pts, served 8:00-11:00. **Restaurant** Independent on the hotel - Service 1:00PM-4:00PM, 8:30PM-11:00PM; mealtime specials 1,500Pts, also à la carte. Regional cooking. **Credit cards** Diners, Visa, Eurocard, MasterCard. **Pets** Dogs not allowed. **Nearby** Palacio de San Ildefonso - Segovia - Puerto de Navacerrada - Villecastin. **Open** All year.

About ten kilometers from Segovia at the foot of the Sierra de Guadarrama is La Granja, a town visited principally for its palace. The village offers local charm with its white, low-slung buildings whose narrow doors and windows ensure protection from the summer heat. The exterior of Las Fuentes is painted yellow and surrounded by a pleasant lawn. A kind of British coziness pervades the house with Scottish fabrics and a comfortable lounge that has a fireplace most welcome in winter. The rooms are equally cozy with large beds and eiderdowns. no. 1 is our favorite as it has space, grace and also the highest pricetag. In no. 8, another good choice, the large window directly over the bathtub frames the mountain like a vast photo enlargement. You will certainly want a view of the sierra. The restaurant in the garden is under different management but has the advantage of its location.

How to get there *(Map 13): 11km southeast of Segovia via N601.*

Hostal de Buen Amor

40170 Sotosalbos (Segovia)
Tel. 921-40 30 20 - Fax 921-40 30 22
Sr Victorio Lopez

Rooms 12 with telephone, bath, TV. **Price** Single 4,500-7,000Pts, double 8,500-10,500Pts, attic room 12,000Pts, suite 15,000Pts. **Meals** Breakfast 1,500Pts, served 8:00-11:00. **Restaurant** Service 1:00PM-3:00PM, 8:30PM-11:00PM, also à la carte. Regional cooking. **Credit cards** Diners, Visa, Eurocard, MasterCard. **Pets** Dogs not allowed. **Nearby** Romanesque chuch of Sotosalbos - Segovia - Naturel Park of las Hoces del Ouaron. **Open** All year.

Scarcely fifteen kilometers from Segovia, Sotosalbos is a village lying at the foot of the mountain where citizens of Madrid enjoy spending weekends of horseback riding and day trips on foot or bicycle. Victorio Lopez is particularly expert in arranging all of these activities. The owner has done an excellent job in restoring this house, having kept its lovely wooden architecture and beams which enliven the interior. Each room is different with unpretentious antique furniture that gives them all a very elegant character. We prefer the ones under the roof, particularly no. 7 where the roof over the bed in the alcove slopes very impressively. The suite offers, in addition, a lounge and an efficient wood stove. The house is truly adorable and its attentive owner creates a genuinely friendly atmosphere that you find also in the restaurant which enjoys a fine reputation for its regional cooking.

How to get there *(Map 13): 15km north of Segovia via N110 towards Soria; after Torrecaballeros, turn left towards Sotosalbos.*

El Zaguán

40370 Turégano (Segovia)
Plaza de España, 16
Tel. 921-50 11 65 - Fax 921-50 11 56 - Sr Mario Garcia
E-mail: zaguan@ctv.es - Web: www.ctv.es/USERS/zaguan

Category ★★ **Rooms** 15 with telephone, bath, WC, TV; elevator. **Price** Single 4,500-7,000Pts, double 7,000-10,000Pts, suite 12,000-15,000Pts. **Meals** Breakfast 1,500Pts, served 8:00-11:00. **Restaurant** Service 1:00PM-4:00PM, 8:30PM-11:00PM, also à la carte. Regional cooking. **Credit cards** Diners, Visa, Eurocard, MasterCard. **Pets** Dogs not allowed. **Nearby** Segovia - La Granja. **Open** All year.

With a visit to Turégano, you get even closer to the true Castillian soul. It is very close to Segovia and you can find no excuse for neglecting this picturesque village with pre-Roman era origins which later underwent Arab occupation and was finally given by the Spanish crown to the Archbishop of Segovia. The vast castle overlooking the plain with its towers and the two imposing walls surrounding it is nearly entirely taken up by the San Miguel Church. The town is laid out in typical fashion, built at the foot of the *castillo* with houses giving way to the town's main square and its more noble residences. The hotel, opposite the *Ayuntamiento*, skillfully weds wooden beams, stone and brick, and the restaurant's high ceiling allows the use of a large fireplace which produces excellent grilled dishes. The rooms are charming, each personalized by different fabrics and popular art works. This is also a good place for a one-day visit.

How to get there *(Map 13): 35km north of Segovia via N110 (towards Soria) to Torrecaballeros; then turn left towards Brieva and Turégano.*

El Hotel de la Villa

40172 Pedraza della Sierra (Segovia)
Calle Calzada, 5
Tel. 921-50 86 51 - Fax 921-50 86 53
Sres Martín

Category ★★★ **Rooms** 22 and 2 suites with air-conditioning, telephone, bath, WC, satellite TV, minibar; elevator. **Price** Double 13,600-14,100Pts, suite 18,300Pts. **Meals** Breakfast 1,000-1,600Pts, served 7:30-11:00. **Restaurant** Service 1:00PM-4:00PM, 8:30PM-11:00PM; mealtime specials 4,100Pts, also à la carte. **Credit cards** All major. **Pets** Dogs not allowed. **Nearby** Pedraza: the Old Town - Hiking and riding in Sierra of Guadarramaand in the Naturel Park of Hyedo de Tejera Negra - Canoeing on the Río Duratón. **Open** All year.

Located in the north of the triangle formed by Segovia, Madrid and Burgos, Pedraza is a city well worth a detour where you will find a medieval village with well-preserved 15th-century architecture which includes the castle of the Velasco nobles where the French king François I was imprisoned. The Hotel de la Villa, located in one of the impressive houses in this attractive ochre-colored village, is at once refined, traditional and modern, something you recognize immediately in the lounges on the ground floor. The dining room is a pure delight where you can see meals prepared on an impressive stove dating back to the Arab invasion. The rooms are spacious and elegant, each one different and each superb. It is difficult to choose among them as all have identical comfort, exceptional decoration and beautifully appointed bathrooms. This is a hotel which, while quite expensive, lives up to its well-deserved reputation.

How to get there *(Map 13): 36km Northeast of Segovia via N110 to Matabuena (towards Soria) then on left to Pedraza.*

La Posada de Don Mariano

40172 Pedraza della Sierra (Segovia)
Calle Mayor, 14
Tel. 921-50 98 86 - Fax 921-50 98 87 - Sr Mariano

Category ★★ **Rooms** 18 with telephone, bath, WC, TV. **Price** Single 11,000Pts, double 13,000Pts, suite 17,000Pts. **Meals** Breakfast 950Pts, served 8:00-11:00. **Restaurant** Service 2:00PM-4:00PM, 9:00PM-11:00PM, closed Mon from Jan 15 - 25 and Jun 15 - 25; mealtime specials 2,950Pts, also à la carte. Regional cooking. **Credit cards** All major. **Pets** Dogs not allowed. **Nearby** Segovia - Castle Castilnovo - Sepúlveda. **Open** All year.

Behind a discreet facade, La Posada de Don Mariano reveals a real jewel decorated throughout by the director of the Spanish version of "House & Garden". Pedraza is a small medieval village straight off a postcard, situated on a huge rock and surrounded by walls. Preserved admirably, you can admire aristocratic homes with their shields and coats of arms along with the Plaza Mayor and its porched houses. The owner of La Posada has created an original style based on the typical elements: Castillian ceramics, furniture from Andalucia and Extremadura, mixed with creations such as fabrics from Canovas found on the beds, curtains and wall hangings. The tones vary with the rooms. White, and with a superb canopied bed, no. 101 is a magnificent bridal chamber. Along the corridors and in the patio, a host of green plants create a charming atmosphere which is never precious or affected. In the restaurant the white-covered tables promise romantic "tête-à-têtes" by candlelight. This is a true hotel of charm in a village that has attracted and inspired many an artist.

How to get there *(Map 13): 36km northeast of Segovia via N110 towards Soria until Matabuena, then Pedraza.*

Molino de Río Viejo

40170 Collado Hermoso (Segovia)
Carretera N-110, km 172
Tel. 921-40 30 63 - Fax 921-40 30 51
Sr Antonio Armero

Rooms 6 with bath, WC. **Price** Double 9,000Pts, double the weekend 10,000Pts. **Meals** Breakfast 700Pts, served 7:00-11:00. **Restaurant** (weekend only). Service 1:00PM-3:30PM, 8:30PM-10:30PM; à la carte 3,000-4,000Pts. Regional cooking. **Credit cards** Visa, Eurocard, MasterCard. **Pets** Dogs not allowed. **Facilities** Riding (for 3 hours - 1 week), parking. **Nearby** Segovia - Castilnovo castle - Sepúlveda. **Open** All year.

When asked to describe El Molino in terms of its being a restaurant or a hotel, its owner prefers to leave it to you, saying that it will, over time, become something very much like your own home. Standing in the middle of the imposing Sierra de Guadarrama, this old mill, already enjoying a long and often colorful past, has been resuscitated and is now a warm and friendly hotel. Relics of its past are on display in the large dining room, among them old farm tools and wheat sheaves, side by side with elegant wicker furniture. The low ceilings create a cozy atmosphere which permeates the entire house, especially the rooms located under the roof. Of these, your best choice would be those at the rear. The food is flawless and all the more pleasant on summer weekends when you can eat under the poplars and oaks that line the river. This, however, is by no means all of the Molino's attractions. If you enjoy riding horses, there are unforgettable trails in the region, where you will be accompanied by the Molino's owners who have been riding them for twenty years. Antonio Armero's slogan is simple: "Get to know Spain on horseback!"

How to get there *(Map 13): 15km north of Segovia via N110 to km 172. The town is near Collado Hermoso.*

Posada de Sigueruelo

Sigueruelo (Segovia)
Calle Badén, 40
Tel. 921-50 81 35 - Fax 921-50 81 35
Sra Concepcíon Alarcos Rodriguez

Rooms 6 with shower, WC. **Price** Double 9,700Pts. **Meals** Breakfast 800Pts, served 7:30-11:00; half board 12,000Pts (per pers.). **Evening meals** Mealtime specials 1,200Pts (lunch), 1,500Pts (dinner). **Credit cards** Visa, Eurocard, MasterCard. **Pets** Small dogs allowed. **Facilities** Parking. **Nearby** Pedraza - Hiking and riding in Sierra of Guadarramaand in the Naturel Park of Hyedo de Tejera Negra - Canoeing on the Río Duratón (4,500Pts the day with lunch). **Open** All year.

In the heart of a wild and sunny landscape sits the tiny village of Sigueruelo between the Sierra de Guadarrama and Ayllón. The Posada has a shady terrace where you can have lunch or a quiet drink and enjoy the life of the inn that includes hiking and horseback riding in the neighboring natural parks as well as canoeing with experienced guides on the Río *Duratón*. Here you see beams, stone walls, regional furniture and works of naïve art while enjoying the comfort of its rooms which are not altogether spacious. Among them, the best are upstairs, ideally the ones with a view. After putting in a strenuous day, you are sure to appreciate the traditional cooking as well as the friendly family atmosphere that always is part of your stay here.

How to get there *(Map 13): 50km northeast of Segovia via N110 (towards Soria) to Sigueruelo.*

Hotel Mesón Leonor

42005 Soria
Paseo del Mirón
Tel. 975-22 02 50 - Fax 975-22 99 53
Sr Pedro Heras Varca

Category ★★★ **Rooms** 32 with air conditioning, telephone, bath or shower, WC, satellite TV, safe, minibar. **Price** Single 5,600-6,650Pts, double 8,950-9,975Pts, double with terrace 9,900-10,500Pts, suite 11,500-12,600Pts. **Meals** Breakfast 600Pts, served 8:00-11:00; half board +2,700 Pts, full board +4,000Pts (per pers.). **Restaurant** Service 1:00PM-4:00PM, 9:00PM-11:00PM; mealtime specials 2,100Pts, also à la carte. Specialties: Meat dishes. **Credit cards** All major. **Pets** Dogs allowed in the rooms. **Facilities** Garage (1,500Pts). **Nearby** In Soria: cathedral San Pedro, churches of Santo Domingo - Vinuesa - Agreda - Sierra de Urbión: road of Laguna Negra de Urbión to Laguna egra de Neila. **Open** All year.

Soria is one of those towns from "Lands of Castille" about which Antonio Machado has spoken so well. The large house sheltering the hotel is austere, while the interior is in Castillian style. The rooms however are more welcoming and comfortable; some of them, with mezzanines, are more spacious and will cost you a few extra pesetas. This is a very pleasant halt for those planning to walk in the beautiful Sierra de Urbión.

How to get there (Map 14): 106km south of Logroño via N3.

La Casa del Cura

Herreros 42145 Soria
Calle Estacion
Tel. 975-27 04 65 - Fax 975-27 04 64

Rooms 12 with telephone, bath. **Price** Single 6,000Pts, double 8,300-9,800Pts. **Meals** Breakfast 800Pts, served 9:00-11:00. **Restaurant** Service 9:00PM-11:00PM; à la carte. **Credit cards** Not accepted. **Pets** Dogs not allowed. **Facilities** Parking. **Nearby** In Soria: cathedral San Pedro, churches of Santo Domingo - Vinuesa - Agreda - Sierra de Urbión: road of Laguna Negra de Urbión to Laguna egra de Neila. **Open** All year.

A few short kilometers from Soria and in the heart of Castille lies Herreros, a picturesque mountain village. Originally an old farm, La Casa del Cura has recently been transformed into a comfortable posada. The skill of the architects is plainly visible in their remarkable work which has preserved all the nobility of existing buildings and their original raw materials while at the same time adding what is necessary in terms of good taste and modernization for a Hotel of Charm. The result may be seen in the lounge-bar where wood, terracotta, stone and brick harmonize nicely with locally produced objects and comfortable sofas. The rooms are charming with wrought-iron beds, quilted bedspreads and refined regional furniture. Those upstairs have the best view of the surroundings. In all, an excellent example of beautiful and successful renovation.

How to get there *(Map 14): 20km west of Soria towards Burgos on N234.*

Casa Grande de Gormaz TR

42313 Quintanas de Gormaz (Soria)
Camino de las Fuentes
Tel. 975-34 09 82 - Sra Maria Jose Marco

Rooms 11 with telephone, bath. **Price** Single 6,000Pts, double 8,500-10,000Pts. **Meals** Breakfast 700Pts, served 7:30-10:30; full board +3,500Pts. **Restaurant** Only for residents. Service 9:00PM-11:00PM; mealtime specials 2,000Pts, also à la carte. **Credit cards** All major. **Pets** Dogs not allowed. **Facilities** Parking. **Nearby** In Soria: cathedral San Pedro, churches of Santo Domingo - Vinuesa, Rello, Berlanga de Duero, Calatañazor - Natural Park: El Cañon del rio Lobos - Agreda - Sierra de Urbión: road of Laguna Negra de Urbión to Laguna egra de Neila. **Closed** May - Nov (except weekends and National holidays).

In the Soria region, the Casa Grande de Gormaz is located in a large property devoted to agriculture. The surroundings are astonishing, suggesting a setting in a western movie. The house stands in the center of an almost desert-like plateau where an old and no-longer-used railway runs nearby and a visitor can easily imagine that its next stop is some phantom train station. It is a large house built at the beginning of the century topped by two symmetrical towers. Here in the main lounge, the glass roof and rustic decor inevitably recall the house of James Dean in *Giant*. The tidy and rustic atmosphere has unquestionable charm, and a long bay window frames the flat-lying countryside like a Flemish painting. The rooms are upstairs, and those on the right side are preferable as they give on the garden. The decoration is pleasant and simple, and what is in questionable taste only adds to the place's strange quality. The two most beautiful rooms - duplexes - are in the towers, each with a truly panoramic view. A curious address taking you straight into the soul of this Castillian land.

How to get there *(Map 13): 54km southwest of Soria via N122 towards San Esteban to El Burgo de Osma; then turn left towards Quintanas.*

Parador Rey Fernando II de León

49600 Benavente (Zamora)
Paseo de Ramón y Cajal
Tel. 980-63 03 00 - Fax 980-63 03 03
Sr Don Pedro Hernande Muñoz

Category ★★★★ **Rooms** 30 with air-conditioning, telephone, bath, WC, satellite TV, minibar.
Price Double 15,000-16,500Pts. **Meals** Breakfast 1,300Pts, served 8:00-11:00. **Restaurant**
Service 1:00PM-4:00PM, 8:30PM-11:00PM; mealtime specials 3,500Pts, also à la carte. **Credit cards**
All major. **Pets** Dogs not allowed. **Facilities** Garage (1,000Pts). **Nearby** Villalpando - Monastery of
Moreruela - Church of Santa María de Tera. **Open** All year.

B uilt in the 12th-century, this chateau was the residence of King Fernando
II who installed his court here in 1176. But later it was practically
destroyed during a battle between the French and English; only the imposing
Torre del Caraco remains today. To build the parador, it was necessary to build
one wing for the rooms and a second for the dining room and reception. The
lounge is in the tower with its magnificent *mudéjar* ceiling in wood marquetry.
In addition to the comfort, one may also appreciate the terraces with their
splendid panorama of the countryside.

How to get there *(Map 3): 69km south of León via N630.*

Parador Condes de Alba de Aliste

49001 Zamora
Plaza Viriato, 5
Tel. 980-51 44 97 - Fax 980-53 00 63
Sra Pelegrín

Category ★★★★ **Rooms** 47 with telephone, bath, WC, satellite TV, minibar; elevator. **Price** Double 15,000-18,500Pts. **Meals** Breakfast 1,300Pts, served 8:00-10:30. **Restaurant** Service 1:00PM-4:00PM, 8:30PM-11:00PM; mealtime specials 3,500Pts, also à la carte. Castillian cooking. **Credit cards** All major. **Pets** Dogs allowed. **Facilities** Swimming pool, garage (600Pts). **Nearby** In Zamora: the cathedral, Museo Catedralicio (Flamencos tapestries) - Church of Arcenillas - Church of San Pedro de la Nave - Colegiata de Toro - Carbajales de Alba. **Open** All year.

This 15th-century palace is right in the heart of Zamora on the edge of the old quarter. Largely destroyed during the revolt of the "Comuneros" in the 16th century, it was then restored by the Counts of Alba and of Aliste and became a hospital in the 18th century. The magnificent Renaissance cloister still survives today, along with a double gallery, the balcony and the grand monumental staircase at the foot of which one can admire a superb coat of arms. Lounges and dining room succeed each other to the garden with its swimming pool. The rooms are very well furnished but the suite, facing the square, deserves a special mention for its comfort and reasonable price. The personnel are friendly and the lady director charming, doing everything to ensure that your stay is one of the happiest times of your journey.

How to get there (Map 11): 62km north of Salamanca via N630.

Hostería Real de Zamora

49000 Zamora
Cuesta de Pizarro, 7
Tel. 980-53 45 45 - Fax 980-53 45 22
Sr Ramón

Category ★★★★ **Rooms** 18 with telephone, bath or shower, WC, TV, minibar. **Price** Single 8,185Pts, double 10,675Pts. **Meals** Breakfast included; half board 13,400Pts, full board 16,000Pts (per 2 pers. 3 days min.). **Restaurant** Pizarro, service 2:00PM-4:00PM, 9:00PM-11:30PM; mealtime specials 1,975Pts, also à la carte. Basque and Castillian cooking. **Credit cards** All major. **Pets** Dogs allowed. **Facilities** Parking. **Nearby** In Zamora: the cathedral, Museo Catedralicio (Flamencos tapestries) - Church of Arcenillas - Church of San Pedro de la Nave - Colegiata de Toro - Carbajales de Alba. **Open** All year

The hotel occupies a former palace of the Inquisition, itself built on an earlier Jewish building that legend links with the famous discoverer of Peru, Francisco Pizarro. A beautiful stone staircase leads to the rooms arranged around a refreshing patio. Some of them, the largest, have a view of the River Ebro: the only nuisance is the noise from the street, but other rooms look onto the patio. All are attractive and fresh with their tiled floors and light walls. The bathrooms are above reproach and some remarkable ancient Jewish baths have been conserved where the water comes from natural sources. A small staircase takes you to the garden and a terrace up against the medieval walls of the town where you can look out over the river. During Holy Week, a series of classical music recitals is given in the patio or the lovely restaurant.

How to get there *(Map 11): 62km north of Salamanca via N630.*

Hospederia Señorio de Briñas

26290 Briñas-Haro (La Rioja)
Travesia de la Calle Real, 3
Tel. 941-30 42 24 - Fax 941-30 43 45 - Sr Pedro Ortega
E-mail: hsbrinas@arrakis.es - Web: www.tecntel.com/briñas

Category ★★★ **Rooms** 14 with telephone, bath or shower, satellite TV. **Price** Single 9,500Pts, double 14,000Pts, suite 18,500Pts. **Meals** Breakfast included, served 9:00-11:30. No restaurant. **Credit cards** Diners, Visa, Eurocard, MasterCard. **Pets** Dogs allowed. **Facilities** Parking. **Nearby** Villages and vineyard of Briones, San Vincente de la Sonsierra and Casalarreina - Balcon de La Rioja. **Closed** Dec 15 - end Jan.

Briñas is a small village close to the Rio Ebro. On the edge of the village stands an 18th-century palace that once belonged to the Count of Haro. The building is of laudable architectural sobriety, usually rare in aristocratic residences, and Angela Gomez and Pedro Ortega have completely restored the interior with taste and experience making this a very attractive Hotel of Charm. The lounges are spread around a central atrium made up of elegant brick arcades. There are numerous areas where guests may enjoy the warmth of the fireplace, the conviviality of the bar or the intimate breakfast nook. Comfort is everywhere, especially in the rooms where attractive antique furniture harmonizes nicely with the floors, both parquet and hemp-covered. Four rooms have terraces. The bathrooms offer refreshing shades of terracotta and white tiles, contributing to decoration that is both comfortable and tasteful. The suites are superb. Our hands-down favorite is the duplex offering a fine setting that includes lovely wooden arcades. Haro is an important wine-growing region and a fine place to visit where you should not miss out on a meal at one of the local bodegas: La Vieja Bodega, Toni, Beethoven II.

How to get there *(Map 5): 4km northeast of Haro.*

Hotel Los Agustinos

26200 Haro (La Rioja)
Calle San Agustin, 2
Tel. 941-31 13 08 - Fax 941-30 31 48
Sr de Miguel Luengo

Category ★★★★ **Rooms** 62 with air-conditioning, telephone, bath, WC, satellite TV, minibar; elevator. **Price** Single 8,800-10,600Pts, double 11,000-13,300Pts, suite 24,200Pts. **Meals** Breakfast 1,100Pts, served 7:30-10:30; half board +2,800 Pts, full board +5,700Pts (per pers.). **Restaurant** Service 1:30PM-3:30PM, 8:30PM-11:00PM; closed Sun and Aug; mealtime specials 2,800Pts. Specialties: Patatas a la riojana - Cordero. **Credit cards** All major. **Pets** Dogs allowed (except in restaurant). **Nearby** Villages of Briones, San Vicente de la Sonsierra and de Casalareina - Balcón de Rioja. **Open** All year.

A 14th-century convent, and then a military hospital, prison, bus station and now a hotel, this is a real pleasure for us because the restoration here has been made with taste. Our greatest delight was in the terrace formed around the cloister which is also the setting for a patio where the former torture chamber of the prison once stood! The cloister arcades aligned the prisoners' cells and on the stonework one can still read their scribblings, which are sometimes very amusing. The church has become the lounge. As for the rooms, they are very classical. The restaurant cellars offer a particularly wide choice of regional wines. An excellent stop-over for a trip through this area of renowned wines.

How to get there (Map 5): 90km south of Bilbao via A68.

Parador de la Mancha

02000 Albacete
Al Sureste
Tel. 967-24 53 21 - Fax 967-24 33 71
Sr Carmelo Martinez Grande

Category ★★★ **Rooms** 69 with air-conditioning, telephone, bath or shower, WC, TV, minibar. **Price** Double 13,500-15,000Pts. **Meals** Breakfast 1,300Pts, served 8:00-10:30. **Restaurant** Service 1:00PM-4:00PM, 8:30PM-11:00PM; mealtime specials 3,500Pts, also à la carte. Specialties: Bacalão a la manchega - Pimientos rellenos - Pierna de cabrito al romero. **Credit cards** All major. **Pets** Dogs not allowed. **Facilities** Swimming pool, tennis, parking. **Nearby** In Albacete: Archeological Museum (Roman ivory dolls), Feria (Sept 7 - 17) - Alcaraz. **Open** All year.

For a visitor coming from Madrid, the Parador is a starting point for discovering the vast plain of La Mancha, the setting for Don Quixote's adventures. The Parador de la Mancha will meet your needs as it is a comfortable hotel in country style, built around a large patio with its fountain. It offers large and cool rooms, each with its own small terrace. The swimming pool is always welcome in summer, and you will also appreciate the hotel's cuisine featuring specialties of La Mancha, famous, among other things, for its cheese.

How to get there *(Map 21): 183km southwest of Valencia via N430, and 5km from Albacete.*

Parador de Almagro

13270 Almagro (Ciudad Real)
Ronda de San Francisco
Tel. 926-86 01 00 - Fax 926-86 01 50
Sra Lope de Santo

Category ★★★★ **Rooms** 55 with air-conditioning, telephone, bath, WC, satellite TV, minibar. **Price** Double 15,000-17,500Pts. **Meals** Breakfast 1,300Pts, served 8:00-10:30. **Restaurant** Service 1:30PM-4:00PM, 9:00PM-11:00PM; mealtime specials 3,700Pts, also à la carte. Specialties: Pisto manchego - Mojete - Migas. **Credit cards** All major. **Pets** Dogs not allowed. **Facilities** Swimming pool, tennis, parking. **Nearby** In Almagro: Plaza Mayor - Bolaños de Calatrava - Church of Moral de Calatrava - Calzada de Calatrava - National Park of Lagunas de Ruidera. **Open** All year.

The parador is built on the ancient convent of San Francisco dating from 1506. Almagro rises out of the vast La Mancha plain – on the route of Cervantes. It is the town of lace and the center of the Order of Calatrava. It is also interesting for its Plaza Mayor, which is a real jewel with its extensive uninterrupted glazed windows and the Corral de Comedias, the only surviving theater of the Siglo de Oro. The parador has no fewer than sixteen patios with galleries where the flowers and fountains combine to create a magic atmosphere. Terracotta and faience are often used in decorating the pretty rooms and the magnificent cellar next to the bar. The hotel is in the heart of town with private parking – and the service is very good.

How to get there *(Map 19): 22km east of Ciudad Real via C415.*

Parador Marqués de Villena

16213 Alarcón (Cuenca)
Avenida Amigos del Castillo
Tel. 969-33 03 15 - Fax 969-33 03 03
Sra Aurora Lozana

Category ★★★★ **Rooms** 13 with telephone, bath, WC, satellite TV, minibar; elevator. **Price** Double 18,500-19,000Pts. **Meals** Breakfast 1,300Pts, served 8:15-11:00. **Restaurant** Service 1:15PM-4:00PM, 9:00PM-11:00PM; mealtime specials 3,700Pts, also à la carte. Specialties: Bacalão a la Manchega. **Credit cards** All major. **Pets** Dogs not allowed. **Nearby** Motilla del Palancar - Valverde - Minglanilla - Puebla del Salvador - Yémeda. **Open** All year.

The parador is in the chateau of the little fortified town of Alarcón and it may well be the most beautiful and best conserved in the province of Cuenca. Set on the edge of the town on a huge rock almost entirely surrounded by the River Jucar, it enjoys a perfect tranquility. The rooms are pleasantly decorated and the bathrooms comfortable. Go for those in the tower, for even if they are rather sombre, their tiny windows – sometimes loopholes – give them an added attraction. A special mention goes to Room 105 from which you can walk the circular pathway with its unmatched view of the surrounding country. Breakfast is perfect, both generous and excellent and served in the imposing restaurant hall.

How to get there *(Map 20): 85km south of Cuenca via N320 to Motilla del Palencar, then N3 towards Madrid.*

Posada de San José

16001 Cuenca
Calle Julián Romero, 4
Tel. 969-21 13 00 - Fax 969-23 03 65 - Sra Morter and Sr Cortinas
E-mail: psanjose@arrakis.es - Web: www.arrakis.es/psanjose

Category ★★ **Rooms** 31 (21 with bath or shower, WC, 9 with basin). **Price** Single 2,500-2,800Pts (with basin), 4,100-4,700Pts (with bath), double 4,100-4,700Pts (with basin), 8,200-9,100Pts (with bath or shower), triple 5,500-6,300Pts (with basin), 11,100-12,300Pts (with bath or shower), 4 pers. 13,200-14,600Pts (with bath or shower). **Meals** Breakfast 550Pts, served 8:00-11:00. **Bar-Restaurant** Service 5:30PM-10:30PM, closed Mon; à la carte. Specialties: Tapas - Morteruedo - Trucha escabechada. **Credit cards** All major. **Pets** Dogs allowed in the rooms. **Nearby** In Cuenca: the cathedral, las Casas Colgadas (Hanging Houses), Museo de Arte Abstractado (Museum of Spanish Abstract Art) - La Ciudad Encantada (The Enchanted City) - Las Torcas - Hoz del Huecar (views). **Open** All year.

The Pposada occupies the former residence of the painter Martinez del Mazo, which is now a hotel full of charm with a magnificent view over the cliffs and gardens. Cuenca has been famous since the 14th century for its houses suspended above the Júcar gorges and, more recently, for its modern art museum. You will like this hotel for its simplicity and the comfortable rooms with a few exceptions, notably no. 9, and all are imbued with that same atmosphere of a well-run house. The furniture and floor tiles are well-polished, the curtains the work of the seamstresses of Cuenca, cotton napkins and towels, and so on. Those rooms with bathrooms also have a beautiful view, and Rooms 15, 21, 32 and 33 also have terraces. A pretty garden and a friendly welcome are good reasons for choosing this posada, which also offers very reasonable prices.

How to get there *(Map 14): 63km southeast of Madrid.*

Hotel Cueva del Fraile

16001 Cuenca
Hoz del Huecar
Tel. 969-21 15 71 - Fax 969-25 60 47 - Sr de la Torre
Web: cuevadelfraile@estancias.es

Rooms 63 with telephone, bath, WC, TV. **Price** Single 8,675-13,675Pts, double 10,250-15,650Pts, triple 14,125-21,425Pts, 4 pers. 17,300-26,200Pts. **Meals** Breakfast (buffet) included, served 8:00-11:00; half board +2,850Pts, full board +4,100Pts (per pers.). **Restaurant** See p. 310. **Credit cards** All major. **Pets** Dogs allowed. **Facilities** Swimming pool, tennis (500Pts), minigolf, parking. **Nearby** In Cuenca: the cathedral, las Casas Colgadas (Hanging Houses), Museo de Arte Abstractado (Museum of Spanish Abstract Art) - La Ciudad Encantada (The Enchanted City) - Las Torcas. **Open** All year.

It is seven kilometers from Cuenca, in the midst of mountainous outcrops, that the "Cueva del Fraile" is to be found. Before being converted some ten years ago into a welcoming and quiet hotel, this 15th-century building was first a convent and then a farm. The rooms are nothing extraordinary, their Castillian furnishings and lighting are not very welcoming. The most attractive are those reached via the covered gallery and overlooking the pretty interior courtyard. One will appreciate the dining room with its large open fireplace, or the bar with its mezzanine, for their rustic atmosphere. A friendly welcome and quality regional cuisine add to the charm of this peaceful establishment without any pretensions.

How to get there *(Map 14): 170km southeast of Madrid to Cuenca, then the road to Palomera for 6km, then to the left on the road to Buenache for 1.2km.*

Parador de Sigüenza

19003 Sigüenza (Guadalajara)
Tel. 949-39 01 00 - Fax 949-39 13 64
Sr Jose Menguiano

Category ★★★★ **Rooms** 81 with air-conditioning, telephone, bath, WC, satellite TV, minibar; elevator. **Price** Double 13,500-15,000Pts. **Meals** Breakfast 1,300Pts, served 8:00-11:00. **Restaurant** Service 1:30PM-4:00PM, 8:30PM-11:00PM; mealtime specials 3,700Pts, also à la carte. Regional cooking. **Credit cards** All major. **Pets** Dogs not allowed. **Facilities** Parking. **Nearby** In Sigüenza: the cathedral (Tomb of Don Martín Vásquez de Arca in the Chapel of the Doncel, the sacristy, Chapel of Santa Librada). **Open** All year.

At the summit of the fortified town of Sigüenza, which rises in terraces on the side of the hill, stands the imposing Moorish fortress which became a Bishop's Palace, and is now a parador. The restoration and reconstruction work has been careful to respect the proportions of this enormous four-sided building of 7,000 m2. To soften the austerity of the site, courtyards and gardens have been laid out. Two immense rooms shelter the lounge and dining room with their sober Castillian furniture. The rooms, whether giving onto the courtyard or valley, are all comfortable. Some have terraces with long reclining chairs. From the large tiled courtyard, one has a magnificent view over the pink roofs of Sigüenza and can trace out the maze of tiny streets. In the marvellous cathedral do not miss the 15th-century funeral monument of Doncel and one of the most beautiful sculptures in the history of Spanish art.

How to get there *(Map 14): 130km northeast of Madrid; at 70km from Guadalajara via N11 to Alcolea del Pinar, then C204 towards Sigüenza.*

Parador de Oropesa

45460 Oropesa (Toledo)
Plaza del Palacio, 1
Tel. 925-43 00 00 - Fax 925-43 07 77

Category ★★★★ **Rooms** 48 with air-conditioning, telephone, bath, WC, satellite TV, minibar; elevator. **Price** Double 15,000Pts. **Meals** Breakfast 1,300Pts, served 8:00-10:30. **Restaurant** Service 1:00PM-4:00PM, 8:00PM-11:00PM; mealtime specials 3,700Pts, also à la carte. Specialties: Cordero del campo - Perdiz de tiro a la toledana. **Credit cards** All major. **Pets** Dogs not allowed. **Facilities** Parking. **Nearby** "Ceramic road" from Talavera de la Reina, via Puente de Arzobispo, Valdeverdeja - Lake of Azután - Lagartera. **Open** All year.

The magnificent feudal "château" of Oropesa was the first historic building to be converted into a parador in 1930. This is a superb gothic-*mudéjar* building, square in plan, and flanked with towers and keeps that look out over the valley of the Campo Arañuelo. The plain of Gredos is in the far distance. It shares the site with a renaissance palace that one can visit. In the interior the large forms and original floors have been preserved, which give a lot of charm and character to the well-furnished reception rooms. The rooms have terraces, some of which overlook the valley, and all the comforts of a grand hotel. At the foot of the historic building is a magnificent swimming pool, bordered by lawns, which also offers a superb panorama. A very beautiful address that should not be missed.

How to get there *(Map 12): 70km south of Madrid via N401; close to the Puerta de Bisagra.*

Hostal del Cardenal

45004 Toledo
Paseo de Recaredo, 24
Tel. 925-22 49 00 - Fax 925-22 29 91 - Sr Gonzalez Luis Gozalbo
E-mail: cardenal@macom.es - Web: www.cardenal.macom.es

Category ★★★ **Rooms** 27 with air-conditioning, telephone, bath, WC, satellite TV, minibar (suite). **Price** Single 5,870-11,650Pts, double 9,450-12,600Pts, triple 12,250-16,350Pts, suite 12,450-17,150Pts. **Meals** Breakfast 900Pts, served 7:15-11:00. **Restaurant** Service 1:15PM-4:00PM, 8:30PM-11:00PM, closed Dec 24; mealtime specials 2,650Pts, also à la carte. Specialties: Cochinillo y cordero asado - Sopa de ajo - Perdiz estofado a la toledana. **Credit cards** All major. **Pets** Dogs allowed. **Nearby** In Toledo: Cathedral, Church of Santo Tomé ("El Entierro del Conte de Orgaz" by Greco), El Tránsito Synagogue, Museum of Santa Cruz - Aranjuez - "Don Quixote country": (N301,south of Aranjuez): Consuegra, Corral de Almaguer, Quintanar de la Orden, El Toboso, Mota del Cuervo Belmonte, Tomelloso, Argamasillo de Alba. **Open** All year.

In Toledo there are many reasons for staying at the Hostal del Cardenal: its location, in the heart of the imperial city, facing the Puerta de Bisagra, one of the jewels of Toledo; its site in a Toledan palace of the 18th century, former summer residence of Cardinal Lorenzana, archbishop of the city; the calm of its Moorish gardens where only the birdsong and fountains are to be heard. There are also its comfort and good cuisine, its summer dinners in the garden. Take a last evening stroll around the circular pathway of the 11th-century bastion of walls.

How to get there *(Map 13): 70km south of Madrid via N401; near to the Porte de Bisagra.*

Hotel Residencia La Almazara

45080 Toledo
Carret de Arges in Polan
Tel. 925-22 38 66 - Fax 925-25 05 62 - Sr Villamor
Web: www.frontpage-98.com/hotelalmazara/home.htm

Category ★★ **Rooms** 21 with telephone, bath, WC. **Price** Single 3,700Pts, double 5,500Pts, double with the view 6,300Pts. **Meals** Breakfast 500Pts, served 8:00-11:00. **Restaurant** See p. 309. **Credit cards** All major. **Pets** Dogs not allowed. **Facilities** Parking. **Nearby** In Toledo: Cathedral, Church of Santo Tomé (El Entierro del Conte de Orgaz od Greco), El Tránsito Synagogue, Museum of Santa Cruz - Aranjuez - "Don Quixote country": (N301, south of Aranjuez): Consuegra, Corral de Almaguer, Quintanar de la Orden, El Toboso, Mota del Cuervo Belmonte, Tomelloso, Argamasilla de Alba. **Open** Mar 7 - Dec 10.

Protected by 500 hectares of olive trees, oaks and junipers, this hotel was the former vacation home of Cardinal Quiroza in the 16th century. It is the oldest hotel in the city and it was featured in the El Greco painting, "General view of Toledo". The rooms are simple but very attractive, with their brand new bathrooms. Rooms 1 to 9 also have terraces with a breathtaking view. The countryside around and the softness of the light make this place a real haven that one is always happy to return to after a tiring visit to Toledo or its surroundings.

How to get there *(Map 13): 73.5km south of Madrid to Toledo via N401; then 3.5km on the road to Arges, near to the restaurant Monterrey-Aire de Cigarrales*

Parador Conde de Orgaz

45001 Toledo
Cerro del Emperador
Tel. 925-22 18 50 - Fax 925-22 51 66
Sra Ester Lope

Category ★★★★ **Rooms** 76 with air-conditioning, telephone, bath, WC, satellite TV, minibar; elevator. **Price** Double 18,500Pts, double with a view 21,000Pts. **Meals** Breakfast 1,300Pts, served 8:00-10:30. **Restaurant** Service 1:00PM-4:00PM, 8:30PM-11:00PM; mealtime specials 3,700Pts, also à la carte. Specialties: Duelos y quebrantos - Perdiz a la toledana - Ponche toledano. **Credit cards** All major. **Pets** Dogs not allowed. **Facilities** Swimming pool. **Nearby** In Toledo: Cathedral, Church of Santo Tomé ("El Entierro del Conte de Orgaz" Greco), El Tránsito Synagogue, Museum of Santa Cruz - Aranjuez - "Don Quixote country": (N301,south of Aranjuez): Consuegra, Corral de Almaguer, Quintanar de la Orden, El Toboso, Mota del Cuervo Belmonte, Tomelloso, Argamasillo de Alba. **Open** All year.

The parador, which takes its name from the famous painting by El Greco, "The Burial of the Count of Orgaz", is on the "Emperor's Hill" in the privileged quarter of Cigarrales. This quarter dominates Toledo, and offers an unmatched view between the Alcántara and San Martin bridges. This remarkable site has conditioned the layout of the buildings. With its completely Toledan character, the hotel is very comfortable and air-conditioned, and also has a swimming pool, both major bonuses when visiting Toledo in summer.

How to get there *(Map 13): 70km south of Madrid via N401; facing the city on the other side of the River Tagus (Tajo).*

Hotel Doménico

45002 Toledo
Cerro del Emperador
Tel. 925-28 01 01 - Fax 925-28 01 03
Sra Eva-Maria Maeso

Category ★★★★ **Rooms** 48 and 2 suites with air-conditioning, telephone, bath, WC, satellite TV, safe, minibar; elevator. **Price** Single 10,810-11,250Pts, double 15,610-16,380Pts, superior double 18,100-18,975Pts, special double 24,860-26,075Pts. **Meals** Breakfast 1,200Pts, served 8:00-10:30; half board +4,200Pts, full board +6,200Pts (per pers., 2 days min.). **Restaurant** Service 1:00PM-4:00PM, 8:30PM-11:00PM; mealtime specials 3,250Pts, also à la carte. Regional cooking. **Credit cards** All major. **Pets** Dogs allowed. **Facilities** Swimming pool, parking. **Nearby** In Toledo: Cathedral, Church of Santo Tomé ("El Entierro del Conte de Orgaz", Greco), El Tránsito Synagogue, Museum of Santa Cruz - Aranjuez - "Don Quixote country": (N301, south of Aranjuez): Consuegra, Corral de Almaguer, Quintanar de la Orden, El Toboso, Mota del Cuervo Belmonte, Tomelloso, Argamasilla de Alba. **Open** All year.

The Hotel Doménico is not in the town center but on the high ground close by, which allows you to admire this ancient city as El Greco painted it. The architecture of the hotel has all the rigor of the arid mineral countryside surrounding it. The interior is very ordinary, the decor modern but without style, but certain rooms - the 38 with "standard" design - have terraces offering magnificent views of the countryside and, even better, of the Old Town. The lounge and bar are very lively areas, while the swimming pool, with its shady corner terraces, is much appreciated. The site, services and quality of facilities all quickly make you forget the banality of the decor.

How to get there *(Map 13): 70km south of Madrid via N401; facing the town on the other bank of the Tagus.*

Hotel Ritz

08010 Barcelona
Gran Via de les Corts Catalanes, 668
Tel. 93-318 52 00 - Fax 93-318 01 48
Web: www.ritzbcn.com

Category ★★★★★ **Rooms** 113 and 12 suites with telephone, bath, WC, satellite TV, safe, minibar; elevator. **Price** Single 36,000Pts, double 45,000Pts, suite 50,000-325,000Pts. **Meals** Breakfast 2,700Pts, served 7:00-11:00. **Restaurant** Service 1:30PM-4:00PM, 8:30PM-11:00PM; à la carte 5,500Pts. Specialties: Pollo con langostinas - Escudella i carn d'olla. **Credit cards** All major. **Pets** Dogs not allowed. **Facilities** Parking. **Nearby** Cimenterie became the Taller de arqutectura de Ricardo Bofill and Walden 7 in Sant Just Desvern - Sitges - Monastery of San Cugat del Valle - Montserrat - Vich; Prat golf course (9-and 18-Hole), San Cugat golf course (18-Hole). **Open** All year.

The hotel is in the heart of the city, a few steps from the Paseo de Gracia, the Ramblas and the barrio gótico. After undergoing extensive renovation, the Ritz of Barcelona has regained its name and luster. If the hotel has remained equal to itself since its opening in 1919, the rooms live up to the renown associated with its prestigious name. It is, after all, the Ritz. Both the outside and the interior have enormous allure as the guest enters via a grand double staircase to discover a vast lobby, where the special attention paid to each guest makes it very clear that this is truly a palace. As with most palaces, the rooms lack the charm of the lounges, but all are nonetheless very comfortable. The hotel restaurant offers international cuisine and a good variety of Catalan dishes. The terrace of the small interior garden is also a pleasant spot for having a drink, while a visit to the subterranean bar is obligatory.

How to get there *(Map 8): On the Gran Via near the Plaza de Catalunya.*

Gran Hotel Havana

08010 Barcelona
Gran Via de les Corts Catalanes, 647
Tel. 93-412 11 15 - Fax 93-412 26 11

Category ★★★★ **Rooms** 145 with air-conditioning, telephone, bath, satellite TV, minibar, safe, outlet for fax; elevator. **Price** Single 21,000Pts, double 23,000Pts, suite 26,000-55,000Pts. **Meals** Breakfast 1,300Pts, served 7:00-11:00. **Restaurant** Service 1:30PM-4:00PM, 8:30PM-11:00PM; à la carte 2,500Pts. **Credit cards** All major. **Pets** Dogs not allowed. **Facilities** Garage (1,700Pts). **Nearby** Cimenterie became the Taller de arqutectura de Ricardo Bofill and Walden 7 in Sant Just Desvern - Sitges - Monastery of San Cugat del Valles - Montserrat - Vich - Prat golf course (9- and 18-Hole) - San Cugat golf course (18-Hole). **Open** All year.

The palaces of Barcelona are being renovated. The Gran Hotel Havana, opened in 1991, is among the grand hotels of the Eixample upon which the interior architects of Catalunya deployed their talent. This large and comfortable building is typical of those built at the end of the 19th century; its lobby occupies practically the entire ground floor. The interior courtyard has been covered with a bean-shaped ceiling, creating a virtual shaft of light stretching up to the roof. Similar rounded forms are present on the ground floor as well as in the hotel's contemporary furniture. Luxury is plainly the goal of the spacious and comfortable rooms here. The decor is elegantly modern and classic with a few whimsical touches, such as the attractive woven decoration on the bedsteads. The gray marble bathrooms are the essence of refinement, and those on the top floor have an excellent view. The hotel is ideally located and the service is perfect.

How to get there *(Map 5): On the Gran Via; near the Plaza de Catalunya.*

Hotel Claris

08007 Barcelona - Pau Claris, 150
Tel. 93-487 62 62 - Fax 93-215 79 70 - Sr P. Bouisset
E-mail: claris@derbyhotels.es - Web: www.derbyhotels.es

Category ★★★★★ **Rooms** 82, 18 junior-suites, 18 duplex and 2 suites with air-conditioning, telephone, bath, WC, satellite TV, minibar, safe; elevator. **Price** Single 36,000Pts, double 42,900Pts, suite 55,000-120,000Pts. **Meals** Breakfast 2,800Pts. Served 7:00-11:00. **Restaurant** Beluga, service 8:30PM-1:00PM, closed Sun. Specialty: caviar. Claris, service 1:30PM-3:30PM, 8:00PM-11:00PM. Ampurda specialties. Barbecue-Terrasse, service 8:00PM-11:30PM. **Credits cards** All major. **Pets** Dogs allowed (except in restaurant). **Facilities** Swimming pool, sauna, garage. **Nearby** Cimenterie became the Taller de arqutectura de Ricardo Bofill and Walden 7 in Sant Just Desvern - Sitges - Monastery of San Cugat del Valle - Montserrat - Vich; Prat golf course (9- and 18-Hole), San Cugat golf course (18-Hole). **Open** All year.

The Claris is near the Barrio Gotic and a short distance from the celebrated buildings designed by Antonio Gaudi (1852-1926). It was built in the 19th century and has retained its Neo-Gothic facade while adding a metallic gray extension which nicely weds the two styles. This architecture is a prelude to the interior decoration which skillfully plays on the contrasts of its building materials and the refinement of its furnishings. You find large concrete pillars, an extensive use of marble plus exotic wood superbly put to use in the hotel's modern chairs and 1930-style light fixtures. In addition, there are mosaics from the Roman era. The same luxury is present in the rooms, resolutely modern although some have very attractive antiques. Art and culture are everywhere and the hotel houses a small museum with a fine collection of Egyptology. This is one of the most beautiful hotels in the Catalan capital.

How to get there *(Map 8): On the Diagonal.*

St-Moritz Hotel

08007 Barcelona
Diputacíon, 262/264
Tel. 93-412 15 00 - Fax 93-412 12 36

Category ★★★★ **Rooms** 92 with air-conditioning, telephone, bath, WC, satellite TV, minibar, safe; elevator - Wheelchair access. **Price** Single 20,900-27,600Pts, double 24,900-32,900Pts. **Meals** Breakfast 2,300-2,500Pts, served 7:00-11:00. **Restaurant** Service 1:30PM-4:00PM, 8:30PM-11:00PM, mealtime specials 2,950Pts, also à la carte. **Credits cards** All major. **Pets** Dogs allowed (except in restaurant). **Facilities** Garage. **Nearby** Cimenterie became the Taller de arqutectura de Ricardo Bofill and Walden 7 in Sant Just Desvern - Sitges - Monastery of San Cugat del Valle - Montserrat - Vich; Prat golf course (9- and 18-Hole), San Cugat golf course (18-Hole). **Open** All year.

The St. Moritz is located on the periphery of the Barrio Gotic, which came into existence as a result of 19th-century urban planning. Today, as numerous offices occupy its renovated buildings, it stands to reason that an efficient and luxurious hotel should be among them. This is an impressive building dating from 1883 and classed as a "historical landmark" by the Ministry of Tourism. For this reason its architecture has been preserved and includes an immense entry in gray marble leading to a huge staircase with a glass roof assuring very pleasant light. The decor is sober and elegantly modern, and this equally applies to the rooms which, in addition to standard comfort and elegant bathrooms, offer a mini-gymnasium equipped with a bicycle-exerciser. On the second floor is the *St. Gallen*, the hotel's restaurant which enjoys the esteem of the residents and businessmen of Barcelona. On the roof is a terrace where you can have lunch.

How to get there (Map 8): On the Diagonal.

Hotel Gran Vía

08007 Barcelona
Gran Vía, 642
Tel. 93-318 19 00 - Fax 93-318 99 97
Sr Garcia

Category ★★★ **Rooms** 53 with air-conditioning, telephone, bath, WC, TV, minibar. **Price** Single 10,000Pts, double 14,000Pts. **Meals** Breakfast (buffet) 1,100Pts, served 7:00-11:00. **Restaurant** See pp. 310-314. **Credit cards** All major. **Pets** Dogs not allowed. **Facilities** Parking (2,300Pts). **Nearby** Cimenterie became the Taller de arqutectura de Ricardo Bofill and Walden 7 in Sant Just Desvern - Sitges - Monastery of San Cugat del Valle - Montserrat - Vich; Prat golf course (9- and 18-Hole), San Cugat golf course (18-Hole). **Open** All year.

In the heart of Barcelona, the Hotel Gran Vía has been here since 1936. It was first of all a beautiful private hotel of which a large part of the furniture and original pictures still remain. Without being luxurious, the Gran Vía still has that charm of all cozy establishments, and one is rapidly won over by the snug atmosphere. After an attractive hall, the arcaded gallery and the colonnade of the first floor, one is a little disappointed by the lack of character of the rooms. Though comfortable, they lack the glory of the public rooms with their rococo style. The very beautiful dining room is now only used for breakfast, which in summer is served on the sunny terrace behind the building. The quieter rooms are also on this side. All in all, the welcome is warm.

How to get there *(Map 8): On the Diagonal, close to the Paza de Catalunya.*

Hotel Condes de Barcelona

08008 Barcelona
Paseo de Gracia, 75
Tel. 93-488 22 00 - Fax 93-488 06 14
E-mail: cb.hotel@condesdebarcelona - Web: www.condesdebarcelona.com

Category ★★★★ **Rooms** 183 with air-conditioning, telephone, bath, WC, satellite TV, video, minibar; elevator. **Price** Double 29,000Pts (1 pers.), 31,000Pts; suite "Gaudí" 60,000Pts, suite "Barcelona" 70,000Pts. **Meals** Breakfast 2,200Pts, served 7:00-11:00. **Restaurant** Service 1:00PM-10:30PM; mealtime specials 2,700Pts, also à la carte. Catalan and international cooking. **Credit cards** All major. **Pets** Dogs not allowed. **Facility** Swimming pool, garage (2,200Pts). **Nearby** Cimenterie became the Taller de arqutectura de Ricardo Bofill and Walden 7 in Sant Just Desvern - Sitges - Monastery of San Cugat del Valle - Montserrat - Vich; Prat golf course (9- and 18-Hole), San Cugat golf course (18-Hole). **Open** All year.

A few meters away from the famous house of Gaudí, La Pedrera, there stood another Art Nouveau house, La Casa Batllo, which is now one of the best hotels in Barcelona. The interior architecture is very pure, with modern black furniture, halogen lighting and a very refined setting for a select clientele patronizing the lounges and bar. Whatever the layout of the rooms, they are comfortable: those on the courtyard look out onto a beautiful terrace and gardens; the rooms on the street are well-insulated from the noise; and in the older building, all those on the upper floor have been renovated. We recommend the Gaudí or Barcelona suites, very fashionable and slightly sophisticated, yet in no way pretentious. If access to the swimming pool is high on your list of priorities, ask for information regarding its hours which are not altogether regular.

How to get there *(Map 8): On the Diagonal; Plaza de Catalunya, then Paseo de Gracia.*

Hotel Turó de Vilana

08017 Barcelona
Calle Vilana, 7
Tel. 93-434 03 63 - Fax 93-418 89 03 - Sr Orteu
E-mail: hotel@turodevilana.com - Web: www.turodevilana.com

Category ★★★ **Rooms** 20 with air-conditioning, telephone, bath with hydromassage, satellite TV, minibar, safe; elevator. **Price** Single 12,500-15,100Pts, double 15,600-18,900Pts. **Meals** Breakfast 1,300Pts, served 7:30-11:00. **Restaurant** See pp. 310/314. **Credit card** All major. **Pets** Dogs not allowed. **Facilities** Parking, garage (1,300Pts). **Nearby** Cimenterie became the Taller de arqutectura de Ricardo Bofill and Walden 7 in Sant Just Desvern - Sitges - Monastery of San Cugat del Valles - Montserrat - Vich - Prat golf course, 9- and 18-hole - San Cugat golf course, 18-hole. **Open** All year.

The hotel is located in Barcelona's residential section, known for its medical center, the Dexeus and Teknon Clinics at the foot of the Tibidabo. Architect-designer Diez Gascon supervised its building and the brick facades, while unremarkable, nonetheless set it off from surrounding buildings. The interior is more interesting, with a lobby that makes tasteful use of wood, glass and travertine and has nicely furnished areas with modern sofas. The rooms have an elegant sobriety warmed by beige or ochre fabrics, wooden floors and paneling. The bathrooms, in marble and travertine, offer every comfort. Certain rooms on the upper floors have terraces, some of them with a view of the mountain. It would be criminal not to enjoy your breakfast here as the buffet is copious, varied and delicious.

How to get there *(Map 5): On the Gran Via; near the Plaza de Catalunya.*

Astoria Hotel

08036 Barcelona
Calle Paris, 203
Tel. 93-209 83 11 - Fax 93-202 30 08

Category ★★★ **Rooms** 117 with air-conditioning, telephone, bath or shower, WC, satellite TV, safe, minibar; elevator. **Price** Single 18,700Pts, double 22,200Pts. **Meals** Breakfast 1,500Pts, served 7:00-11:00. **Restaurant** See pp. 310-314. **Credit cards** All major. **Pets** Dogs allowed. **Facilities** Parking. **Nearby** Cimenterie became the Taller de arqutectura de Ricardo Bofill and Walden 7 in Sant Just Desvern - Sitges - Monastery of San Cugat del Valle - Montserrat - Vich; Prat golf course (9 and 18-Hole), San Cugat golf course (18-Hole). **Open** All year.

This beautiful hotel with its Art Déco facade, even though only built in the 1950s, is in the residential quarter of Barcelona, the Eixample. A very solemn hallway, marble columns and large mirrors, all set the tone. The rooms, with double-glazing and air-conditioning, are quiet and decorated simply, while offering all the comforts. In the bathrooms, some elements have been covered with marble. Some rooms are duplexes offering a lounge and a terrace. There is no restaurant, but the bar with pleasant lamps has a snug atmosphere along with an attractive rest lounge. The general ambiance is discreet and elegant. Depending on the season, weekend rates may be available.

How to get there (Map 8): On the Diagonal.

Hotel Duques de Bergara

08002 Barcelona
Calle Bergara, 11
Tel. 93-301 51 51 - Fax 93-317 34 42
Sra Dolores Hurtado

Category ★★★★ **Rooms** 149 with air-conditioning, telephone, bath, WC, satellite TV, minibar; elevator. **Price** Single 32,900Pts, double 35,900Pts. **Meals** Breakfast 1,900Pts, served 7:00-10:30. **Restaurant** Service 1:00PM-4:00PM, 8:00PM-11:00PM; mealtime specials 2,500Pts. International cooking. **Credit cards** All major. **Pets** Dogs not allowed. **Facilities** Swimming pool, parking. **Nearby** Cimenterie became the Taller de arqutectura de Ricardo Bofill and Walden 7 in Sant Just Desvern - Sitges - Monastery of San Cugat del Valle - Montserrat - Vich; Prat golf course (9-and 18-Hole), San Cugat golf course (18-Hole). **Open** All year.

This is a private house built in 1903 and converted into a hotel a few years ago. The entrance is beautiful enough to take your breath away: its caisson ceiling of incredible height opens onto a glass roof that fills the hotel with the sort of light that photographers dream about. Marble covers all of the staircase right up to the magnificent doors. Alas, like almost all older hotels trying to keep abreast of the demands of the modern visitor, nothing in the bedrooms recalls the past of such an attractive building. This being said, even if they are modern, it does not make them any less pleasant. The bathrooms are especially functional. The dining room, although sadly neglected, is still a comfortable staging post that deserves noting.

***How to get there** (Map 8): On the Diagonal.*

Hotel Méridien Barcelone

08002 Barcelona
La Rambla, 111
Tel. 93-318 62 00 - Fax 93-301 77 76

Category ★★★★ **Rooms** 195 and 11 suites with air-conditioning, telephone, bath, WC, satellite TV, video, minibar; elevator - Wheelchair access. **Price** Single 34,000-38,000Pts, double 38,000-42,000Pts, suite 90,000Pts. **Meals** Breakfast 2,500Pts. **Restaurant** Service 1:00PM-3:30PM, 8:00PM-10:30PM; à la carte. Mediterranean cooking. **Credit cards** All major. **Pets** Dogs not allowed. **Facilities** Garage. **Nearby** Cimenterie became the Taller de arqutectura de Ricardo Bofill and Walden 7 in Sant Just Desvern - Sitges - Monastery of San Cugat del Valle - Montserrat - Vich; Prat golf course (9- and 18-Hole), San Cugat golf course (18-Hole). **Open** All year.

Here again the "Ramblas" has been chosen to modernize an old hotel. The services are those of a grand hotel intended for a clientele of wealthy tourists or businessmen. One must however recognize the special effort that has been made in matters of decor. The lounges are luxurious. The rooms with their immense beds are furnished in the style of the 1930s, with an abundance of fabrics in soft colors that create an elegant and subtle atmosphere. If you would like to reserve a suite, then ask for 918. This is a hotel for staying to see the lights of the town while also profiting from its voluptuous comfort. The interesting rates for weekends should be noted.

How to get there *(Map 8): On the Ramblas.*

Hotel Colón

08002 Barcelona
Avenida de la Catedral, 7
Tel. 93-301 14 04 - Fax 93-317 29 15 - Sr Espejo Melero
E-mail: colon@ncsa.es - Web: www.nexus.es/colon/index.htm

Category ★★★★ **Rooms** 147 with air-conditioning, telephone, bath, WC, satellite TV, minibar; elevator. **Price** Single 17,500Pts, double 26,300Pts, superior double 41,200Pts, suite 46,350Pts. **Meals** Breakfast (buffet) 1,900Pts, served 7:00-11:00. **Restaurant** Service 1:00PM-3:00PM, 8:00PM-10:30PM; mealtime specials 3,500Pts, also à la carte. Catalan and international cooking. **Credit cards** All major. **Pets** Dogs allowed. **Nearby** Cimenterie became the Taller de arqutectura de Ricardo Bofill and Walden 7 in Sant Just Desvern - Sitges - Monastery of San Cugat del Valle - Montserrat - Vich; Prat golf course (9- and 18-Hole), San Cugat golf course (18-Hole). **Open** All year.

The Hotel Colón has an unequaled site: in the heart of the gothic quarter and facing the 13th-century cathedral. This is an institution for foreign tourists, and even if some fittings and equipment are now rather dated, it still remains a very agreeable hotel to stay in. The ambiance is cozy, as with any good old hotel, making the lounges and bar a nice place to visit in the evenings. The rooms vary, but one goes first for those on the top floor with their superb terraces. With the "Ramblas" a few paces away, this is the ideal spot in Barcelona!

How to get there *(Map 8): Facing the cathedral.*

Hotel Regencia Colón

08002 Barcelona
Avenida de la Catedral, 7
Tel. 93-318 98 58 - Fax 93-317 28 22
Sr Espejo Rafael

Category ★★★ **Rooms** 55 with air-conditioning, telephone, bath or shower, WC, TV, safe, minibar; elevator. **Price** Single 9,800-13,000Pts, double 16,500Pts, triple 20,000Pts. **Meals** Breakfast (buffet) 1,250Pts, served 7:00-11:00. **Restaurant** See pp 310-314. **Credit cards** All major. **Pets** Dogs allowed. **Facilities** Parking (2,500Pts). **Nearby** Cimenterie became the Taller de arqutectura de Ricardo Bofill and Walden 7 in Sant Just Desvern - Sitges - Monastery of San Cugat del Valle - Montserrat - Vich; Prat golf course (9- and 18-Hole), San Cugat golf course (18-Hole). **Open** All year.

Situated just next to its "big brother", the Regencia Colón is very much less expensive but offers the same convenient site, along with comfortable and well-equipped rooms. Nothing is very original but with its vast and rather solemn entry hall this is a "well-meaning" hotel, very relaxing after a long walk through the small lanes of the gothic quarter or along the "Ramblas".

How to get there *(Map 8): Facing the cathedral.*

Nouvel Hotel

08002 Barcelona
Calle Santa Ana, 18-20
Tel. 93-301 82 74 - Fax 93-301 83 70

Category ★★★ **Rooms** 54 with air-conditioning, telephone, bath or shower, WC, satellite TV, (some with safe and minibar); elevator. **Price** Single 12,125Pts, double 18,000Pts, triple 22,125Pts. **Meals** Breakfast 1,000Pts, served 7:00-11:00. **Restaurant** See pp. 310/314. **Credit cards** All major. **Pets** Dogs not allowed. **Nearby** Cimenterie became the Taller de arqutectura de Ricardo Bofill and Walden 7 in Sant Just Desvern - Sitges - Monastery of San Cugat del Valles - Montserrat - Vich - Prat golf course (9- and 18-Hole), San Cugat golf course (18-Hole). **Open** All year.

The Nouvel Hotel is an attractive, early-20th-century building close to the cathedral, which is to say near the *barrio gotico* and the Ramblas. The ground floor area is magnificent with vaulted openings, Art Nouveau woodwork and an Art Deco marquee of tinted glass on the facade. The entrance has also retained a certain look one associates with comfortable wealth; guests are received in what was once a luxurious gallery and proceed to a vast stone staircase with beautifully worked wrought iron. The rooms, while spacious and well-maintained, are rather ordinary but offer the comfort expected in a three-star hotel. The best of them give onto the street. This is an interesting address for anyone wanting to be in the heart of the city and enjoy the life of this quarter. As for exciting city life, everyone knows there is plenty of that in Barcelona.

How to get there *(Map 8): Near the Cathedral.*

Hotel Metropol

08002 Barcelona
Carreer Ample, 31
Tel. 93-310 51 00 - Fax 93-319 12 76
Sra Gema Mal

Category ★★★ **Rooms** 68 with air-conditioning, telephone, bath or shower, WC, satellite TV, minibar; elevator. **Price** Single 11,700Pts, double 13,200Pts. **Meals** Breakfast 1,100Pts, served 7:30-10:30. **Restaurant** See pp. 310-314. **Credit cards** All major. **Pets** Dogs not allowed. **Nearby** Cimenterie became the Taller de arqutectura de Ricardo Bofill and Walden 7 in Sant Just Desvern - Sitges (beach) - Monastery of San Cugat del Valle - Montserrat - Vich - Prat golf course (9 and 18-Hole golf), San Cugat golf course (18-Hole). **Open** All year.

Among the small hotels in the *barrio gótico*, the Metropol is one of the best, nicely located close to the Plaza Real and the port. The lobby, on the patio, is all in pink, a tradition in Spanish houses, and the rooms are large but very pleasant and enjoy good light; we prefer the ones on the street side. The decor is modernistic, dating from the Olympic Games held in Barcelona, and is marked by sober, elegantly contemporary furniture and marble bathrooms. The hotel has no restaurant, but you can enjoy Catalan specialties in the small bars and restaurants in the nearby streets.

How to get there (Map 8): In the Old Town.

Hotel Gravina

08001 Barcelona
Calle Gravina, 12
Tel. 93-301 68 68 - Fax 93-317 28 38
E-mail: gravina@smc.es

Category ★★★ Rooms 85 with air-conditioning, bath with hydromassages, satellite TV, minibar; elevator. **Price** Single 12,500-15,000Pts, double 18,000Pts, suite 20,000-32,000 Pts. **Meals** Breakfast 1,000-1,500Pts, served 7:30-11:00. **Restaurant** Service 1:00PM-3:00PM, 8:00PM-10:30PM; à la carte. Regional and international cooking. **Credit cards** All major. **Pets** Dogs not allowed. **Nearby** Cimenterie became the Taller de arquitectura de Ricardo Bofill and Walden 7 in Sant Just Desvern - Sitges - Monastery of San Cugat del Valles - Montserrat - Vich - Prat golf course (9- and 18-Hole golf), San Cugat golf course (18-Hole). **Open** All year.

A relatively new hotel, the Gravina is at the top of the Ramblas and west of the Plaza de Catalunya. The building is an attractive one dating from the 19th century, where the guest enters through a facade bearing a lion's head. There are numerous and attractive wrought iron balconies. The Modernist spirit prevails in the interior decoration as Spanish designers, to avoid a cold and often sterile look, have skillfully used marble, wood and artful metallic structures. The rooms are identical, spacious and with up-to-date comfort. The decoration is, however, banal with lifeless, hotel-style mahogany-inspired furniture and fabrics range from blue to orange. The bathrooms are perfect and feature hydromassage. A good address in the center of Barcelona.

How to get there *(Map 8): Near the Old Town.*

Hotel Jardí

08001 Barcelona
Plaça Sant Josep Oriol, 1
Tel. 93-301 59 00/58 - Fax 93-318 36 64
E-mail: sgs110sa@encomix.es

Rooms 39 with telephone, bath or shower, WC (10 with TV). **Price** Single 4,000-6,800Pts, double 6,800-7,800Pts, triple 9,500Pts. **Meals** Breakfast 750Pts. Served 8:30-11:30. Restaurant See pp. 310-314. **Credit cards** All major. **Pets** Dogs not allowed. **Nearby** Cimenterie became the Taller de arqutectura de Ricardo Bofill and Walden 7 in Sant Just Desvern - Sitges (beach) - Monastery of San Cugat del Valle - Montserrat - Vich - Prat golf course (9- and 18-Hole golf), San Cugat golf course (18-Hole). **Open** All year.

The Jardí is included in this guide only because of its location on one of the prettiest squares in the neighborhood, one that is about as typical and popular as you could ask for and where amateur painters gather at the nearby *Cafe del Pi*. It is in a small, 19th-century building with a yellow exterior, simple and without much charm. The rooms are sober and undistinguished but very well kept-up. It is advisable to reserve one offering a view on the shady terraces of the Plaza del Pi or overlooking the Plaza Sant Josep Oriol.

How to get there (Map 8): In the Old Town near the Ramblas.

Hotel San Sebastián Playa

08870 Sitges (Barcelona)
Port Alegre, 53
Tel. 93-894 75 00 - Fax 93-894 04 30
Sr José Llauradó

Rooms 51 with air-conditioning, telephone, bath, WC, satellite TV, video, safe, minibar; elevator. **Price** Single 13,000-19,800Pts, double 15,500-23,800Pts, suite 22,000-30,900Pts; view on the sea +3,750-5,000Pts. **Meals** Breakfast (buffet) 1,500Pts, served 7:00AM-12:00PM; half board +2,100-2,500Pts. **Restaurant** La Concha, service 1:30PM-4:00PM, 8:30PM-11:00PM; à la carte 3,200-6,500Pts. **Credit cards** All major. **Pets** Dogs not allowed. **Facilities** Swimming pool, garage, parking. **Nearby** Barcelona - Costa Daurada; Terramar golf course (18-Hole). **Open** All year.

The Hotel San Sebastián Playa is relatively new and built in a neo-classical style recalling the architecture of palaces from the early years of the century. Its site, in the seaside resort of Sitges, is incomparable at only a hundred meters from the historic center. Facing the sea, it promises its clientele in the front rooms some exceptional morning awakenings. Prices vary with room location, with higher prices for those facing the sea. In the reception rooms, the decor is modern and uses beautiful and elegant materials. One finds the same sobriety in the rooms which gives them a rather cold atmosphere, but all are very comfortable. The beach is close by, but the hotel has its own attractive and well-sheltered swimming pool. A very good hotel in this tourist town, very animated in summer, which allows you to alternate calm and distractions.

How to get there *(Map 8): 39km south of Barcelona via C246, corniche road along the sea.*

Hotel Romántic

08870 Sitges (Barcelona)
Sant Isidre, 33
Tel. 93-894 83 75/894 29 53 - Fax 93-894 81 67 - José Manuel Vendrell
E-mail: romantic@arrakis.es

Rooms 55 with telephone, bath or shower, WC, ventilator. **Price** Single 7,400-8,900Pts, with terrasse 8,300-10,000Pts; double 10,400-12,200Pts, with terrasse 11,500-13,200Pts; extra bed +3,400-4,100Pts. **Meals** Breakfast included, served 7:00-11:00. **Restaurant** See p. 314. **Credit cards** All major. **Pets** Small dogs allowed on request. **Nearby** Barcelona - Costa Dorada; Terramar golf course (18-Hole). **Open** Apr - Oct 15.

This is a charming hotel in a beautiful house in the town of Sitges, some forty kilometers away from the Catalan capital, and very much the fashionable beach. All the trendy crowd of Barcelona is to be found here, and the atmosphere in summer is exceptional, especially in the evenings at aperitif- and tapas-time, when all the parties start– only to finish in the wee hours of the morning! The rooms are indeed well-kept but rather basic and only fitted with showers. On the other hand, the atmosphere is very lively. Painters staying at the hotel have left their frescoes on the walls, while from 6pm onwards one can have a drink, with classical music in the bar. The shaded garden has many small corners for reading or unwinding in full peace and quiet. The welcome is very friendly and the atmosphere very informal, but the hotel is better suited for bachelors than for family groups.

How to get there (Map 8): 29km south of Barcelona via the C246, the corniche along the sea coast.

Termes La Garriga

08530 La Garriga (Barcelona)
Banys, 23
Tel. 93-871 70 86 - Fax 93-871 78 87
Sr Monné - Sr Vilá

Category ★★★★ **Rooms** 22 with air-conditioning, telephone, bath, WC, TV, minibar, safe; elevator. **Price** Single 11,300-17,800Pts, double 16,800-26,800Pts, suite 37,800-58,600Pts; extra bed 6,300Pts. **Meals** Breakfast 1,500Pts, served 8:30-10:00; half board +5,400Pts, full board +6,200Pts. **Restaurant** Service 1:30PM-3:00PM, 8:30PM-10:00PM; mealtime specials and also à la carte. Regional and international cooking. **Credit cards** Amex, Visa, Eurocard, MasterCard. **Pets** Dogs not allowed. **Facilities** Swimming pool, sauna, health center, bikes, parking and garage (900Pts). **Nearby** Barcelona - Costa Daurada; Muntanyá golf course (18-Hole). **Open** All year.

If the idea of getting back in shape should suddenly appeal to you, the Termes La Garriga would be an excellent choice. It neatly combines all that is necessary for doing just that in a setting and atmosphere reminiscent of the glorious days of Biarritz and Baden Baden. Nothing here even smacks of a clinical ambience; this a place where executives can get plenty of exercise both indoors and out for a few days while the ladies can get themselves ready for the summer. The rooms are elegant and each is decorated differently. The garden has a swimming pool for those not interested in the hotel's fitness programs. A few kilometers from Barcelona, this is a useful place to know as it offers a base from which to visit the Catalan region and also to take advantage of the art of relaxation which La Garriga so skillfully practices.

How to get there *(Map 8): 35km north of Barcelona via A7 or N152. Take the La Garriga exit. The hotel is well-indicated in the city center.*

Fonda Europa

08400 Granollers (Barcelona)
Anselm Clavé, 1
Tel. 93-870 03 12 - Fax 93-870 79 01
Sr Font

Category ★★★ **Rooms** 7 with air-conditioning, telephone, bath, WC, satellite TV, minibar, safe; elevator. **Price** Single 9,300Pts, double 12,500Pts. **Meals** Breakfast included, served 8:00-11:00. **Restaurant** Service 1:00PM-3:30PM, 9:00PM-11:15PM; à la carte: 3,000-4,000Pts. **Credit cards** All major. **Pets** Dogs allowed. **Facilities** Garage (1,000Pts). **Nearby** Barcelona - Costa Daurada; Terramar golf course (18-Hole). **Open** All year.

This is one of the old hotels that everyone in the province of Barcelona knows, especially for its restaurant which is both highly popular and very much in keeping with local traditions. The Perellada family has been in this lovely building, with its orange facade adorned with eye-catching friezes, since 1714. Here you find rooms very nicely furnished, offering refinement and good taste plus particularly efficient service. We especially liked Room 7 with its bathroom reminiscent of old Pompeii. In addition, two days a week, Thursdays and Sundays, are market days here in this small and friendly city.

How to get there *(Map 8): 28km north of Barcelona via A7 or N152. Take the La Garriga exit. The hotel is well-indicated in the city center.*

Parador Duques de Cardona

08261 Cardona (Barcelona)
Castillo de Cardona
Tel. 93-869 12 75 - Fax 93-869 16 36
Sr Juan Yepe

Category ★★★★ **Rooms** 60 with air-conditioning, telephone, bath, WC, TV, (50 with minibar); elevator. **Price** Double 15,000-17,500Pts. **Meals** Breakfast 1,300Pts, served 8:00-11:00. **Restaurant** Service 1:30PM-4:00PM, 8:30PM-10:30PM; mealtime specials 3,500Pts, also à la carte. Catalan cooking. **Credit cards** All major. **Pets** Dogs not allowed. **Facilities** Parking. **Nearby** In Cardona: Church of Sant Vicenç - Salt mountain of Salina. **Open** All year.

R aised by the Dukes of Cardona, this fortress was built at the very beginning of the Middle Ages and modified over the course of the centuries, and for a long time served as military barracks. Despite its rather impressive proportions, the new occupants have learned how to make the place welcoming: ceilings with caissons and numerous copper-colored carpets all help warm the public rooms. The bedrooms are attractive and well-furnished. The view, superb in earler times, is now somewhat compromised since Cardona is one of the major mining towns in the northern part of the country.

How to get there *(Map 8): 97km northwest of Barcelona to Manresa, then C1410.*

Hotel Llicorella

08880 Cubelles (Barcelona)
Carretera C 246 - Camino de San Antonio, 101
Tel. 93-895 00 44 - Fax 93-895 24 17 - Sra de Adria

Category ★★★★ **Rooms** 16 with air-conditioning, telephone, bath, WC, satellite TV, safe, minibar. **Price** Single 11,000Pts, double 14,000-20,000Pts, suite 20,000Pts. **Meals** Breakfast 1,100Pts. **Restaurant** Service 1:30PM-4:00PM, 8:30PM-11:00PM; à la carte. Specialties: Pimientos del piquillo rellenos de gambas - Higado de pato sobre cebolla y manzana confitadas - Tocinillo de cielo sobre coulis de frambuesa. **Credit cards** All major. **Pets** Dogs allowed (except in the restaurant) (+530Pts). **Facilities** Parking. **Nearby** Sitges - Villafranca del Penedes - Barcelona - Beaches. **Open** All year.

Hardly have you left the many lights of Barcelona than you come into the heart of Catalonia, where stretches of countryside ever more beautiful than what has come before follow one another. In one of these privileged little corners you will find the Hotel Llicorella, a handsome stone residence with a careful recipe of elegance and sobriety. The owner is known to a large number of Catalans as he ran a well-known picture gallery in Barcelona, and has remained in contact with many artists. Still a lover of the arts, he has filled his hotel with many works of recognized artists. All details are aesthetic. The kitchen is run by Renata Dabbert, whose excellent cooking is an original interpretation of traditional Catalan culinary tradition combined with touches of French cuisine. The rooms are each dedicated to a different painter, and mix a taste for art with refined comfort. There is also a very good restaurant.

How to get there *(Map 8): 54km southwest of Barcelona via A7, exit Villafranca (no. 29), then C244 and C246.*

Hotel San Bernat

08460 Montseny (Barcelona)
Tel. 93-847 30 11 - Fax 93-847 32 20
Sr Jorge Riera

Category ★★★ **Rooms** 21 with telephone, bath, WC, TV. **Price** Single 13,500Pts, double 17,000Pts. **Meals** Breakfast included, served 8:00-11:00. **Restaurant** Service 1:30PM-4:00PM, 8:30PM-10:00PM; à la carte. Catalan cooking. **Credit cards** All major. **Pets** Dogs not allowed. **Facilities** Parking. **Nearby** Sierra of Montseny from San Celoni to Massanet de la Selva, 120 km (Ermitage de Santa Fe, Brull, Tona, Viladrau). **Open** All year.

A small, winding road surrounded by very pleasant greenery leads to this hotel, situated on the high ground above Montseny. The entrance to this ivy-covered building is the first pleasant surprise, with two resident Saint Bernards romping on the lawn. Next, there is a small pond reflecting the surrounding willow trees. The rooms, small and simple, are pleasant and in good taste, the bathrooms are a delight, the best among them looking out on the valley. The lawn behind the hotel is an ideal place to have a cup of tea, offering at once a splendid view of the valley and the nearby mountains. A matchless feeling of peace can be found here. The small and pretty church is where San Bernat – Saint Bernard – once stopped. Although guests are welcomed somewhat haphazardly, this is an ideal spot for a restful and bucolic stay.

How to get there *(Map 8): 70km northeast of Barcelona; 8km northwest of Montseny, on the road to Tona.*

Hotel Sant Marcal

Sant Marcal 08460 Montseny (Barcelona)
Careterra de San Celoni
Tel. 93-847 30 43 - Fax 93-847 30 43 - Sr Jordi Tell
E-mail: tellhotels@arquired.es - Web: www.arquired.es/user/tellhotels

Category ★★★ **Rooms** 10 with bath, WC, satellite TV. **Price** With half board and full board 12,350Pts, 14,600Pts. **Meals** Breakfast included, served 8:00-11:00. **Restaurant** Servlce 1:30PM-4:00PM, 8:30PM-10:00PM; mealtime specials 4,500Pts, also à la carte. Regional cooking. **Credit cards** All major. **Pets** Dogs not allowed. **Facilities** Sauna (1,500Pts), croquet, parking. **Nearby** Sierra de Montseny de San Celoni in Massanet de la Selva, 120km (Ermitage de Santa Fe, Brull, Tona, Viladrau). **Open** All year.

The Sierra de Montseny sits astride the provinces of Barcelona and Gerona. This is why neighboring villages such as Viladrau and Sant Marcal are officially in different regions in the eyes of the Administration. When you leave the highway at Sant Celoni, you find yourself in the mysterious Catalan mountains. The air becomes sweet and humid, the vegetation dense, an ideal place for exploring the valley. The Tell family has converted the village's old Roman monastery into a hotel of charm. Below is a small chapel, and a broad flagstone walk leads to the reception area. The lounge and dining room take up the ground floor, the latter offering a fine view and the chance to enjoy excellent Catalan cooking. The rooms have wooden beams, natural stone and antique furniture, nicely set off by attractive plaid fabrics. Here is comfort and tranquillity in an authentic natural setting.

How to get there (Map 8): 86km northeast of Barcelona via A7 La Jonquera, exit 11 at Sant Celoni towards Santa Fe and Sant Marcal.

Parador de Vich

08500 Vich (Barcelona)
Tel. 93-812 23 23 - Fax 93-812 23 68
Sr Francisco Casas

Category ★★★★ **Rooms** 36 with air-conditioning, telephone, bath, WC, TV, minibar; elevator. **Price** Double 13,500-15,000Pts. **Meals** Breakfast 1,300Pts, served 8:00-10:30. **Restaurant** Service 1:30PM-4:00PM, 8:30PM-10:30PM; mealtime specials 3,500Pts, also à la carte. Specialties: Zarzuela de pescado y mariscos, semi-tomba. **Credit cards** All major. **Pets** Dogs not allowed. **Facilities** Swimming pool, tennis, garage, parking. **Nearby** In Vich: Cathedral and Episcopal museum - Rupit - Monastery of Santa Maria in Estany and Monastery of Poblet in Santes Creus - Monserrat. **Open** All year.

The architecture and decor of this parador are not its major strengths, and the building put up in 1972 under the Franco regime is massive and hardly welcoming. The interior arrangements are not in the best taste either. But its greatest quality is its site. For, apart from its isolated setting 14 kilometers from Vich which makes it quiet and restful, it also has the advantage of a magnificent panorama over the Pantana de Sau lake and the Guilleries massif. It is imperative to ask for a front room with a balcony. The swimming pool is very delightful, facing the lake and in the midst of a well-kept garden.

How to get there *(Map 8): 69km north of Barcelona via N152; 15km from Vich, towards Roda de Ter.*

Hotel Mas Pau

17742 Avinyonet de Puigventós (Gerona)
Carretera de Figueres a Olot
Tel. 972-54 61 54 - Fax 972-54 63 26 - Sr T. Gerez
Web: www.maspau.com - E-mail: maspau@grn.es

Category ★★★★ **Rooms** 20 with air-conditioning, telephone, bath, WC, satellite TV, minibar.
Price Double 11,500-13,000Pts, junior-suite 13,000-15,000Pts., suite 18,000-20,000Pts. **Meals**
Breakfast 1,200Pts, served 7:15-10:00. **Restaurant** Service 1:00PM-4:00PM, 8:00PM-11:00PM;
closed Sun night and Mon; in summer closed Mon lunch; à la carte 4,000-5,500Pts. **Credit cards**
All major. **Pets** Dogs not allowed. **Facilities** Swimming pool, parking. **Nearby** In Figueres Museu
Dali (Salvador Dali museum) - Cadaqués - Monastery of Sant Pere de Rodes - Massanet de Cabrenys
- Torremirona golf course. **Closed** Jan 15 - Mar 15.

If you decide to stop at Figueres to visit the famous Salvador Dali museum,
a detour via Avinyonet is a must. This is where the *Mas Pau* is to be found,
one of the best known gastronomic establishments in the area. A hotel has
recently been added, and its charm is only equalled by its quality. This ancient
farm, built in the 16th century, is right in the country and surrounded by fields.
The rooms have been arranged in a new annex, in the same spirit as the public
rooms of the main building. More modern, they also bear witness to the
exquisite taste of the owners. It is beautiful, functional and comfortable, with
friendly and stylish personnel.

How to get there *(Map 9): 58km south of Perpignan; 42km from Gerona via
A7, exit Figueres, then take the road to Olot.*

Mas Falgarona ^{TR}

17742 Avinyonet de Puigventós (Gerona)
Tel. and Fax 972-54 66 28
Severino Jallas Gándara - Brigitta Schmidt

Rooms 9 with telephone, shower, TV. **Price** Double 12,000-20,000Pts. **Meals** Breakfast 1,300Pts, served 7:30-11:00. **Restaurant** Service 1:00PM-4:00PM, 8:00PM-11:00PM; mealtime specials 2,950Pts. Mediterranean cooking. **Credit cards** All major. **Pets** Dogs not allowed. **Facilities** Swimming pool, parking. **Nearby** Salvador Dali Museum in Figueres - Cadaques - Monastery of Sant Pere de Rodes - Massanet de Cabrenys - Torremirona golf course (3km) and Peralada golf course (8km). **Open** All year.

With this new address in the refined *turismo rural* category, Avinyonet may boast of an excellent new inn. The Mas Falgarona is on a very attractive property close to the French border - Collioure is a scant fifty kilometers away - and the Costa Brava. The restoration is exemplary; the various buildings have attractive stone exteriors and are centered around a courtyard, the oldest bearing the dates of their construction - 1450 and 1550 - engraved over their entrances. The lobby has a magnificent vaulted ceiling of large red bricks with an authentic terracotta floor and a natural stone staircase, the finishing touch being added by large antique jars. The upstairs lounge pays equal respect to historic architectural traditions. The decoration in the rooms is clean and spare, with large beds, very pretty rustic furniture and art works by local artists contributing to the rural yet refined atmosphere so enjoyable here. The bathrooms are brightened by colorful handmade ceramics, and have excellent showers. Brigitta excels in the art of Mediterranean cooking, enough in itself to convince you to visit the Mas Falgarona.

How to get there *(Map 9): 58km south of Perpignan (France); 42km from Gerona via A7, exit Figueres, then the road to Olot.*

Hotel Aigua Blava

Aigua Blava 17255 Begur (Gerona)
Playa de Fornells
Tel. 972-62 20 58 - Fax 972-62 21 12
E-mail: hotelaiguablava@.com - Web: www.aiguablava.com

Category ★★★★ **Rooms** 85 with telephone, bath or shower, WC, TV, minibar. **Price** Single 9,700-12,500Pts, double 12,300-21,000Pts, suite 18,400-26,000Pts. **Meals** Breakfast 1,650Pts, served 8:00-10:30; half board +9,800-16,700Pts, full board +10,800-19,500Pts (per per., 3 days min.). **Restaurant** With air-conditioning, service 1:30PM-3:30PM, 8:30PM-10:30PM; mealtime specials 3,800Pts, also à la carte. Spanish and international cooking. **Credit cards** Amex, Visa, Eurocard, MasterCard. **Pets** Small dogs allowed (1,500Pts). **Facilities** Swimming pool, tennis, volley ball, hairdresser, parking, garage (1,500Pts). **Nearby** Pals - Costa Brava - Barcelona - Gerona - Pals golf course (18-Hole). **Closed** Nov 8 - Feb 22.

At the head of a charming creek where rocks covered with pine trees surround the limpid sea, the Aigua Blava enjoys a truly beautiful site. It is made up of a group of buildings set around a very attractive small and flowered park. Go for a room with a terrace looking over the sea. With their bright carpeting and white walls, the rooms are both comfortable and welcoming. As night falls the swimming pool is floodlit, and its glow mixes with the lights of the villas all around, thus creating a magic atmosphere. Alas, the cuisine does not live up to the standards of the rest.

How to get there (*Map 9*): *On the coast north of Barcelona; 46km east of Gerona via A7, exit no. 6.*

Hotel Jordi's

17255 Begur (Gerona)
Apartado, 47
Tel. 972-30 15 70 - Fax 972-61 01 12
Jordi y Maria

Category ★★ **Rooms** 8 with bath. **Price** Double 10,300Pts. **Meals** Breakfast included. No restaurant. **Credit cards** Amex, Visa, Eurocard, MasterCard. **Pets** Dogs allowed. **Facilities** Parking. **Nearby** Pals - Costa Brava - Barcelona - Gerona - Pals golf course (18-Hole). **Open** All year.

A very good location, well away from the surrounding confusion and run personally by Jordi. This beautiful house is on the high ground overlooking the surrounding countryside, and is set among cypresses and pine trees that give a welcome shade and cool. Eight rooms have been arranged on two levels with great care; they are beautifully simple, their wood furniture married with cooling floor tiles, and their bathrooms impeccable. On the ground floor, the rooms all have terraces, but those on the upper floor (the house is built on a slope) have smaller windows. Whether in the restaurant around the open fireplace or on the large, shaded terrace, you can feel the authentic atmosphere of a Catalan home. The welcome here is very friendly.

How to get there (Map 9): On the coast north of Barcelona; 46km east of Gerona via A7, exit no. 6.

Chalet del Golf

17463 Bolvir-Puigcerda (Gerona)
Tel. 972-88 09 62 - Fax 972-88 09 66
Sr Lucarini

Category ★★★ **Rooms** 18 and 8 suites with telephone, bath, WC, TV; elevator. **Price** Single 11,000-14,000Pts, double 13,500-17,000Pts. **Meals** Breakfast 1,350Pts, served from 8:30; half board +3,750Pts, full board +6,000Pts (per pers.). **Restaurant** Service 1:30PM-4:00PM, 8:30PM-10:30PM; mealtime specials 3,000Pts, also à la carte. **Credit cards** All major. **Pets** Dogs allowed (except in the restaurant). **Facilities** Swimming pool, tennis, squash, golf course (18-Hole), parking. **Nearby** Cerdanya Valley - Andorra (a duty free principality) - Bellver de Cerdaña (fishing in the rio Segre) - Skiing (La Molina and Maranges) - Llivia; Cerdaña golf course (18-Hole). **Open** All year except fifteen days before Christmas.

Naturally there is a beautiful golf course, and the house that serves as hotel and restaurant is no less charming. Woodlands nearby make timber easily available, and great use of it has been made in decorating the hotel, giving it a very warm atmosphere. All the rooms look out over the golf course, and they are simple, but that doesn't matter much—they are mainly used by sports lovers, who spend most of their days outside. In contrast, the management has fitted out a snug restaurant and lounges that make one think of Great Britain.

How to get there (Map 8): 172km north of Barcelona via N152, then at Puigcerdá via C1313.

Hotel Torre del Remei

17539 Bolvir de Cerdanya (Gerona)
Camí Reial
Tel. 972-14 01 82 - Fax 972-14 04 49 - Sr Boix

Category ★★★★★ **Rooms** 4 and 7 suites with air-conditioning, telephone, bath with jacuzzi, WC, satellite TV, safe; elevator. **Price** Double 28,000-33,000Pts, suite 45,000-70,000Pts. **Meals** Breakfast 2,500Pts, served 8:00AM-12:00PM. **Restaurant** Service 1:00PM-4:00PM, 9:00PM-11:00PM; à la carte 7,000Pts. Specialties: Carpaccio de vemado - Vieiras salteadas con puré de berengereias - Liebre royale - Soufflé de torrón. **Credit cards** All major. **Pets** Dogs allowed (except in restaurant). **Facilities** Swimming pool, parking. **Nearby** Cerdanya Valley - Andorra (a duty free principality) - Bellver de Cerdaña (fishing in the rio Segre) - Skiing (La Molina and Maranges) - Llivia; Cerdaña golf course (18-Hole). **Open** All year.

Only fifteen minutes from the border at Bourg-Madame in a superb country of vast prairies and mountains in the real heart of Catalonia, the Hotel Torre del Remei has been installed in a beautiful aristocratic residence dating from the beginning of the century. Despite renovation the building has lost nothing of its original character, while the decor is remarkable, allying luxury, charm and comfort. Here are polished floors, crystal lamps and caisson ceilings, alongside contemporary art and furniture with studied lines. One has to salute the restaurant and the personnel, stylish yet efficient, and attentive to your slightest request. Thanks to its exceptional situation, the Torre del Remei, open summer and winter, attracts both sports lovers (close to a golf course and to ski resorts) and lovers of the outdoors and good food.

How to get there (Map 8): 154km north of Barcelona via N152, then 2km from Puigcerdá via N260.

Playa Sol

17488 Cadaqués (Gerona)
Playa Pianc, 3
Tel. 972-25 81 00/25 81 40 - Fax 972-25 80 54
E-mail: playasol@publintur.es

Category ★★★ **Rooms** 49 and 1 suite with air-conditioning, telephone, bath, WC, TV; elevator. **Price** Double 11,900-19,500Pts. **Meals** Breakfast 1,300Pts, served 8:00-11:00. **Restaurant** at lunch from Jun. to Sept near the swimming pool; à la carte (small) or see p. 314. **Credit cards** All major. **Pets** Dogs not allowed. **Facilities** Swimming pool, tennis, parking (950-1,200Pts). **Nearby** In Cadaqués: museum Perrot Moore and Church - Port-Lligat (Dali house) - Costa Brava. **Closed** Dec 20 - Feb 20.

You travel a magnificent road overlooking the sea with wind-blown vegetation on either side and finally arrive at Cadaqués. Along with Port Lligat, Cadaqués had its illustrious ambassador in the person of Salvador Dalí who made this small fishing port world famous. This fact may explain why it has retained a certain authenticity with its small white houses lining the bay and its brightly colored, old fishing boats. The hotel was built quite recently but fits into its surroundings very nicely and its location is exceptional as it faces the port and the small beach. The rooms offer more comfort than charm, but most have a balcony looking out on the sea. This surely explains why it is usually full to capacity in the summertime. For this reason you are advised to reserve well in advance. Seven kilometers from Rosas is an exceptional restaurant, El Bulli, where the tapas-style menu has a total of twenty items, as unexpected as they are extraordinary. True, this place may seem located at the end of the world, so if you don't enjoy driving at night, head for El Bulli at lunchtime.

How to get there *(Map 9): 69km north of Gerona.*

Hotel Edelweiss

17867 Campródon (Gerona)
Carretera Sant Joan, 28
Tel. 972-74 06 14 - Fax 972-74 06 05
Sra Marga Cabo

Category ★★★★ **Rooms** 21 with telephone, bath, hairdryer, WC, satellite TV; elevator. **Price** Double 10,850-14,400Pts. **Meals** Breakfast (buffet) included, served 8:30-11:00. **Restaurant** Open weekends and National Holidays. Service 9:00PM-11:00PM. **Credit cards** All major. **Pets** Dogs allowed. **Facilities** Room service (24h), parking. **Nearby** In Camprodón: Monastery of Sant Pere - Beget - Llanars (Church of San Esteve) - Molló (Church of Santa Cecília) - San Juan de las Abadesas - Collado de Ares road; Camprodón golf course (18-Hole). **Closed** Dec 24 and 25.

The facade is welcoming, and one step inside you immediately notice the refinement of this place. The owner claims he decorated his hotel just as if it were his own home. The pieces of furniture are only copies but not one fault can be found with them. The bathrooms are harmonious. In the dining room, only breakfasts and dinners are served. They feature a buffet our grandmothers would be proud of: local cold cuts and cheeses along with the traditional *pamb tomáquet*. A warm welcome and plenty of attention mean you will certainly want to take careful note of this hotel's address.

How to get there *(Map 8): 133km north of Barcelona via N152 to Ripoll, then C151.*

La Mère Michelle

17121 Corça (Gerona)
Calle Mayor, 5
Tel. 972-63 05 35 - Fax 972-63 05 35
Sra Michelle Amram

Rooms 4 with bath, WC. **Price** Double 15,000Pts. **Meals** Breakfast 1,200Pts, served 8:00AM-1:00PM. **Restaurant** Service 12:30PM-4:30PM, 8:30PM-11:30PM; mealtime specials 3,500-4,000Pts, also à la carte. French and mediterranean cooking. **Credit cards** Not accepted. **Pets** Small dogs allowed. **Nearby** Pubol (Gala and Dali castle) - Gerona - Figueres (Salvador Dali Museum) - Ceramics and a flea market in La Bisbal; 10 golf courses. **Open** Aug and all weekends and National Holidays out of season.

Nearly everyone around Gerona knows the small restaurant La Mère Michelle, opened by a French woman living in Spain. The small village of Corça is very well situated for vacations, just a few kilometers away from the regional capital of Gerona, surrounded by golf courses and about twenty kilometers from the beaches. All the conviviality of a family home has been retained, with beams and old furniture giving a lot of warmth to the decor. It is the same in the restaurant, very small, where you must hurry to reserve if you wish to try the good French specialties of the house: not only the scents of Mediterranean cuisine but also all the generosity of the cooking of Alsace. The rooms are attractively decorated and comfortable, more in the spirit of a boarding house than a traditional hotel - no TV, no direct phone but, on the other hand, a small fridge in each room along with tea– and coffee-making facilities along with room service. This is a friendly and untypical address for Spain.

How to get there *(Map 9): 30km from Gerona via E15 exit Gerona North, then towards La Bisbal.*

Hotel Grévol

17869 Llanars (Gerona)
Careterra de Camprodón a Setcases
Tel. 972-74 10 13 - Fax 972-74 10 87 - Sr Sole
E-mail: info@hotelgrevol.com - Web: www.hotelgrevol.com

Category ★★★★ **Rooms** 36 with telephone, bath, WC, TV, minibar; elevator. **Price** Double 16,500-19,500Pts. **Meals** Breakfast (buffet) 1,475Pts, served from 8:30; half board 12,350-13,850Pts, full board 14,975-16,475Pts (per pers., 3 days min.). **Restaurant** Service 1:00PM-3:30PM, 9:00PM-10:30PM; closed Mon, 15 days in May and Nov; mealtime specials 3,850Pts, also à la carte. Specialties: regional and international cooking. **Credit cards** All major. **Pets** Dogs not allowed. **Facilities** Covered swimming pool, parking, garage. **Nearby** In Llanars: Church of San Esteve - Camprodón (Church of San Pedro) - Molló (Church of Santa Cecilia) - Beget - Collado de Ares road; Camprodón golf course (18-Hole). **Open** All year.

The recently built and very well equipped Grévol recalls those large Austrian chalet-hotels. The Camprodón region attracts a family clientele wanting to get some fresh air in the refreshing setting of the Pyrenees, and to engage in an open air sport such as golf, skiing or horseback riding. The hotel rooms are charming with panelled walls, furniture in wood and oak in Tyrolian style, which is also found in the main room of the restaurant around an open fireplace. All this creates a very comfortable atmosphere. With a more than complete games room-hall (bowling, table football, billiards, etc.), children will be more than happy. After a day's hiking the family can then swim in the covered pool or unwind in the huge jacuzzi.

How to get there (Map 8): 129km north of Barcelona via N152 to Rjpoll, then C151. At 3km on the road from Camprodón to Setcases.

Hotel Santa Marta

17310 Lloret de Mar (Gerona)
Playa de Santa Cristina
Tel. 972-36 49 04 - Fax 972-36 92 80 - Sr Noguera
E mail: hstamarta@grn.es

Category ★★★★ **Rooms** 78 with air-conditioning, telephone, bath, WC, satellite TV, minibar; elevator. **Price** Single 13,500-21,000Pts, double 19,000-31,000Pts, suite 29,000-49,000Pts. **Meals** Breakfast 1,850Pts, served 8:00-11:00; half board +8,100Pts, full board +11,500Pts (per pers.). **Restaurant** Service 1:30PM-3:30PM, 8:30PM-10:30PM; mealtime specials 6,250Pts, also à la carte. Specialties: Rollitos de salmon con cangrejos - Suquet de mero. **Credit cards** All major. **Pets** Dogs allowed except in restaurant (+800Pts). **Facilities** Swimming pool, tennis (1,000Pts), beach, windsurfing, parking. **Nearby** Botanical garden Pinya de Rosa and Mar i Murtra (Blanes, 5km) - Road from Lloret del Mar to Tossa del Mar (12km) - Gerona - Beaches. **Closed** Dec 15 - Feb 1.

This was the most fashionable hotel on the Costa Brava thirty years ago. It is certainly modern, and with an exceptional location that is unique in the region. It is surrounded by woodland, clinging to the rocks and facing the sea. There is also a fully equipped private beach, and all this in such divine peace and quiet. The rooms, all recently renovated, are very comfortable, the decoration classic and the hospitality is all one could ask for.

How to get there (Map 9): 39km south of Gerona via A7, exit no. 9; 3km from Lloret.

Cal Borrell

17539 Meranges (Gerona)
Regreso, 3
Tel. 972-88 00 33 - Fax 972-88 01 44 - Sr Forn
E-mail: info@canborell.com - Web: www.canborell.com

Category ★★ **Rooms** 8 with telephone, bath, WC. **Price** Double 11,000-12,000Pts. **Meals** Breakfast included, served 9:00-11:00; half board +3,500Pts, full board +6,000Pts. **Restaurant** Service 1:00PM-4:00PM, 9:00PM-11:00PM; à la carte 3,500-5,500Pts. Specialties: Pork, game. **Credit cards** Visa, Eurocard, MasterCard. **Pets** Dogs not allowed. **Facilities** Snowshoe treks in winter organized by the hotel. **Nearby** Skiing (La Molina and Maranges) - Andorra (a duty free principality) - Bellver de Cerdaña (fishing in the rio Segre); Cerdaña golf course (18-Hole). **Open** Jan - Apr and the weekends all the year - Closed from Mon afternoon to Wed except in summer an Easter.

Cal Borrell is a former farmhouse refurbished and transformed into a hotel in the heart of a picture-perfect mountain village. The rooms have magnificent wooden ceilings and beams, and all have a view over the valley. Try to get the room called "The house on the prairie", with its mezzanine and superb panorama. There is a guaranteed warm mountain atmosphere, perfect for relaxing and rest. One also appreciates the good cuisine served in the restaurant as the Cal Borrell is known for its excellent table.

How to get there (Map 8): 191km north of Barcelona via N152 to Puigcerdá, then C1313 for about 7km; take the small road to the right.

Hotel Carles Camós Big-Rock

17250 Playa de Aro (Gerona)
Barri de Fanals, 5
Tel. 972-81 80 12 - Fax 972-81 89 71
Sr Camós

Category ★★★★ **Suites** 5 with air-conditioning, telephone, bath, WC, TV, minibar. **Price** Suite 12,000-22,000Pts. **Meals** Breakfast 1,200Pts, served 8:30-11:00. **Restaurant** Service 1:00PM-3:30PM, 8:30PM-10:30PM; à la carte 3,600-4,800Pts. Specialties: Lomo de merluza con patatitas - Suquet de rape y langostinos - Capriccio de crema con fresitas. **Credit cards** All major. **Pets** Dogs allowed. **Facilities** Swimming pool, parking. **Nearby** In Gerona: Cathedral, chapel of Sant Feliu and Monastery of Sant Pere de Galligants - Beaches; Costa Brava golf course (18-Hole). **Closed** In Jan, Mon and Sun night in winter.

Known primarily for its restaurant, Big-Rock also has a few rooms. Isolated in the country, this is a large and ancient building which was refurbished with taste in the last century. The owner is an excellent chef and great personality, as he founded the "Brotherhood of Happy Joy", and everything with him is genuine and simply breathes fun. The flowered terraces glory in the sun while the furniture sweetly smells of polished wood. The rooms are in fact all suites, and deserve a special mention for their luxurious amenities. Tasteful pictures decorate the walls, so why be surprised if the King of Spain himself sometimes passes by here?

How to get there *(Map 9): 37km southeast of Gerona via C250.*

Castell de Peratallada

17113 Peratallada (Gerona)
Plaça del Castell, 1
Tel. 972-63 40 21 - Fax 972-63 40 11 - Sr Jesus Torrent

Category ★★★★ **Rooms** 7 and 1 suite with air-conditioning, telephone, bath, WC, minibar. **Price** Double 25,000Pts, suite 40,000Pts. **Meals** Breakfast included, served 8:30-11:00. **Restaurant** Service 1:00PM-4:00PM, 8:30PM-11:00PM, closed Sun all year and Mon in winter. **Credit cards** All major. **Pets** Dogs not allowed. **Nearby** Gerona - Costa Brava. **Open** All year.

To the north of Barcelona between Girona and the Mediterranean is a region known as the Ampudán where villages dating from the Middle Ages proudly maintain Catalan traditions. Peratallada, classed as a national monument, is a genuine treasure of medieval architecture. There you will find innumerable examples, among them a vast trench dug in the rock surrounding the city. The city's name - Peratallada - is, literally translated, "carved stone." The hotel, nicely located in a pedestrians-only zone, is in an 11th-century castle. The ground floor has two long hallways with high vaulted ceilings, a splendid decor for the lounge bar and restaurant. There are few rooms in this luxurious hotel and the furniture, rugs and paintings are absolutely authentic period pieces. It is an ideal place for receptions, although the hotel could make an effort to diminish the guests' inconvenience while they are going on. The village is truly historic but at the same time very lively with art galleries, handicraft shops and antiques stores lining a number of its small streets.

How to get there *(Map 9): 120km north of Barcelona via A7 (Barcelona/La Jonquera), take the northern Girona exit; then C-255 towards La Bisbal; 1km after La Bisbal, turn left for Peratallada which is 4km further.*

El Moli

17706 Pont de Molins (Gerona)
Carretera las Escaules
Tel. 972-52 92 71 - Fax 972-52 91 01 - Familia Lladó

Category ★★ **Rooms** 8 with telephone, bath, WC. **Price** Double 10,500Pts. **Meals** Breakfast served 8:00-10:00. **Restaurant** Service 12:30PM-3:30PM, 7:30PM-10:30PM, closed Dec 15 - Jan 15; à la carte 3,000-4,000Pts. **Credit cards** All major. **Pets** Dogs allowed in the restaurant. **Facilities** Tennis (800Pts), parking. **Nearby** Figueres (Salvador Dali museum) - Massaner de Cabrenys - Gerona. **Open** Holy Week - Oct.

Set back from a country road stands a former 18th-century mill, restored and converted into a hotel-restaurant some ten years ago. Here it is clear that someone loves secondhand objects: the mill stones now serve as low tables; all the sideboards, cupboards, troughs and beds were bought from local antique dealers. Five meters in front of the hotel terrace flows the River Monje, lined with magnificent trees. The restaurant has a good reputation and attracts a French clientele since the border is only some twenty kilometers away. The rooms are charming, while no. 102 is the largest and overlooks the river. Taking count of the very reasonable prices as well, El Moli certainly merits a detour.

***How to get there** (Map 9): 43km north of Gerona via A7, exit no. 2.*

Hostal de la Gavina

17248 S' Agaró (Gerona)
Plaza de la Rosaleda
Tel. 972-32 11 00 - Fax 972-32 15 73 - Sra Requena
E-mail: gavina@iponet.es
Web: www.lhw.com/costabrava/delagavina.html

Category ★★★★★ **Rooms** 74 with air-conditioning, telephone, bath, WC, TV, video, safe, minibar; elevator. **Price** Single 20,800-28,500Pts, double 24,000-41,000Pts, junior-suite 32,000-45,500Pts, suite 36,500-110,000Pts. **Meals** Breakfast 2,500Pts, served 7:00-11:30; half board +8,400Pts, +12,100Pts (per pers.). **Restaurant** Service 1:30PM-3:30PM, 8:30PM-11:00PM; mealtime specials 5,900Pts, à la carte. "Grill Candlelight", open in the evening; à la carte 5,000-7,000Pts. Specialties: Scampi candlelight. **Credit cards** All major. **Pets** Dogs not allowed. **Facilities** Swimming pool, sauna, paddle-tennis, parking, garage (2,500Pts). **Nearby** In Gerona: Cathedral, chapel of Sant Feliu and Monastery of Sant Pere de Galligants - Beaches; Costa Brava golf course (18-Hole). **Closed** Oct 20 - Holy Week.

This is an old house that the owners transformed little by little into a hotel and then a hotel "de luxe". It enjoys an enviable situation: all the rooms, the flowery terrace and the patio have a superb view of the sea. The rooms are also all different and personalized. If your budget permits, go for the royal suite, but only if your taste in decoration leans towards Louis XV. The region is well-supplied with golf courses with no fewer than three very close to the hotel.

How to get there (Map 9): 34km southeast of Gerona via C250.

Balneario Termas Orión

17430 Santa Colomá de Farnés (Gerona)
Tel. 972-84 00 65 - Fax 972-84 04 66
Sr Campeny

Category ★★★ **Rooms** 66 with telephone, bath or shower, WC, TV; elevator. **Price** With half board per pers. single 9,100Pts, double 7,100Pts, triple 6,550Pts. **Meals** Breakfast included, served 8:30-10:00. **Restaurant** With air-conditioning. Service 1:30PM-3:00PM, 8:30PM-10:00PM; mealtime specials 2,300-2,400Pts, also à la carte. Specialties: Gaspacho - Catalan cooking. **Credit cards** Visa, Eurocard, MasterCard. **Pets** Dogs not allowed. **Facilities** Covered swimming pool, tennis, parking. **Nearby** Thermal station - In Gerona: Cathedral, chapel of Sant Feliu and Monastery of Sant Pere de Galligants. **Closed** Jan 15 - Feb 15.

On leaving the village and at the end of an alley of huge trees, you come upon this gleaming white building with stone columns. Built in the last century, the hotel has kept all its allure and atmosphere: everything here has the feel of times past. A gramophone, a magic lantern, a collection of old spectacles, everything seem to have always been here. There is even a lounge-theater (the former owner was a great actress). The natural springs have been completely refurbished in recent times, and only the mosaics of the earlier swimming pool remain; the former marble baths serve as flower pots. The rooms are simple and the bathrooms have an unmatched comfort. Choose the newer rooms or those looking out on the vast stone terrace on the park. It is all very romantic.

How to get there (Map 9): *23km southwest of Gerona, and 2km from Santa Colomá.*

Hotel Mas Torrellas

17246 Santa Cristina de Aró (Gerona)
Carretera Santa Cristina a Playa de Aro, km 1,713
Tel. 972-83 75 26 - Fax 972-83 75 27
Familia Carrera

Category ★ Rooms 17 with air-conditioning, telephone, bath, WC, TV, minibar. **Price** Double 8,500-11,500Pts. **Meals** Breakfast included, served 8:00-11:00; half board +2,100Pts, full board +4,200Pts (per pers.). **Restaurant** Service 1:00PM-4:00PM, 7:30PM-11:30PM; mealtime specials 2,100Pts, also à la carte. Specialties: Pastel de esparragos - Zarzuela - Capricho de la casa. **Credit cards** All major. **Pets** Dogs not allowed. **Facilities** Swimming pool, tennis, riding, sauna, parking. **Nearby** In Gerona: Cathedral, chapel of Sant Feliu and Monastery of Sant Pere de Galligants - Beaches - Costa Brava golf course (18-Hole). **Closed** Oct 15 - Mar 15.

A real discovery... A few years ago the owners spotted and bought a residence in the midst of ten hectares of land, then restored it and fitted it out as a hotel. It is not luxurious: they have opted for personality and atmosphere. The famous Catalan vaultings are everywhere, above all in the former stables now converted into the dining room. A mention for the cellar-bar with its original old beams and wine barrels from all regions of the country! The rooms are neat—the best choice is no. 18, which looks out on the countryside and mountain, and was a round bath. For the moment this hotel has only a one-star rating but, given all the advantages on offer, take advantage of this quickly before its prices rise to those of a three-star.

How to get there (Map 9): 31km southeast of Gerona via C250.

Can Felicia

Segueró 17851 Beuda (Gerona)
Tel. 972-59 05 23
Sr and Sra Llimona
E-mail: canfelicia@beuda.com - Web: www.beuda.com/canfelicia

Rooms 6 with bath. **Price** 3,000Pts (per pers.). **Meals** Breakfast included, served 7:30-10:00; half board 4,500Pts, full board 6,000Pts. **Evening meals** Mealtime specials 1,500Pts. Familial and regional cooking. **Credit cards** Not accepted. **Pets** Dogs not allowed. **Facilities** Parking. **Nearby** Besalú - Santa Pau - Naturel Park de la Garrotya - Gerona. **Open** All year.

Segueró is a spot quite far out in the country, yet only ten kilometers from Besalú, a small city known for its numerous and impressive remains of bygone eras, Roman and Gothic among them. Very recently, Marta opened her property to *turismo rural*, and Can Feliciá offers several comfortable lodgings designed for families along with the possibility of living at one's own rhythm. The meals all bear the mark of home cooking, and this is a very friendly place where you can genuinely make yourself at home

How to get there *(Map 9): 30km northwest of Gerona; 10km north of Besalú.*

Mas de Torrent

17123 Torrent (Gerona)
Tel. 972-30 32 92 - Fax 972-30 32 93
Sr Gregori Berengüi
E-mail: mtorrent@intercom.es - Web: www.mastorrent.com

Category ★★★★★ **Rooms** 30 with air-conditioning, telephone, bath, WC, satellite TV, video, safe, minibar. **Price** Double 32,000-40,000Pts, suite Jardín 32,000-40,000Pts, suite Masia 39,000-45,000Pts; extra bed 10,000Pts. **Meals** Breakfast 2,600Pts; half board +7,800Pts (per pers.). **Restaurant** Service 1:30PM-3:30PM, 8:30PM-11:30PM; à la carte 3,500-6,000Pts. Regional and international cooking. **Credit cards** All major. **Pets** Dogs allowed except in suite and restaurant (2,500Pts). **Facilities** Swimming pool, tennis, squash, bikes, parking. **Nearby** Gerona - Costa Brava - Empordá golf course (27-Hole). **Open** All year.

In the heart of Catalonia, nine kilometers from the most fashionable beaches of the Costa Brava (Aigua Blava, Bégur, etc.), a large 18th-century farm building, now completely restored, has been offering its cuisine and suites for some years. The appeal is to a clientele sensitive to comfort and gentle manners. Everything has been arranged in exquisite taste; all the rooms are different and decorated with a lot of finesse. Twenty bungalows have been built for families in a private garden. The restaurant is delightful and one should take note of a collection of prints in the dining room in honor of Picasso. The ambiance is very calm and relaxed. What more could one want?

How to get there *(Map 9): 36km east of Gerona via A7, exit no. 6, towards Palamós; at the crossroads, go towards Pals; Torrent is 800 meters further on.*

Hotel Can Marlet

17404 Riells de Montseny (Gerona)
Tel. 972-87 09 03 - 972-87 09 43 - Fax 972-87 09 43
E-mail: canmarlet@gm.es - Web: www.montseny.net/canmarlet

Rooms 11 with air-conditioning, telephone, bath, WC, satellite TV, minibar. **Price** Single 10,000Pts, double 11,000Pts, suite 16,000Pts. **Meals** Breakfast 900Pts, served 8:00-11:00; half board 8,700Pts, full board 9,900Pts (per pers.). **Restaurant** Service 1:30PM-3:00PM, 8:30PM-10:00PM; à la carte. Regional cooking. **Credit cards** All major. **Pets** Dogs not allowed. **Facilities** Swimming pool, parking. **Nearby** Sierra de Montseny de San Celoni in Massanet de la Selva, 120km (Ermitage de Santa Fe, Brull, Tona, Viladrau). **Closed** Oct - Mar (except weekends).

Here is an excellent address in the back country of Catalunya with the sea only thirty-odd kilometers away. You leave the highway, and once past the village of Breda, you take the small road leading to Riells. You will soon find yourself in Montseny's beautiful natural park. Paying close attention - the entrance to the hotel is only discreetly marked - you next make a right turn. The hotel itself is equally discreet, nestled among pine trees, willows, magnolias and hydrangea. Of recent construction, it has a charming pink stucco exterior, and the calm, quiet lobby offers small lounges classically furnished with comfortable chairs and a thick rug. Gay colors have been chosen here with red and blue dominants. The rooms have great personality with wooden floors, modern lamps and floral engravings, all contributing to a warm, country-like atmosphere. The nicest of them have small balconies overlooking the swimming pool. The restaurant opens on the garden and serves excellent Catalan dishes. Golf, horseback riding and day trips make this an ideal hotel.

How to get there *(Map 8): 76km from Barcelona; 61km southwest of Gerona. On A7, exit Breda, then 6.5km to Breda.*

Xalet La Coromina

17406 Viladrau (Gerona)
Carretera de Vic
Tel. 938-84 92 64 - Fax 938-84 81 60
Sra Gloria Rabat

Rooms 8 with telephone, bath, satellite TV. **Price** Single 8,200Pts, double 10,400Pts. **Meals** Breakfast 6,200Pts per pers., served 7:30-11:00; half board 8,000Pts, full board 9,600Pts (per pers.). **Restaurant** Service 1:30PM-3:30PM, 8:30PM-11:30PM; mealtime specials and also à la carte. Regional cooking. **Credit cards** All major. **Pets** Dogs not allowed. **Facilities** Parking. **Nearby** Natural Park of Montseny: Granollers road in Gerona - Ermitage de Santa Fe - Barcelona- Gerona - Rack-railway to Vall de Núria. **Closed** Jan 8 - 31.

Adjacent to Montseny's natural park, this region, close to the Costa Brava and Barcelona, is the center of "greenery" tourism in Catalunya. It offers walks through forests of pines, oaks and beeches, plus a fishing zone highly reputed for its trout. When you leave the coast, the road twists around the mountainside, giving you a foretaste of the region's natural beauty. The Xalet is just at the entrance to the village, an attractive house dating from the early part of the century with an ivy-covered facade and surrounding beds of hydrangea. The interior is elegant and comfortable in a British style, with a dining room decorated in *trompe-l'œil* which opens on a French-style garden you reach through a large bay window. There is a genuine coziness in the rooms which are nicely appointed with pastel prints. Those looking out on the garden are the most quiet, and our preference is the attic-room just under the eaves. A refined establishment, something not lost on Barcelona natives.

How to get there (Map 8): 76km from Barcelona; 61km southwest of Gerona.

Hostal de la Glória

17406 Viladrau (Gerona)
Calle Torreventosa, 12
Tel. 938-84 90 34 - Fax 938-84 94 65 - Sr Eudal Formatje
E-mail: hostalgloria@informail.lacaixa.es

Category ★★★ **Rooms** 22 with telephone, bath, TV. **Price** Double 9,800Pts. **Meals** Breakfast 850Pts, served 7:30-11:00; half board +3,500Pts, full board +4,000Pts (per pers.). **Restaurant** Service 1:30PM-3:30PM, 8:30PM-11:30PM; mealtime specials 1,850Pts, also à la carte. Regional and international cooking. **Credit cards** All major. **Pets** Dogs not allowed. **Facilities** Swimming pool, parking. **Nearby** Natural Park of Montseny: Granollers road in Gerona - Ermitage de Santa Fe - Barcelona - Gerona - Rack-railway to Vall de Núria. **Closed** Dec 15 - Jan 15.

A simple and friendly hotel offering a large terrace overlooking the valley. Its rustic decoration and furniture are not long on refinement but the warmth of the decor, centered around hunting trophies and attractive prints with fishing themes. remind the guest that this is indeed a mountainous region. The dining room is well-appointed, the rooms are large and comfortable without much effort spent on decoration and in the summertime, the swimming pool is a definite plus.

How to get there *(Map 8): 76km from Barcelona; 61km southwest of Gerona. On A7, exit Breda.*

Hotel Besiberri

25599 Arties (Lérida)
El Fuerte, 4
Tel. and Fax 973-64 08 29
Sra Carmen Lara Aguilar

Rooms 16 and 1 suite with telephone, bath, TV. **Price** Double 8,000-12,000Pts, suite 14,000Pts. **Meals** Breakfast included, served 8:00-11:00. **Restaurant** See p. 315. **Credit cards** Visa, Eurocard, MasterCard. **Pets** Dogs not allowed. **Nearby** In Arties: Church of Santa Maria Viella - Vall d'Aran - Skiing in Baqueira-Beret (10km). **Closed** May and Nov.

Arties is one of thirty-nine villages that make up the Val d'Aran, geographically part of France's Upper Garonne Valley but belonging to Spain since 1308. Here you hear Spanish along with the local dialect and French. The village has carefully preserved its old stone and slate houses built on both sides of the river that runs through it. This is a small and adorable hotel that takes up two houses, one with a very traditional appearance, the other with a pink painted exterior. The interior is wholly charming, having a lounge with a friendly fireplace and a breakfast nook on the ground floor. The decoration is equally charming with rooms done in warm colors to make them even cozier. Some have a nice view of the river, but there is a strong current that produces a sound some guests might not appreciate. The other rooms give on Monte Arco. A small lawn-garden slopes down to the water's edge. Hiking and skiing provide year-round leisure activities.

How to get there (Map 7): 175km north of Lérida.

Hotel Caldas

25528 Caldas de Bohi (Lérida)
Tel. 973-69 62 30 - Fax 973-69 60 30
Sr Moriscot Pidemunt

Category ★★ **Rooms** 104 (31 with bath, WC; 73 with WC and 14 with TV). **Price** Single 3,485-4,495Pts, double 3,615-14,435Pts, triple 12,200-18,915Pts, 4 pers. 15,765-24,830Pts. **Meals** Breakfast 595-745Pts, served 8:00-10:30; half board +2,945Pts, full board +4,400Pts (per pers.). **Restaurant** Service 2:00PM-3:30PM, 9:00PM-10:00PM; mealtime specials 2,350Pts, also à la carte. Specialties: Truchas de la casa - Carn dolla. **Credit cards** Not accepted. **Pets** Small dogs allowed. **Facilities** Thermal swimming pool, tennis (800Pts), sauna (1,100Pts), garage (500Pts). **Nearby** Bohí Valley from Pont de Suert to Caldes de Bohi (Romanesque churches of Durro, Erill-Aval, Sant Climent de Taúll, Santa Maria) - Excursions in the Aigües Tortes National Park (San Maurici lake) and Vall d'Aran. **Closed** Oct - Jun 23.

The green and winding mountain road ends with a group of hotels at an altitude of 1,500 meters. It was on this site more than sixty years ago that the most important thermal spa in Spain opened. A rare environment and divine peace surround this complex of hotels with its 37 natural springs. A remarkably equipped sporting complex naturally makes this site even more attractive. Our choice has fallen on the very smallest hotel in the complex, which is full of charm. There is a terrace with climbing plants to welcome you, an adorable patio and attractive little corner spots. The ceilings of all the rooms retain their ancient beams. But make no mistake about it: the whole place is as simple as the people running it. The prices are equally unpretentious.

How to get there *(Map 7): 145km north of Lérida via N230; 3km after the Suert bridge, take small road to the right.*

Hotel El Castell

25700 La Seu d'Urgell (Lérida)
Carretera N 60
Tel. 973-35 07 04 - Fax 973-35 15 74
Sr Jaume Tápies Travé - Sr Jaume Tápies Ibern

Category ★★★★ **Rooms** 32 and 5 suites with air-conditioning, telephone, bath, WC, satellite TV, safe, minibar. **Price** Single 17,500Pts, double 23,000Pts, junior-suite 34,000Pts. **Meals** Breakfast included, served 7:30-10:30. **Restaurant** Service 1:00PM-3:30PM, 8:00PM-10:30PM; à la carte 5,500-8,000Pts. Specialties: Raviolis de cigalas con mousse de calabacin - Risotto de bogavente con moixernons y trufa. **Credit cards** All major. **Pets** Dogs allowed in the rooms. **Facilities** Swimming pool, parking. **Nearby** In Seu: Santa María Cathedral - Monastery Sant Serni de Tavérnoles in Anserall - Castellciutat - Excursions into the Vall d'Aran - The Cerdanya: Bellver de Cerdanya, Llivia, Puigcerdá - Andorra (Duty Free Principality). **Open** All year.

It is on the summit of a gently sloping hill, at the foot of which lies the medieval town of Seo d'Urgel, that El Castell is to be found. In this hotel protected by its mountain (the Sierra del Cadí), everything is organized to take advantage of such a privileged site. A remarkable comfort characterizes the place with the ground floor rooms enjoying a terrace or private garden, while those on the upper floor have just been renovated. In addition, all display a personalized decor. The restaurant is gastronomic. Truly a hotel for those insisting on style, nature and good living.

How to get there (Map 8): 133km northeast of Lérida via C1313.

Parador Castillo de la Zuda

43500 Tortosa (Tarragona)
Castillo de la Zuda
Tel. 977-44 44 50 - Fax 977-44 44 58 - Sr Esteban
E-mail: tortosa@parador.es

Category ★★★★ **Rooms** 75 with air-conditioning, telephone, bath, WC, TV, minibar; elevator. **Price** Double 13,500-15,000Pts. **Meals** Breakfast 1,300Pts, served 8:00-10:30. **Restaurant** Service 1:30PM-3:15PM, 8:00PM-10:15PM; mealtime specials 3,500Pts, also à la carte. **Credit cards** All major. **Pets** Dogs not allowed. **Facilities** Swimming pool, parking. **Nearby** In Tortosa: Cathedral - Morella - Hunting and fishing in the Ebro Delta (Sant Carles de la Rapida; cray fish). **Open** All year.

The château of La Zuda takes its name from the well which, according to Arab sources, was sunk within the walls in the year 944, and which can still be seen today. This ancient Roman town has had a tumultuous history, becoming in turn a Arab fortress, a prison in the 12th century, and then a royal residence before being ceded to the Templars. Inside, the dining room has kept four huge windows and three open fireplaces as witnesses of such a past. The rooms have terraces with a magnificent panorama. But it is from the swimming pool that one has the best view over Tortosa and over the fertile valley of the Ebro, all with a backdrop of the mountains of Tortosa and Beceite, a huge hunting reserve.

How to get there (Map 16): 83km southwest of Tarragona via A7.

Parador Via de la Plata

06800 Mérida (Badajoz)
Plaza de la Constitución, 3
Tel. 924-31 38 00 - Fax 924-31 92 08
Sr Victor Teodosio

Category ★★★★ **Rooms** 82 with air-conditioning, telephone, bath, WC, satellite TV, minibar; elevator. **Price** Double 16,500Pts. **Meals** Breakfast 1,300Pts, served 7:30-11:00. **Restaurant** Service 1:00PM-4:00PM, 8:30PM-11:00PM; mealtime specials 3,500Pts, also à la carte. Specialties: Gazpacho extremeno - Criadillas de la tierra - caldereta - gigues de Almoharím - chuleta de vacuno - cordero asada. **Credit cards** All major. **Pets** Dogs not allowed. **Facilities** Swimming pool, fitness center, sauna, garage (1,100Pts), parking. **Nearby** Roman Mérida: Roman Art Museum, Roman Theater, Roman Amphitheater, Roman bridge - Montijo - Embalse de Proserpina - Medelin. **Open** All year.

Mérida is a major tourist center where one comes to see the numerous Roman, Visigoth and Arab remains, and the parador is installed in an 18th-century convent, itself built on the ruins of a Roman temple. It has experienced diverse fortunes, even having been a prison! But have no fear, no traces remain of this former occupation. The hotel has two large lounges, one particularly elegant and intimate in the former chapel. There is a bright and sunny dining room with spotless white linen where you can taste the delicious *Extremeño* specialties. The rooms are spacious, comfortable and tastefully decorated in regional style. There is also a delightful patio and a garden decorated with the Roman sculptures brought to light during the building work.

How to get there (Map 17): 68km south of Cáceres via N630.

Parador de Zafra

06300 Zafra (Badajoz)
Plaza Corazon de Maria, 7
Tel. 924-55 45 40 - Fax 924-55 10 18 - Sr Antonio Atalaya

Rooms 45 with air-conditioning, telephone, bath, WC, satellite TV, minibar. **Price** Double 15,000-17,500Pts. **Meals** Breakfast 1,300Pts, served 7:30-11:00; half board +4,700Pts, full board +6,970Pts (per pers., 3 days min.). **Restaurant** Service 1:30PM-4:00PM, 8:30PM-11:00PM; mealtime specials 3,600Pts; also à la carte. **Credit cards** Amex, Visa, Eurocard, MasterCard. **Pets** Dogs not allowed. **Facilities** Swimming pool, parking. **Nearby** In Zafra: Colegiata Ntra. Sra. de la Candeleria, Hospidal de santiago, convento de Sta Clara, Casa palacio de Marqués de Solanda, Bodegas Medina - "Ducado de Feria" road and "Ruta de los Templarios". **Open** All year.

This parador is in the center of a lovely *alcazar* in this charming little city whose name has not changed since the Moorish invasion. An imposing turret survives from that period, and to it has been added a building in Andalusian Moorish style with an eye-catching facade of nicely-blended white and gray. Once past the vast entrance way, you discover a magnificent patio in white marble. The lounges are quite luxurious, and a magnificent staircase leads to the rooms, most of which have balconies overlooking the patio. The rooms are large with furniture that evokes the charm of the era of the Spanish *conquistadores*. Those in the annex are smaller but equally comfortable. The swimming pool enjoys the shade of the historic walls surrounding it, a true oasis, especially in the summertime. The immense dining room is equally cool. Here is a fine hotel, one that brings to mind the glorious days of the Spanish Empire.

How to get there (Map 17): 68km south of Badajoz.

Hotel Huerta Honda

06300 Zafra (Badajoz)
Lopez Asme, 30
Tel. 924-55 41 00 - Fax 924-55 25 04

Rooms 45 with air-conditioning, telephone, bath, WC, satellite TV, minibar. **Price** Single 8,700-15,200Pts, double 10,900-20,000Pts. **Meals** Breakfast 1,000Pts, served 7:30-11:00. **Restaurant** Service 12:30PM-4:00PM, 8:30PM-11:30PM; mealtime specials 4,000Pts; also à la carte. **Credit cards** All major. **Pets** Dogs not allowed. **Facilities** Swimming pool, parking. **Nearby** In Zafra: Colegiata Ntra. Sra. de la Candeleria, Hospidal de santiago, Convento de Sta Clara, Casa palacio de Marqués de Solanda, Bodegas Medina - "Ducado de Feria" road and "Ruta de los Templarios". **Open** All year.

R ight next to the Parador, the Hotel Huerta Honda is part of a group of 17th-century buildings that have been renovated over centuries to become a hotel today. Its concept is typical of certain Spanish hotels: there are three restaurants, two bars and a nightclub all at your disposal. The interior decoration is nothing if not surprising; it ranges from blatant bad taste to extreme refinement. You can find rooms which are at the same time exquisite and kitsch. On the other hand, the hotel's restaurant, *La Barbacana*, is magnificent with its antique furnishings and a kitchen run by the Hotel School of San Sebastian with truly remarkable results. A good hotel, located nicely between Madrid and Sevilla.

How to get there *(Map 17): 68km south of Badajoz.*

Hotel Meliá Cáceres

10003 Cáceres
Plaza de San Juan, 11
Tel. 927-21 58 00 - Fax 927-21 40 70
E-mail: melia.caceres@solmelia.es

Category ★★★★ **Rooms** 86 with air-conditioning, telephone, bath, WC, satellite TV, trouser-press, safe, minibar; elevator. **Price** Single 16,700Pts, double 21,000Pts, suite 25,900Pts; extra bed +4,600Pts. **Meals** Breakfast (buffet) 1,500Pts, served 7:30-11:00. **Restaurant** La Indias, service 1:00PM-4:00PM, 8:30PM-11:00PM; mealtime specials 3,500Pts, also à la carte. **Credit cards** All major. **Pets** Dogs not allowed. **Nearby** In Cáceres: Barrio Monumental, Plaza de Santa Maria, Palacio de los Golfines de Abajo; Sanctuario de la Virgen de la Montaña - Arroyo de la Luz. **Open** All year.

Asuperb town and admirably preserved, the Old Town - el Barrio Monumental - of Cáceres is a real museum of Spanish Gothic town architecture. The Meliá Cáceres is in a former palace of the aristocratic Ovendo family which made its fortune in America, and had a number of such palaces built. All the original structure has been preserved and one enters through a heavy wooden door opening onto the Plaza de San Juan. A large central patio allows a soft light to enter the hall which gives access to the reception rooms. Seating and tables have been arranged around ancient wells to enhance the serene atmosphere. The bar has been installed in the former stables, covered with magnificent brick vaulting. The rooms are decorated with taste, and we recommend those giving on the square shaded by bay trees and palms. Comfort is exemplary and the breakfasts delicious. The restaurant is also much appreciated, having won for the second consecutive year the *Plato de oro de la gastronomía española*. A very good hotel where one is served by a delightful and competent staff.

How to get there *(Map 17): 300km west of Madrid.*

Hospederia del Real Monasterio

10140 Guadalupe (Cáceres)
Plaza Juan Carlos I
Tel. 927-36 70 00 - Fax 927-36 71 77
Sr Dominguez

Category ★★ **Rooms** 47 with air-conditioning, telephone, bath, WC; elevator. **Price** Single: 5,350Pts, double 7,900Pts, suite 20,000Pts. **Meals** Breakfast 875Pts, served 8:30-10:30; half board 6,900Pts, full board 9,450Pts (per pers. 2 days min.). **Restaurant** Service 1:30PM-3:30PM, 9:00PM-10:30PM, mealtime specials 2,800Pts, also à la carte. Specialties: Sopa de tomate - Cabrito asado - Migas estremeñas - Criadillas de tierra - Cardillos salvajes perfecto de nueces - Biscuit de higos - Pudding de castañas. **Credit cards** Visa, Eurocard, MasterCard. **Pets** Dogs not allowed. **Facilities** Parking. **Nearby** Monastery of Guadalupe - Ermitage de Humilladero - Caramero - Logrosán. **Closed** Jan 12 - Feb 12.

An impressive and grandiose ensemble, built both for monastic purposes and those of war, this monastery was an important cultural center, and the Franciscan Community occupying it today has chosen to open a hotel in one part of the monastery. From the hallway one has a very beautiful view on one of the most enchanting corners of the edifice, *Los Caídos*. Lounges, a dining room and large rooms are spread around the cloister, a small Gothic masterpiece, which is covered with a canopy in summer. Naturally you should visit the monastery with its facade on the town square, and the *mudéjar* cloister and church that has conserved an impressive collection of works of art, including several exceptional pictures by Zurbarán in the sacristy.

How to get there (Map 18): 139km east of Cáceres via N521, then C524 and C401.

Parador Zurbarán

10140 Guadalupe (Cáceres)
Marqués de la Romana, 10
Tel. 927-36 70 75 - Fax 927-36 70 76
Sr Florentino Garcia

Category ★★★★ **Rooms** 41 with telephone, bath, WC, TV, minibar; elevator. **Price** Double 12,500-13,500Pts. **Meals** Breakfast 1,300Pts, served 8:00-11:00. **Restaurant** Service 1:00PM-4:00PM, 9:00PM-11:00PM; mealtime specials 3,200Pts, also à la carte. Specialties: Cabrito asado - Sopa de arroz cacereña - Bacalao monacal - Caldereta de Cordero. **Credit cards** All major. **Pets** Dogs not allowed. **Facilities** Swimming pool, tennis, garage, parking. **Nearby** Monastery of Guadalupe - Ermitage de Humilladero - Caramero - Logrosán. **Open** All year.

Guadalupe was an important center of pilgrimage, and today the grandiose monastery, the Zurbarán and the museum (with a very beautiful collection of lace, among others things) all merit a stop here. The ancient St. John the Baptist hospital from the 18th century now houses the hotel. It certainly does not have the prestige of the monastery, but its interior layout has a lot more charm. The lounges and dining room are once again arranged around the patio, whose arcades are invaded by orange trees, and in the summer one lunches in the shade of the gallery. The rooms are very prettily decorated but it is preferable to ask for those in the new building which have a view over the mountains, village. The incredible monastery situated right in front. On the rear side is the swimming pool in the midst of a very flowery garden, much appreciated in the summer.

How to get there (Map 18): *139km east of Cáceres via N521, then C524 and C401.*

Parador Carlos V

10450 Jarandilla de la Vera (Cáceres)
Tel. 927-56 01 17 - Fax 927- 56 00 88
Sr Tomas Caldo Arena

Category ★★★ **Rooms** 53 with air-conditioning, telephone, bath, WC, satellite TV, minibar. **Price** Double 15,000-17,000Pts. **Meals** Breakfast 1,300Pts, served 8:00-11:00. **Restaurant** Service 1:00PM-4:30PM, 8:30PM-11:00PM; mealtime specials 3,700Pts, also à la carte. Specialties: Cabrito - Calderetas. **Credit cards** All major. **Pets** Dogs not allowed. **Facilities** Swimming pool, tennis, parking. **Nearby** Cuacos de Yuste and Monastery of Yuste - Garganta la Olla - Cathedral of Plasencia. **Open** All year.

In the north of Extremadura in the wild country of the Vera, this 14th- and 15th-century chateau is to be found. The very well preserved edifice still has its beautiful surrounding wall, elegant angle towers and a drawbridge. The building is built around a flowered patio, and one facade consists of two arcaded galleries and a stone balcony worked in the oriental style. It is here that Charles V lodged before retiring to the Yuste monastery. The dining room occupies the ground floor while on the upper floor the lounge opens onto a balcony dominating the patio. The furniture is simple but the caisson ceilings, size of the rooms, lamps, medallions and trophies a contribute to the chateau spirit. The rooms are both perfect and comfortable.

How to get there *(Map 11): 141km northeast of Cáceres via N630 to Plasencia, then C501.*

Parador de Trujillo

10200 Trujillo (Cáceres)
Plaza de Santa Clara
Tel. 927-32 13 50 - Fax 927-32 13 66
Sr Fuertes

Category ★★★★ **Rooms** 46 with air-conditioning, telephone, bath, WC, satellite TV, minibar.
Price Double 15,000Pts. **Meals** Breakfast 1,300Pts, served 7:45-11:00. **Restaurant** Service
1:30PM-4:30PM, 9:00PM-11:00PM; mealtime specials 3,700Pts, also à la carte. Specialties: Tenca,
cordero asado. **Credit cards** All major. **Pets** Dogs not allowed. **Facilities** Garage, parking. **Nearby**
In Trujillo: Plaza Mayor and Church of Santa Maria la Mayor - Santa Cruz de la Sierra - Cáceres -
Guadalupe - National Park of Monfrague. **Open** All year.

Trujillo was the home base of the Conquistadors, as recalled by the
equestrian statue of Francisco Pizarro on the Plaza Mayor, and is a
beautiful town with a host of medieval and Renaissance monuments. The
parador is in what was once a convent founded in the 16th century by the
Order of the Immaculate Conception. Built around a courtyard, the cloister is
planted with orange trees and has three facades in Renaissance style topped by
a gallery with small Tuscan columns. The interior decoration is rather
impersonal, particularly in the rooms which, however, are perfectly
comfortable. Some have terraces entirely covered with a trellis, the traditional
manner in this region of protecting against the heat. The hotel is air-
conditioned.

How to get there *(Map 18): 47km east of Cáceres via N521; the parador is
located in the lower part of town.*

Posada Finca Santa Marta

Pago de San Clemente
10220 Trujillo (Cáceres)
Tel. and Fax 927-31 92 03 - Fax 91-350 22 17 (in Madrid)
Sr Henri Elink - Sra Marta Rodriguez-Gimeno
E-mail: henri@facilnet.es - Web: www.fincasantamarta.com

Rooms 12 with bath. **Price** Double 9,500Pts. **Meals** Breakfast included. **Evening meals** On request; mealtime specials 2,500-3,000Pts. **Credit cards** All major. **Pets** Dogs allowed. **Facilities** Swimming pool, parking. **Nearby** In Trujillo: Plaza Mayor and Church of Santa Maria la Mayor - Santa Cruz de la Sierra - Cáceres - Guadalupe - National Park of Monfrague. **Open** All year.

On the national highway linking Madrid and Lisbon, Trujillo is a good stop where one can visit its Plaza Mayor, famous for its arcades and Renaissance palace. One can try the regional tomato soup with figs, and its braised pork - la *morada* - or, even better, stay in the countryside at the Finca de Santa Marta, a rare *cortijo* converted for "greenery tourism". This farm-manor house, known in the region as a *lagar*, where oil and wine are produced, provides eight beautiful rooms. A long and rigorous restoration has preserved all the authenticity of the buildings; you can still visit the mill, now converted into a vast lounge-dining room, the wine press, cellars, stables, sheepfolds and even the little chapel. The rooms have been subjected to all the care of the owner-decorator and have very refined decors: old wood and tiles have been restored to mix harmoniously with the regional furniture while providing the most up-to-date comfort. The garden is delightful, complete with a swimming, pool and surrounded by many acres of olive, cherry and almond trees, making for beautiful spring days in white and pink.

How to get there *(Map 18): On the highway N-V (Madrid to the Portuguese border), to Trujillo, then 14km towards Guadalupe via C524.*

Pazo da Merced

15510 Neda (La Coruña)
Tel. 981-38 22 00 - Fax 981-38 01 04
Sra Marinela Medina
E-mail: pazomerced@arrakis.es

Category ★★★★ **Rooms** 5 with telephone, bath, WC, TV, minibar. **Price** Single 10,400Pts, double 13,000Pts. **Meals** Breakfast 1,200Pts, served 9:00-11:00. **Restaurant** Only for residents, on request. **Credit cards** All major. **Pets** Dogs not allowed. **Facilities** Swimming pool, parking. **Nearby** Les rías. **Open** All year.

On the northwest corner of Spain, the highly indented coastline lets the sea flow inland, forming what the Spanish call rias. Here on the bank of the Ria de Ferrol, you find the Pazo da Merced, an L-shaped, 18th-century house to which has been subtly and harmoniously added new and wholly contemporary architecture. An attractive glass-covered metal staircase leads up to the rooms. These are spacious with antique beams and floors. They have a pleasant combination of Victorian and Biedermeir furniture, while the bathrooms are distinctly modern. On one side there is a small French-style garden, and on the side facing the sea is a landing dock which has been made into a terrace where breakfast - and other meals if you ask for them - is served. A small private beach marks the end of the hotel's property. The Merced is one of the rare attractive hotels in this lovely region which has escaped the industrialization that took place in the 70s and 80s.

How to get there (Map 1): 60km north of La Coruña, to El Ferrol.

Parador de Los Reyes Católicos

15705 Santiago de Compostela (La Coruña)
Plaza del Obradoiro, 1
Tel. 981-58 22 00 - Fax 981-56 30 94 - Sr Morales
E-mail: santiago@parador.es

Category ★★★★★ **Rooms** 136 with telephone, bath, WC, satellite TV, minibar; elevator. **Price** Single 21,200Pts, double 26,500Pts, suite 53,000Pts. **Meals** Breakfast 1,800Pts, served 7:00-11:00. **Restaurant** Service 1:00PM-3:30PM, 9:00PM-11:30PM; mealtime specials 3,800Pts; also à la carte. Specialties: Merluza con almejas - Caldo gallego - Vieiras a la gallega - Solomillo de ternera gallega al queso del cebrero - Tarta de santiago - Filloas rellenas de crema. **Credit cards** All major. **Pets** Dogs not allowed. **Facilities** Garage (2,200Pts). **Nearby** In Santiago: Cathedral, Plaza del Obradoiro, Plaza de la Quintana, Barrio antiguo - Church of Santa Maria la Real del Sarl - Pazo de Oca (manor and gardens) - Monastery of Santa Maria de Conjo. **Open** All year.

It was in 1499 that the Catholic monarchs Isabel and Fernando established this royal hostel to shelter pilgrims. Situated on the very attractive Plaza del Obradoiro, it remains today a testimony to an era when history, religion, art and culture were intimately linked. Today, tourists have replaced the foot-sore pilgrims on the road to Santiago de Compostela, and this parador is one of the best hotels in Spain. The setting is grandiose as are the entry and facade, the four cloistered patios dating from the 16th and 17th centuries and the stables which have become the principal dining room. Another dining room with a terrace looking on the cathedral offers the opportunity of tasting the cooking of Galicia. The rooms are exquisite, in particular Rooms 201, 202 and 204, while the Cardinal Suite and the Royal Suite overlook the square. The service is that of a grand hotel, attentive and discreet.

How to get there *(Map 1): Facing the cathedral.*

Casa Grande de Cornide

Cornide (Calo-Teo) 15886 Santiago (La Coruña)
Tel. 981-80 55 99 - Fax 981-80 57 51
Sra Maria Jesus Castro Rivas

Rooms 10 with telephone, bath, WC, satellite TV, minibar. **Price** Single 10,000-12,000Pts, double 13,000-15,000Pts. **Meals** Breakfast 950Pts, served 8:00-11:00. **Restaurants** See p. 316. **Credit cards** All major. **Pets** Dogs allowed. **Facilities** Swimming pool, parking. **Nearby** Santiago de Compostela route - Church of Santa Maria la Real del Sarl - Gardens and Manor Pazo de Oca - Monastery of Santa Maria de Conja. **Open** All year.

Only nine kilometers from Santiago, the Casa Grande de Cornide is a hotel of incomparable charm. It enjoys an inland location. You enter through a beautiful old stone entrance where you come upon its different wings, all representative of local architecture, and discover a large garden with magnolias, oak and olive trees along with a palm grove. The owners are connoisseurs of Spanish art and this shows in the way they have restored the house and particularly the library. The rooms here are in the wings, three in the old one, two in the more recent one. Each is furnished differently but all have the same enjoyably subtle atmosphere, the result of a predominantly deep red decor along with furniture in very dark wood. The suite is the most spacious, with a glass-covered mezzanine decorated in a style that tastefully combines Victorian architecture with that commonly found in old-fashioned hay barns. This hotel is a true find, one where you are always warmly received and it is a good place to regain your strength after a pilgrimage to Santiago or before setting out for Portugal.

How to get there (Map 1): 9km south of Santiago, on the Vigo road; at the gas station of Casalonga, turn on left and follow the road during 2km; Casa Grande de Cornide is on right.

Parador de Ribadeo

27700 Ribadeo (Lugo)
Amador Fernandez, 7
Tel. 982-12 88 25 - Fax 982-12 83 46

Category ★★★★ **Rooms** 47 with telephone, bath, WC, TV, minibar, safe; elevator. **Price** Double 12,500-15,000Pts. **Meals** Breakfast 1,300Pts, served 8:00-11:00. **Restaurant** Service 1:00PM-4:00PM, 9:00PM-11:00PM; mealtime specials 3,200Pts, also à la carte. Specialties: Pulpo - Filloas - Empanadas - Lacón con grelos. **Credit cards** All major. **Pets** Dogs not allowed. **Facilities** Parking, garage. **Nearby** Fort of S. Damian, Collegiate S. Francisco and Chapel of N.S. del Camino, Bridge dos Santos - Mondoñedo - Foz. **Open** All Year.

This parador is two kilometers from the center of town, built where the Rio Eo's estuary, before arriving at the sea, forms a number of *rias* so characteristic of the countryside in Galicia. The building's exterior is none too impressive but inside, the quality of this parador is immediately apparent. There is a large lounge with a bar and numerous sofas in marine colors, all looking out on the estuary. The classic and elegant dining room includes tables in a gallery with an interesting view. The sun-filled and nicely decorated rooms are a pleasure to behold, and everything devoted to the guest's comfort has been recently renovated. While all are well-situated, the suites offer terraces with deck chairs. Watching the boats on the river is a pleasant diversion, and at night, the luminous reflections of the houses on the opposite bank may be seen on the water.

How to get there *(Map 2): 90km north of Lugo via N640.*

Parador Condes de Villalba

27800 Valeriano Valdesus - Villalba (Lugo)
Tel. 982-51 00 11 - Fax 982-51 00 90
Sr Vazquez Camara

Category ★★★ **Rooms** 6 with telephone, bath, WC, TV, minibar; elevator. **Price** Double 15,000-17,500Pts. **Meals** Breakfast 1,300Pts, served 8:00-11:00. **Restaurant** Service 1:00PM-4:00PM, 9:00PM-11:00PM, mealtime specials 3,500Pts, also à la carte. Specialties: Pulpo - Filloas - Empanadas - Lacón con grelos. **Credit cards** All major. **Pets** Dogs not allowed. **Facilities** Parking. **Nearby** Lugo (cathedral and fortifications) - Chapel of Baamonde - Monastery of Meira. **Open** All year.

It was a very long time ago that the Los Andrade Tower defended Villalba against its attacking enemies. The recognition it deserved was nearly lost, but the Paradores administration saved it, in extremis, from destruction while at the same time providing the region with a good hotel. Recent renovation has taken place and now the very large rooms have all the amenities required. Good regional cuisine is served in the basement dining room. A comfortable stop on the road to Santiago de Compostela.

How to get there *(Map 2): 36km north of Lugo via N6 to Rábade, then C641.*

Parador de Monterrey

32600 Verín (Orense)
Tel. 988-41 00 75 - Fax 988-41 20 17
Sr Oreste Calbo

Category ★★★ **Rooms** 23 with telephone, bath, WC, minibar. **Price** Double 11,500-13,500Pts. **Meals** Breakfast 1,200Pts, served 8:00-10:30. **Restaurant** Service 1:30PM-4:00PM, 9:00PM-11:00PM; mealtime specials 3,200Pts, also à la carte. Regional cooking. **Credit cards** All major. **Pets** Dogs not allowed. **Facilities** Swimming pool, garage. **Nearby** In Verín: Monterrey Castle - Church of Santa Maria of Mijos - Church and Castle of Mezquita. **Closed** Dec and Jan.

Some four kilometers from the town, this parador benefits from the isolation granted to a clientele seeking maximum peace and quiet. Of recent construction but respecting the style of the region, the building dominates the valley of the Tamega, covered with vineyards, and the Château of Monterrey. The rooms all offer equal amenities in a traditional decor, but the prettiest are those looking onto the chateau, so be sure to ask for Rooms 102, 104 and 106.

How to get there (Map 2): 78km southeast of Orense via N525.

Parador Conde de Gondomar

36300 Bayona (Pontevedra)
Tel. 986-35 50 00 - Fax 986-35 50 76
Sr Martín

Category ★★★★ **Rooms** 122 with telephone, bath, WC, satellite TV, minibar. **Price** Double 15,000-20,000Pts. **Meals** Breakfast 1,400Pts, served 8:00-11:00. **Restaurant** Service 1:30PM-4:00PM, 8:30PM-11:00PM, mealtime specials 3,800Pts, also à la carte. Specialties: Fish - Sea food - Empanadas. **Credit cards** All major. **Pets** Dogs not allowed. **Facilities** Swimming pool, tennis, garage, parking. **Nearby** Fortress (Monte Real) - Monte Groba - Faro island - Road from Bayona to La Guardia. **Open** All year.

The hotel rises like an incomparable watchtower on the Monte Real peninsula, surrounded by a wall predating the Roman colonization. It was here that the galley La Pinta touched shore with the first Indians from America aboard. Its sheer size is impressive, as are the space and installations (five lounges, three dining rooms). The rooms all offer every amenity wished for. Its 18 hectares of land and 3 kilometers of walls protect it from any tourist bustle. Its sporting facilities allow one to avoid even leaving the hotel, which can be very convenient for a family vacation.

How to get there *(Map 1): 20km southwest of Vigo via C550.*

Gran Hotel de la Toja

36991 Isla de la Toja (Pontevedra)
Tel. 986-73 00 25 - Fax 986-73 12 01
Sr Alvarez Cordero
E-mail: info@latojagranhotel.com - Web: www.latojagranhotel.com

Category ★★★★★ **Rooms** 197 with telephone, bath, WC, satellite TV, minibar; elevator. **Price** Single 17,000-24,000Pts, double 21,500-30,000Pts, suite 30,000-43,000Pts; extra bed 6,000-8,000Pts - with view +2,700-4,270Pts. **Meals** Breakfast (buffet) 1,900Pts, served from 7:00; half board +7,750Pts, full board +10,800Pts (per pers.). **Restaurant** Service 1:30PM-3:00PM, 9:30PM-11:00PM; mealtime specials 5,850Pts, also à la carte. Specialties: Fish, sea food. **Credit cards** All major. **Pets** Dogs not allowed. **Facilities** Heated swimming pool, tennis, health center, golf course (9-Hole), parking. **Nearby** El Grove (Shellfish festival during the second week of Oct) - Salvora. **Open** All year.

There are the "beach hotels" and the "palaces on the coast", and the Gran Hotel de la Toja is certainly a "palace on the coast". Enjoying a privileged site on a small island of the Ria de Arosa, it has all the extras of a grand hotel: private beach, pine woods, swimming pool, tennis courts and golf. The public rooms are luxurious: vast ceremonial lounges, a more intimate bar, a welcoming dining room. The rooms are very comfortable, although they are more charming in the older part of the building. There is also a casino and a spa close to the hotel, which should please more than one visitor!

How to get there *(Map 1): 73km southwest of Santiago via N550 to Puente Cesures, then signs for La Toja; the hotel is located on the island.*

Hotel Convento de San Benito

36002 La Guardia/A Guarda (Pontevedra)
Plaza San Benito
Tel. 986-61 11 66 - Fax 986-61 15 17
Sr Antonio Baz Gomez

Rooms 24 with telephone, bath, WC, satellite TV, minibar. **Price** Single 4,900-6,300Pts, double 6,900-12,700Pts; extra bed 2,200-2,800Pts. **Meals** Breakfast 700Pts, served 7:30-11:30. **Restaurant** See p. 315. **Credit cards** All major. **Pets** Dogs not allowed. **Facilities** Garage (1,000Pts). **Nearby** Laguardia - Monte Santa Tecla. **Open** All year.

In a fishing port with just a whiff of nostalgia at the mouth of the Rio Miño, the San Benito hotel stands with its back to an ancient wall and occupies an old monastery founded by the Ozore de Sottomayor family. Visible remains include an impressive, solid-wood door, some sculpted stone, aging stained-glass windows and part of a cloister with a fountain. The appearance of the interior may only be qualified as noble, with furniture in 17th-century style and vast carpets. The rooms have wooden floors and flowered bedspreads, relieving the feeling of conventional austerity. Those that look out on the cloister enjoy the serenity this hotel offers, while those on the second floor have a view of the port and the activity going on there. La Guardia is a good stop on the roads to Compostella and Portugal, and here you can seek out a small restaurant on the port and try the famous crabs of Galicia along with some *Albariño*, the region's celebrated white wine.

How to get there (Map 1): 28km southwest of Tuy via C550.

Parador Casa del Barón

36002 Pontevedra
Barón, 19
Tel. 986-85 58 00 - Fax 986-85 21 95
Sr Basso Puga

Category ★★★ **Rooms** 47 with telephone, bath, WC, TV, minibar; elevator. **Price** Double 11,500-15,000Pts. **Meals** Breakfast 1,300Pts, served 8:00-11:00. **Restaurant** Service 1:00PM-4:00PM, 8:30PM-11:30PM; mealtime specials 3,200Pts, also à la carte. Specialties: fish, sea food. **Credit cards** All major. **Pets** Dogs not allowed. **Facilities** Parking. **Nearby** Monastery of Lérez - Castle of Sotomayor - Mirador of Coto Redondo. **Open** All year.

The Parador Casa del Barón occupies the pazo of Maceda. A pazo was an ancient Galician manor house which abandoned the military character of the castles built during the middle Ages and was more inspired by monastic or rural architecture. When this one became a hotel in 1955, it was insisted upon that the original style of this old *pazo* should be conserved and restored. The unusual kitchen, now a lounge, and the elegant staircase of the entry testify to this. The other rooms of the house are also very agreeable. Although the food is hardly out of the ordinaty, the dining room opens onto the terrace and a flourishing garden. All the bedrooms are very refined. The Casa del Barón is located in the ancient barrio of Pontevedra, a very attractive area in this town whose outskirts are rather disappointing.

How to get there *(Map 1): 57km south of Santiago by the highway, Pontevedra-Norte exit; in the old part of the town.*

Parador San Telmo

36700 Túy (Pontevedra)
Avenida de Portugal
Tel. 986-60 03 09 - Fax 986-60 21 63
Sr Rizos Garrido

Category ★★★ **Rooms** 30 with telephone, bath, WC, TV, minibar. **Price** Double 11,500-15,500Pts. **Meals** Breakfast 1,300Pts, served 8:00-11:00. **Restaurant** Service 1:00PM-4:00PM, 9:00PM-11:00PM; mealtime specials 3,500Pts, also à la carte. Specialties: Pulpea Feire - Lacon con grelos. **Credit cards** All major. **Pets** Dogs not allowed. **Facilities** Swimming pool, tennis, parking. **Nearby** In Tuy: Cathedral - Romanesque church of Pexegueiro - Mirador de Aloya - Salvaterra de Miño. **Open** All year.

Built on the model of Galician houses, the hotel rises on a small promontory on the right bank on the Miño in a green and quiet countryside that reminds one of an Irish landscape. The atmosphere reflects the environment: serene and peaceful. The bedrooms are very attractive and no. 105 offers a small gallery with rattan furnishings, and the suite has a large balcony. This is a particularly good hotel for trying local specialties.

How to get there (Map 1): 34km south of Vigo via N550, towards Portugal.

Hotel Pazo El Revel

36990 Villalonga (Pontevedra)
Tel. 986-74 30 00 - Fax 986-74 30 90
Sr Ansorena Garret

Category ★★★ **Rooms** 22 with telephone, bath, WC, TV. **Price** Single 6,850-7,500Pts, double 11,000-13,000Pts. **Meals** Breakfast included, served 9:00-11:00. No restaurant. **Credit cards** Visa, Eurocard, MasterCard. **Pets** Dogs not allowed. **Facilities** Swimming pool, tennis, parking. **Nearby** Monastery of Lérez - Castillo de Sotomayor - Mirador de Coto Redondo - Beaches - A. Toxa golf course. **Open** Jun 1st - Sept 30.

This elegant 17th-century Galician residence has 22 simply appointed rooms: tiling, white walls and furniture limited to what is strictly necessary, but nonetheless providing all the comfort required. The character of the house is shown more by the pretty garden with its swimming pool and tennis court, while on the covered terrace wicker armchairs await you. This place is quiet and one can listen to the birds singing. The beaches nearby and the Romanesque churches of the region well deserve a visit.

How to get there *(Map 1): 23km north of Pontevedra via A9, exit Caldas or Pontevedra; 9km from Cambados.*

La Posada de Alameda

28749 Alameda del Valle (Madrid)
Grande, 34
Tel. 91-869 13 37/869 00 17 - Fax 91-869 01 63
Sr Gregorio Marcos
Web: www.sierranorte/posada-alameda

Category ★★★★ **Rooms** 22 with air-conditioning, telephone, bath, WC, TV. **Price** Double 10,500Pts, suite 12,000Pts. **Meals** Breakfast 750Pts, served 8:00-10:00. **Restaurant** Service 1:00PM-3:30PM, 9:00PM-11:00PM; also à la carte. Castillian cooking. **Credit cards** All major. **Pets** Dogs not allowed. **Facilities** Parking. **Nearby** Valley of Lozoya - Madrid. **Open** All year.

Some fifty kilometers from Segovia, you come across the Lozoya Valley, a place with ever-changing landscapes. The mountaintops are snow-covered in winter and below them lie almond groves, lakes and rivers. It was in this peaceful setting that this wholly traditional inn was built a few years ago. It is, however, totally modern in spirit with excellent contemporary Spanish paintings on its walls. The rooms all look out on the countryside; they are spacious and identically furnished with attractive furniture, either lacquered, white or in natural wood. Rooms 101, 102 and 103 are the largest. The Alameda is a particular favorite of *Madrileños* in quest of a pleasant weekend.

How to get there *(Map 13): 52km east of Segovia, 90km north of Madrid via N1. After 69km, take C604 to Rascafria, then to Alameda.*

Parador de Chinchón

28370 Chinchón (Madrid)
Avenida Generalísimo, 1
Tel. 91-894 08 36 - Fax 91-894 09 08
Sr Jose Rizos

Category ★★★★ **Rooms** 38 with air-conditioning, telephone, bath, WC, TV, minibar. **Price** Double 17,500Pts. **Meals** Breakfast 1,300Pts, served 8:00-11:00. **Restaurant** Service 1:30PM-4:00PM, 8:30PM-11:00PM; mealtime specials 3,500Pts, also à la carte. Castillian cooking. **Credit cards** All major. **Pets** Dogs not allowed. **Facilities** Swimming pool, garage (1,250Pts). **Nearby** Colmenar de Oreja - Nuevo Baztán - Alcalá de Henares - Aranjuez - Madrid. **Open** All year.

Chinchón has a main square *(Plaza Mayor)* which alone is worth a visit, and the parador is not far from it. A serene atmosphere pervades this ancient convent founded by the Augustinians in the 15th century. The main staircase ceiling has retained its original frescoes and the chapel of Santa Maria del Rosario is well-conserved. The simplicity of the decoration, where white and the *azulejos* reign, gives much elegance to the lounges, dining room and bedrooms. Choose for preference suite no. 8 with its terrace. The decor also lends charm to the green and flowered patios. Hidden at the bottom of the garden, where the kitchen garden used to be, is an attractive swimming pool and bar. Both inviting relaxation as do the little corner spots under the trees, bamboos, flowers and fountains.

How to get there *(Map 13): 42km southeast of Madrid via N3 to Puente de Azganda, then C300; close to the Plaza Mayor.*

Ritz Hotel

28014 Madrid
Plaza de la Lealtad, 5
Tel. 91-701 67 67 - Fax 91-701 67 76 - Sr Jordán
E-mail: reservas@ritz.es - Web: www.ritz.es

Category ★★★★★ **Rooms** 156 with air-conditioning, telephone, bath, WC, satellite TV, safe, minibar; elevator. **Price** Single 56,000Pts, double 64,000-78,000Pts, suite 125,000-225,000Pts. **Meals** Breakfast 3,900Pts, served 7:30-11:00. **Restaurant** Service 1:30PM-4:00PM, 8:30PM-12:00AM; mealtime specials 7,500Pts, also à la carte. Specialties: Cocido madrileño - Paella Ritz. **Credit cards** All major. **Pets** Dogs allowed (extra charge). **Facilities** Gymnasium, sauna. **Nearby** Palacio del Prado - Castillo de los duques de l'Infantado in Manzanares el Real - El Paular Monastery - Villages of the Sierra Pobre (Talamanca de Jarama, Torrelaguna, Patones, the Sierra Pobre de Torrelagana towards El Berrueco) - Aranjuez via el Tren de la Fresa, 40mn from May to Sept - Valle de los Caídos - Monastery of the Escorial; Puerta de Hierro golf course (18-Hole). **Open** All year.

Bearing the name that has become the symbol of "grand luxe" hotels, the Ritz of Madrid was built at the initiative of Alfonso XIII. Totally renovated, but more faithful than ever to its initial decoration, the result is striking: the sumptuous carpets from the Real Fábrica that cover all the floors are superb, and so precious that a full-time restorer is employed. The gardens and terrace have been reopened, and the menu and the cellars of the famous restaurant have been further improved. In the rooms one always finds those Ritz details: sumptuous bouquets of flowers, the initialed towels of the hotel (that make one doubt one's honesty !), and the baskets of exquisite fruits. Even if not staying at the Ritz, you can always have tea in the Royal *(Real)* Lounge, lunch in the garden, cocktails on the terrace, or dinner in the most beautiful restaurant in Madrid.

How to get there (Map 13): Facing the Prado Museum.

AC-Santo Mauro Hotel

28010 Madrid
Zurbano, 36
Tel. 91-319 69 00 - Fax 91-308 54 77

Category ★★★★★ **Rooms** 37 with air-conditioning, telephone, bath, WC, satellite TV, minibar, safe; elevator. **Price** Single 34,000Pts, double 44,000-52,000Pts, presidential suite with private chauffeur 125,000Pts. **Meals** Breakfast 2,500Pts, served 8:00-11:00. **Restaurant** Belagua, service 1:30PM-4:00PM, 8:30PM-11:00PM; à la carte 9,000Pts. **Credit cards** All major. **Pets** Dogs allowed. **Facilities** Covered swimming pool, sauna, gymnasium, garage. **Nearby** Palacio del Prado -Castillo de los duques de l'Infantado in Manzanares el Real - El Paular Monastery - Villages of the Sierra pobre (Talamanca de Jarama, Torrelaguna, Patones, the Sierra Pobre de Torrelagana towards El Berrueco) - Aranjuez via el Tren de la Fresa, 40mn from May to Sept - Valle de los Caídos - Monastery of the Escorial; Puerta de Hierro golf course (18-Hole). **Open** All year.

Intimate and luxurious, traditional and modern: these are the attributes that make the Santo Mauro one of the best hotels in Madrid. A palace which was designed by a French architect before it was turned into a hotel, it housed innumerable foreign embassies. Totally renovated, the Santo Mauro has retained all its classic qualities - period woodwork and stucco decoration - and yet enjoys a modern and subtle decor both elegant and refined. This comes notably from a sophisticated use of color and marvelously sober contemporary furniture in a skillfully designed interior which allows you to have you meals in the library, something we found quite unique. The rooms offer the five-star comfort and charm that is the hallmark of this hotel. Here, a spirit of creativity has happily embraced the tradition of a luxury hotel.

How to get there *(Map 13): Near the Paseo de la Castellana.*

Palace Hotel

28014 Madrid
Plaza de las Cortes, 7
Tel. 91-360 80 00 - Fax 91-360 81 00

Category ★★★★★ **Rooms** 354 and 46 suites with air-conditioning, telephone, bath, WC, satellite TV, safe, minibar; elevator - Wheelchair access. **Price** Single 56,000Pts, double 73,000Pts, suite 79,000-195,000Pts. **Meals** Breakfast 3,700Pts, served 7:15-11:00. **Restaurant** Service La Rotonda 1:00PM-4:00PM, La Cupola 8:00PM-12:00AM; mealtime specials, also à la carte. **Credit cards** All major. **Pets** Dogs allowed (except in restaurant, with extra charge). **Facilities** Hairdresser, beauty salon, garage. **Nearby** Palacio del Prado - Castillo de los duques de l'Infantado in Manzanares el Real - El Paular Monastery - Villages of the Sierra Pobre (Talamanca de Jarama, Torrelaguna, Patones, the Sierra Pobre de Torrelagana towards El Berrueco) - Aranjuez via el Tren de la Fresa, 40mn from May to Sept - Valle de los Caídos - Monastery of the Escorial; Puerta de Hierro golf course (18-Hole). **Open** All year.

Admirably well-situated, the Palace deploys its immense facade in the face of the square Canovas del Castillo between the Prado Museum and the Congress. King Alfonso XIII opened it in 1912. Prestigious, it has been selected by many personalities of the century from Mata Hari to Richard Nixon, among many others. Its majestic hallway leads to one of the most beautiful lounges, "*La Rotonda*", where a series of double neo-classical columns supports a magnificent cupola decorated with Art Nouveau tiles. A lamp with its palms of crystal hangs down from the ceiling to complete this superb 1900s decor. The bedrooms are perfect; a luxury of good taste makes every space into an exceptional location. This hotel is for those refined friends who do not flinch at prices!

How to get there (Map 13): Facing the Prado Museum.

Villa Real Hotel

28014 Madrid
Plaza de las Cortes, 10
Tel. 91-420 37 67 - Fax 91-420 25 47 - Sr Garcia
E-mail: info.derbyhotels.es - Web: www.derbyhotels.es

Category ★★★★★ **Rooms** 115 with air-conditioning, telephone, bath, WC, satellite TV, safe, minibar; elevator. **Price** Single 34,900Pts, double 41,600Pts, suite 75,000Pts. **Meals** Breakfast (buffet) 2,500Pts. **Restaurant** Service 1:30PM-3:30PM, 8:30PM-11:30PM; mealtime specials 6,000Pts, also à la carte. **Credit cards** All major. **Pets** Dogs allowed. **Facilities** Garage (1,600Pts). **Nearby** Palacio del Prado - Castillo de los duques de l'Infantado in Manzanares el Real - El Paular Monastery - Villages of the Sierra Pobre (Talamanca de Jarama, Torrelaguna, Patones, the Sierra Pobre de Torrelagana towards El Berrueco) - Aranjuez via el Tren de la Fresa, 40mn from May to Sept - Valle de los Caídos - Monastery of the Escorial; Puerta de Hierro golf course (18-Hole). **Open** All year.

In Madrid, one finds more "de luxe" hotels than those concerned with charm. With its 1900s decor, the Villa Real is well-situated facing the Prado Museum at the very heart of the cultural and financial quarter of the capital. Inside there is the atmosphere of a grand hotel: vast lounges luxuriously decorated and a cozy bar. The huge and classical rooms are very attractive with well-equipped bathrooms, still with that freshness so lacking in certain palace-type hotels. The service is attentive, the welcome friendly and without a trace of haughtiness or ostentation.

How to get there (Map 13): In the city center, facing the Prado Museum.

Hotel Wellington

28001 Madrid
Velásquez, 8
Tel. 91-575 44 00 - Fax 91-576 41 64 - Sr Lobo

E-mail: wellington@hotel-wellington.com
Web: www.hotel-wellington.com

Category ★★★★★ **Rooms** 275 and 25 suites with air-conditioning, telephone, bath, WC, satellite TV, safe, minibar; elevator. **Price** Single 29,750Pts (weekend)-20,500Pts, double 37,500Pts (weekend)-20,500Pts, suite 49,500-95,000Pts. **Meals** Breakfast 2,250Pts, served 7:00-11:00. **Restaurant** El Fogon, service 1:30PM-4:00PM, 9:30PM-10:30PM; à la carte 5,500-6,500Pts. International cooking. **Credit cards** All major. **Pets** Dogs not allowed. **Facilities** Swimming pool (in summer), garage (2,500Pts). **Nearby** Palacio del Prado - Castillo de los duques de l'Infantado in Manzanares el Real - El Paular Monastery - Villages of the Sierra Pobre (Talamanca de Jarama, Torrelaguna, Patones, the Sierra Pobre de Toreralagana towards El Berrueco) - Aranjuez via el Tren de la Fresa, 40mn from May to Sept - Valle de los Caídos - Monastery of the Escorial; Puerta de Hierro golf course (18-Hole). **Open** All year.

The Wellington is a luxurious hotel where a calm and cozy atmosphere reigns. The rooms are spacious and well-equipped, and have beautiful bathrooms in marble. Those with windows over the Via Velásquez are protected with double glazing to assure perfect quiet. Choose first those rooms overlooking the interior garden and swimming pool, or even better those on the top floor with their own small terraces. One will linger happily at the hotel bar with its English style: panelling, copper work and lamps make it a particularly warm corner. The rustic decor of the dining room is perhaps rather surprising in such surroundings: beams, white walls and hunting trophies, but it is nonetheless attractive.

How to get there *(Map 13): Near the Parque del Retiro.*

Hotel Reina Victoria

28012 Madrid
Plaza de Santa Ana, 14
Tel. 91-531 41 00 - Fax 91-522 03 07

Category ★★★★ **Rooms** 201 with air-conditioning, telephone, bath, WC, satellite TV, minibar; elevator. **Price** Double 21,000-26,250Pts, suite 60,000Pts. **Meals** Breakfast 1,800Pts, served 7:00-11:00. **Restaurant** El Ruedo, service 1:30PM-4:00PM, 9:30PM-10:30PM. Local specialties and bullmeat dishes. **Credit cards** All major. **Pets** Dogs not allowed. **Facilities** Garage. **Nearby** Palacio del Prado - Castillo de los duques de l'Infantado in Manzanares el Real - El Paular Monastery - Villages of the Sierra Pobre (Talamanca de Jarama, Torrelaguna, Patones, the Sierra Pobre de Torrelagana towards El Berrueco) - Aranjuez via el Tren de la Fresa, 40mn from May to Sept - Valle de los Caídos - Monastery of Escorial - Puerta de Hierro golf course (18-Hole). **Open** All year.

The hotel is located in a vast Art Deco building, nicely set in the center of Old Madrid, a short walk from the city's tourist sights. When the *corridas* begin, *aficionados* and members of the bullfighting fraternity gather at the *Bar Manolete*, named in honor of the maestro from Córdoba. The restaurant has a menu featuring bull-derived dishes that should not be missed. The ground floor lobby is always lively with business people rubbing elbows with tourists in a relaxed atmosphere. The comfort offered by the rooms is up to international hotel standards, and those facing the front are the sunniest. From the rooms on the upper floors, the view is quite simply breathtaking.

How to get there *(Map 13): Near the Plaza Mayor.*

La Residencia de El Viso

28002 Madrid
C/. Nervión, 8
Tel. 91-564 03 70 - Fax 91-564 19 65
Sra Maria Colmenero Herrero

Rooms 12 with air-conditioning, telephone, bath, satellite TV; elevator. **Price** Single 11,000-14,400Pts, double 18,000Pts. **Meals** Breakfast 750Pts, served 8:00-11:00. **Restaurant** A la carte around 3,500Pts. **Credit cards** All major. **Pets** Dogs not allowed. **Nearby** Palacio del Prado - Castillo de los duques de l'Infantado in Manzanares el Real - El Paular Monastery - Villages of the Sierra Pobre (Talamanca de Jarama, Torrelaguna, Patones, the Sierra Pobre de Torrelagana towards El Berrueco) - Aranjuez via el Tren de la Fresa, 40mn from May to Sept - Valle de los Caídos - Monastery of Escorial - Puerta de Hierro golf course (18-Hole). **Open** All year.

This is the hotel that Madrid, a city remarkably short of hotels of charm at reasonable prices, has long awaited. This is a house built in a 1930s style, nicely located on a quiet and shady street but still close to the center of the city. The lounge and bar are tempting, with a collection of armchairs dating from different periods and upholstered in varied and colorful prints. They open on a pretty interior tree-lined courtyard where breakfast and drinks are served in summer. The dining room is equally charming with green table linen and wicker chairs where appetizing regional dishes are served. The rooms, with a kind of country flavor, are small, but they have complete bathrooms. Those giving on the courtyard are to be preferred. This is a perfect place to stay that allies charm, calm and access to Madrid's city center.

How to get there (Map 13): Near the Plaza República Argentina.

Hotel Inglés

28014 Madrid
Echegaray, 8
Tel. 91-429 65 51 - Fax 91-420 24 23
Sr Antonio Marco

Category ★★★ **Rooms** 58 with telephone, bath or shower, WC, satellite TV; elevator. **Price** Single 8,500-9,900Pts, double 12,000-16,000Pts. **Meals** Breakfast 700Pts, served 7:30-11:00. **Restaurant** See pp. 316-318. **Credit cards** All major. **Pets** Dogs not allowed. **Facilities** Garage (1,300Pts). **Nearby** Palacio del Prado - Castillo de los duques de l'Infantado in Manzanares el Real - El Paular Monastery - Villages of the Sierra Pobre (Talamanca de Jarama, Torrelaguna, Patones, the Sierra Pobre de Torrelagana towards El Berrueco) - Aranjuez via el Tren de la Fresa, 40mn from May to Sept - Valle de los Caídos - Monastery of the Escorial; Puerta de Hierro golf course (18-Hole). **Open** All year.

In the heart of the city and only two paces from Old Madrid, the Calle Echegaray is a very lively street filled with small restaurants. It is here that the Hotel Inglés is to be found. All the bedrooms have been recently renovated and offer full amenities, although one rather regrets their somewhat clinic-like floors. The "British" aspect evoked by the name of the hotel is found in the discreetly lit lounge where deep leather armchairs await you. Another advantage of the hotel is the parking area, and when you know Madrid and its traffic, this is a huge plus factor. Finally, more than 100 years of age, the Hotel Inglés is professional and efficient. The prices are reasonable for Madrid, where charm is to be found especially in the palaces.

How to get there *(Map 13): Near the Puerta del Sol.*

Hotel Bótanico

28200 San Lorenzo de El Escorial (Madrid)
C/. Timoteo Padrós, 16
Tel. 91-890 78 79 - Fax 91-890 81 58 - Sr Jose Luis Muñano Sánchez
E-mail: botanico@itelco.es

Category ★★★ Rooms 17 and 3 suites with air-conditioning, telephone, bath, satellite TV, minibar; elevator. **Price** Single 11,300-14,900Pts, double 14,100-18,700Pts; extra bed 3,500Pts. **Meals** Breakfast 1,100Pts, served 8:00-11:00. **Restaurant** Service 1:30PM-4:00PM, 8:30PM-11:00PM; à la carte. Castillian cooking. **Credit cards** All major. **Pets** Dogs not allowed. **Facilities** Swimming pool, parking. **Nearby** Monastery of Escorial - Valle de los Caidos - Madrid. **Open** All year.

Visiting the Escorial Monastery, built in the reign of Felipe II, is virtually inevitable when visiting Madrid unless you have decided to stop in this village. A very pretty hotel awaits you here - the Botánico. It is surrounded by a large lawn, kept shady by pine and chestnut trees. Its two terraces, where breakfast and other meals are served, offer a fine view of the valley. The interior is warm and elegant with paneled walls and ceilings, parquet floors and soft lighting in a what is not unlike Anglo-Saxon style. The rooms are cozy with attractive antique furniture and bathrooms nicely lined with slate. We particularly like no. 35, nestled in the tower with a 360-degree view. A swimming pool is planned for this summer. In a word, a wonderful address.

How to get there (Map 12): 45km northwest of Madrid via N VI, exit El Escorial.

El Tiempo Perdido

28189 Patones de Arriba (Madrid)
Travesia del Ayuntamiento, 7
Tel. 91-843 21 52 - Fax 91-843 21 48 - Sr Fournier

Category ★★★★ **Rooms** 6 mini-suites and 2 suites (duplex) with air-conditioning, telephone, bath, WC, TV, video, minibar, safe. **Price** 1 pers. 20,000Pts, 2 pers. in mini-suite 25,000Pts, 2 pers. in suite 35,000Pts. **Meals** Breakfast 2,000Pts, served 8:00AM-12:00PM. **Restaurant** El Poleo, service from 2:00PM, 9:00PM; à la carte 4,500-5,000Pts. Specialties: Endivas caramelizadas - Cordero ala miel - Charlotte de frutas del bosco. **Credit cards** Amex, Visa, Eurocard, MasterCard. **Pets** Dogs allowed except in restaurant (2,000Pts). **Facilities** Garage (1,200Pts). **Nearby** Madrid - Castillo de Uceda **Open** From Fri noon to Mon noon, previous day and public holidays (Spanish) - closed Jul 30 - Sept 1; Christmas - Jan 3.

The owner of "El Tiempo Perdido," Pierre Fournier, both a decorator and an antique collector, has lived for many years in Spain. He has opened this attractive hotel in a particularly beautiful little Castillian village some fifty kilometers from Madrid. It is a typical valley house and close to the church. Its interior is a model of refinement with antique furniture, old engravings and Provence-style fabrics, skillfully displayed in all the larger rooms, all of which have an intimate lounge. As if this weren't enough, you may also enjoy croissants direct from the Hôtel du Palais in Biarritz. Just across the street are two excellent restaurants: *El Poleo*, a large and genuinely gastronomic restaurant, and its smaller version under the same management offering a large terrace and a superb panoramic view of the surrounding countryside. While "El Tiempo Perdido" may well translate literally into "Lost Time," a far better name would be "Happy Days".

How to get there *(Map 13): 50km of Madrid via N1, to Torrelaguna then follow the road to Patones de Arriba. Puting your car aside behind the church, the hotel is not very far away.*

Hotel Santa Maria del Paular

28741 Rascafria (Madrid)
Carret. de Cotos, km 26,5
Tel. 91-869 10 11/12 - Fax 91-869 10 06

Category ★★★★ **Rooms** 58 with air-conditioning, telephone, bath or shower, WC, satellite TV.
Price Single 15,900Pts, double 21,000Pts, suite 23,400Pts. **Meals** Breakfast 1,875Pts, served 8:00-
11:00, full board +9,000Pts (per pers., 3 days min.). **Restaurant** Service 1:30PM-4:00PM, 9:00PM-
11:30PM; mealtime specials 5,500Pts, also à la carte. Specialties: Judiones de la Granja con Matanza
- Cordero Lechal - Asado al Horno de leña - Cochinillo frito - Buñuelos al bon - Pastelería. **Credit
cards** All major. **Pets** Dogs not allowed. **Facilities** Heated swimming pool, tennis, bikes, billiards,
parking. **Nearby** Monastery del Paular - Skiing in Puerto de Navacerrada. **Open** All year.

At the foot of the Sierra de Guadarrama beside the River Lozoya, and
scarcely 85 kilometers from Madrid, we find ourselves at the very
picturesque site of Santa Maria del Paular. Even though classified as a
historical monument, this ancient monastery of the Carthusians dating from
1390 was long abandoned. It was only in 1948 that part of it became a parador.
In 1952 Benedictine monks moved into the monastery to give life back to this
beautiful ensemble. When you pass through the main archway, similar to a
triumphal arch, you come to the "Ave Maria" patio surrounded by a colonnade
supporting the red-brick building. Inside, the same sobriety and the same good
taste are to be found. In the back, a garden leads to the swimming pool and
tennis court.

How to get there *(Map 13): 85km north of Madrid via N1; at km 69 take C604.*

Donamaria'ko Benta

31750 Donamaria (Navarra)
Barrio de la Ventas, 4
Tel. 948-45 07 08 - Fax 948-45 07 08
E-mail: donamariako@jet.es

Rooms 5 with bath. **Price** Double 7,000-8,000Pts. **Meals** Breakfast 500Pts, served 9:00-11:00.
Restaurant Service 1:00PM-4:00PM, 8:30PM-11:00PM, closed Sun evening and Mon; à la carte
2,500-3,500Pts. Regional cooking. **Credit cards** Visa, Eurocard, MasterCard. **Pets** Dogs allowed
except in restaurant. **Facilities** Parking. **Nearby** Natural Park of Bértiz - Cuevas de Urdax -
Zugarramurdi - Pamplona. **Open** All year.

This region offer numerous excursions, one of the most interesting being to
the Bértiz Natural Park, an authentic botanical garden which has preserved
a hundred and twenty species of different trees and shrubs. The town of
Donamaria, a *señorial* village, has preserved numerous relics of the Middle
Ages. Of these, two old *caseríos* have recently been transformed: one into a
small hotel, the other into a restaurant some fifty meters away. The rooms are
comfortable and quiet, and the lounge has a very friendly atmosphere, warmed
by the fireplace that is used as soon as the weather turns cold. The restaurant
rapidly gained a good reputation for serving traditional cooking prepared with
taste and imagination. Close to the French border, this region is strongly rooted
in its traditions and superstitions. It has an original culture that the owners of
Donamaria'ko seek to perpetuate either by setting up small conferences or
simply by showing the places that keep those traditions alive.

How to get there *(Map 6): 56km northwest of Pamplona via N121 to Señorio
de Bértiz. Turn left towards Santesteban, then towards Donamaria; 60km from
Biarritz.*

Venta Udabe

01300 Udabe Basaburua (Navarra)
Tel. 948-50 31 05 - Fax 948-50 31 05
Javier Goñi and Laura Ganola

Rooms 8 with telephone, bath. **Price** Double 7,000-8,000Pts. **Meals** Breakfast Included, served 7:30-11:00. **Restaurant** Service 1:00PM-4:00PM, 8:30PM-11:00PM; mealtime specials 1,700Pts, also à la carte. Regional cooking. **Credit cards** Visa, Eurocard, MasterCard. **Pets** Dogs not allowed. **Facilities** Swimming pool, parking. **Nearby** Pamplona - Santiago de Compostella route. **Closed** Dec 20 - Jan 20, open weekends in low season.

The Venta Udabe is in an old postal relay station between Pamplona and San Sebastian, surrounded by pasture land and low hills in the lovely Ultzama Valley. It is a square-built house with balconies alive with flowers. It extends into a small fenced-off pasture overlooked by the mountains. This is truly a charming inn. The lounge and dining room are on the ground floor, and there you may taste excellent local specialties, particularly Udabe cheese. The rooms are a treat with comfortable eiderdown quilts on big rustic beds and regional furniture. Most have a view of the mountains. The owners have several horses that a guest can rent for long and enjoyable rides. This is a small, mountain address with both simplicity and charm, located in an absolutely magnificent setting.

How to get there *(Map 6): 30km northwest of Pamplona towards San Sebastian via the main highway or N130. Turn at Urritza towards Lizaso.*

Hotel Ayestaran

31870 Lekumberri (Navarra)
Calle Aralarso
Tel. 948-50 41 27 - Fax 948-50 41 27
Sr Ayestaran Oquinena

Category ★ **Rooms** 90 (54 with bath or shower); 15 with WC. **Price** Double with shower 5,300-6,400Pts, double with bath 6,300-8,400Pts. **Meals** Breakfast 600Pts, served 8:30-11:00; half board +2,250Pts, full board +3,500Pts (per pers.). **Restaurant** Service 1:30PM-3:30PM, 9:00PM-10:30PM; mealtime specials 1,650Pts, also à la carte. Specialties: Alcachofas al jamón - Meat dishes. **Credit cards** Visa, Eurocard, MasterCard. **Pets** Dogs not allowed. **Facilities** Swimming pool, tennis. **Nearby** Swimming pool, tennis. **Closed** Dec 20 - Jan 20.

As you leave the coast and enter the real Basque country, you come across the Hotel Ayestaran. It is lodged in two buildings, one a residence for summer and a second for winter, on either side of a rather noisy road which, in two years' time, will be diverted. In the meantime, the hotel does not lack for charm. It is all white with red shutters in the summer that change to green in the winter. Its first hundred years have just been celebrated. The hotel corridors are filled with Basque furniture dating from the beginning of the century. The bedrooms are simple and furnished with antique beds of local origin. Bathrooms have been renovated and all the rooms on the road are all double-glazed. The 100-year-old trees in the garden shade the swimming pool and tennis court. The winter hotel is more traditional with its typical dining room and open fireplace, its woodwork and furniture. The bathrooms have also been renovated. The welcome here is among the most friendly.

How to get there *(Map 6): 56km south of San Sebastián via A15 or N1 to Tolosa, then N240.*

Hospederia de Leyre

31410 Monasterio de Leyre (Navarra)
Tel. 948-88 41 00 - Fax 948-88 41 37 - Sr E. Cia
E-mail: info@monasterio-de-leyre.com
Web: www.monasterio-de-leyre.com

Category ★★ **Rooms** 32 with telephone, bath or shower, WC. **Price** Single 4,350-4,725Pts, double 7,625-9,240Pts. **Meals** Breakfast 775Pts, served 8:30-10:00; half board +2,325Pts, +3,100Pts (per pers.). **Restaurant** With air-conditioning. Service 1:00PM-3:30PM, 8:00PM-10:00PM; mealtime specials 1,550Pts, also a la carte. Regional cooking. **Credit cards** Amex, Visa, Eurocard, MasterCard. **Pets** Dogs not allowed. **Facilities** Parking. **Nearby** Monastery of Leyre - Pamplona. **Closed** Dec 9 - Mar 1st.

In the Sierra de Leyre at the end of a winding and steep road, this ancient monastery rises up in the midst of a site of great beauty. The panorama over the artificial lake of Yesa and its environment of small hills is splendid. Considered in the 11th century as the great spiritual center of Navarre and then abandoned in the 19th century, the monastery is now one of the most important historical monuments of the region. The hotel has been installed in the 17th- and 18th-century parts of the building which have been renovated. 30 rooms are available all simply furnished but comfortable. In the lounges you will appreciate the quiet that characterizes this establishment full of charm.

How to get there *(Map 6): 51km southeast of Pamplona via N240 to Yesa, then take small road to the left.*

Hotel Europa

31001 Pamplona (Navarra)
Espoz y Mina, 11
Tel. 948-22 18 00 - Fax 948-22 92 35 - Familia Idoate
E-mail: heuropa@cmn.navarra.net - Web: webs.navarra.net/heuropa

Category ★★★ **Rooms** 25 with air-conditioning, telephone, bath, WC, TV, minibar; elevator. **Price** Double 10,500-15,000Pts. Meals Breakfast 1,000Pts, served 7:30-11:00; full board +6,250Pts (per pers.). **Restaurant** Service 1:00PM-3:30PM, 9:00PM-11:00PM; closed Sun; à la carte 4,300-6,200Pts. Specialties: Mero al horno con vinegreta de ajetes y verduras crujientes - Pechuga de pichon asada con sus muslitos guisados en salsa tradicional - Canutillos de higo con queso, nueces y helado de sagarmine. **Credit cards** All major. **Pets** Dogs not allowed. **Nearby** In Pamplona: Cathedral, Museum of Navarra - Feria (around Jul 6 - 14) - Santiago de Compostella route in Navarra (Roncesvalles, Pamplona, Obanos, Puente la reina, Estella, Los Arcos, Torres del Río) - Ulzama golf course (18-Hole), Gorraiz golf course (18-Hole). **Open** All year.

Pamplona is famous for its festivals and notably its *Encierro*, when bulls are let loose in the streets of the town before the bullfights in the arenas on the same afternoon. Gourmet *aficionados* know the Europa above all for its gastronomic restaurant preparing excellent cuisine with produce fresh from the market. Also for its wine cellar. This fully renovated hotel also makes you appreciate the know-how of the family team. A classical but also modern decor which favors above all comfort and service : everything is impeccable, well-thought-out, discreet, stylish - and also a little bit formal, as so often with the atmosphere of any well-known restaurant. But one would be wrong to complain about too much perfection !

How to get there *(Map 6): 80km south from San Sebastián.*

Mesón del Peregrino

31100 Puente La Reina (Navarra)
Carretera de Pamplona, 11
Tel. 948-34 00 75 - Fax 948-34 11 90
Sr Angel Cambero - Sra Nina Sedano

Category ★★ **Rooms** 13 and 1 suite with air-conditioning, telephone, bath, WC, TV. **Price** Single 9,000Pts, double 12,000-15,000Pts, suite 25,000Pts. **Meals** Breakfast 1,500Pts, served 8:00-10:00. **Restaurant** Service 1:30PM-3:30PM, 8:30PM-11:00PM; mealtime specials 3,500Pts, also à la carte. **Credit cards** Visa, Eurocard, MasterCard. **Pets** Dogs allowed. **Facilities** Swimming pool, parking. **Nearby** In Pamplona: Cathedral, Museum of Navarra - Feria (aroud Jul 6 - 14) - Santiago de Compostella route in Navarra (Roncesvalles, Pamplona, Obanos, Puenta la Reina, Estella, Los Arcos, Torres del Río) - Ulzama golf course (18-Hole), Gorraiz golf course (18-Hole). **Closed** Christmas and New Year.

If you are rather fearful of the too lively nights of the Saint Firmin festival in Pamplona, then take refuge some twenty kilometers away at Puente La Reina, a strategic staging post on the road to Santiago de Compostela. At the Meson del Peregrino everything is done to attract you, and all is conceived to satisfy your well-being: reception, comfort, decor and gastronomy should create that harmony which will satisfy all your senses. It is true that the old stone house is pretty, the large dining room opening onto the garden is inviting and warm, and the cuisine is appetizing. There is also a restful garden with its swimming pool. Nina and Angelo practice the art of entertaining their guest admirably. This is a very attractive address to seek out.

How to get there (Map 6): 24km southwest from Pamplona.

Parador Principe de Viana

31390 Olite (Navarra)
Plaza de los Teobaldos, 2
Tel. 948-74 00 00 - Fax 948-74 02 01
Sr Bertolin Blasco

Category ★★★ **Rooms** 43 with air-conditioning, telephone, bath, WC, TV, minibar; elevator. **Price** Double 14,500-16,500Pts. **Meals** Breakfast 1,300Pts, served 8:00-10:30. **Restaurant** Service 1:00PM-4:00PM, 8:30PM-11:00PM; mealtime specials 3,500Pts, also à la carte. Regional cooking. **Credit cards** All major. **Pets** Dogs not allowed. **Nearby** In Olite: Castle, Church of Santa Maria la Real, Church of San Pedro - Monastery of Oliva. **Open** All year.

Installed in the residential part of the very beautiful chateau of the Kings of Navarre, this parador opens onto a small, quiet and sunny square planted with trees. The decor preserves the medieval character of the building and gives it all its charm. In addition, thanks to the stained glass windows, a soft and warm light gives the house an atmosphere of calm and meditation. The rooms have been installed in a recently rebuilt part of the building. They are sober and comfortable, but unfortunately lack the charm of the lounges.

How to get there (Map 6): 43km south of Pamplona via N120, or via A15.

Irigoienea ^{TR}

31711 Urdazubi/Urdax (Navarra)
Barrio Iribere
Tel. 948-59 92 67 - Fax 948-59 92 43 - Sr Jose Miguel Pardo
E-mail: horigoienea@jet.es

Rooms 12 with telephone, bath or shower, TV. **Price** Double 6,000-8,000Pts. **Meals** Breakfast 600Pts, served 7:30-11:00. No restaurant but snacks available on request. **Credit cards** Visa, Eurocard, MasterCard. **Pets** Dogs not allowed. **Facilities** Video in the sitting room. **Nearby** Beaches of Saint-Jean-de-Luz (25 min.) - Elizondo and Valley of Baztan. **Closed** Christmas.

Two kilometers from the borders of France and Spain sits the small village of Urdax, surrounded by a magnificent region of forest and pasture land where growing interest in "greenery tourism" explains why a number of charming houses, the Irigoiena among them, have opened their doors to guests. This is a typical three-story *caserón* with a white exterior and green shutters and distinguishable from its neighbors by the stonework visible at the corners of each of its façades. A large wooden terrace overlooks the garden, which is awaiting the arrival of a swimming pool. The decoration in the rooms is sober but the atmosphere is warm; the floors are in wood, the beds antique, and flowers abound, especially hydrangea. In addition, classical music is available on an interior sound system. The most attractive rooms give on the garden and the most charming is no. 301, nestled under the roof. Regional specialties are on sale and small snacks are always available. From wherever you look, the view of the valley is magnificent. You mustn't miss visiting the fourteen villages in the Baztan Valley where the rich traditions of Navarra live on.

How to get there (Map 6): 80km north of Pamplona (Pamplona - France) on N121B via Dantxarinea. 25km from Saint-Jean-de-Luz (France).

Parador de Argómaniz

01192 Argómaniz-Vitoria (Alava)
Carret. N 1
Tel. 945-29 32 00 - Fax 945-29 32 87
Sr Jorge Luis Rodriguez Rasco

Category ★★★ **Rooms** 54 with telephone, bath, WC, satellite TV, minibar; elevator. **Price** Double 15,000Pts. **Meals** Breakfast 1,300Pts, served 8:00-11:00. **Restaurant** Service 1:00PM-4:00PM, 8:30PM-11:00PM; mealtime specials 3,500Pts, also à la carte. **Credit cards** All major. **Pets** Dogs not allowed. **Facilities** Parking. **Nearby** In Vitoria: Church of Santa Maria and museum of Vitoria - Salinas de Añana - Sanctuary of Estibaliz. **Open** All year.

Before going into battle against the Spanish and the British at Vitoria, the Emperor Napoleon stayed in this 17th-century building. What was once a promenade with arcades has been transformed into a reception hall, and you can still admire the original columns. Numerous lounges contribute to the hotel's atmosphere of relaxation, allowing you to enjoy the quiet of the building. On the top floor under the eaves, the woodwork has been left uncovered, and it is here that the dining room may be found. The rooms are in the two modern wings and soberly decorated. Comfortable and very bright, they also have small corner lounges. From the windows, the hill and monastery of Estibaliz are visible along with Vitoria, the capital of the province.

How to get there *(Map 5): 12km east of Vitoria on N1.*

Hotel Castillo El Collado

01300 Laguardia (Alava)
Paseo El Collado, 1
Tel. 941-12 12 00 - Fax 941-60 08 78 - Sr Javier Acillona

Rooms 8 with air-conditioning, telephone, bath, satellite TV, minibar. **Price** Single 14,000Pts, double 15,000-17,000Pts, suite 22,000Pts. **Meals** Breakfast 1,200Pts, served 8:00-10:00; half board 11,500Pts (per pers., 4 days min.). **Restaurant** Service 1:00PM-4:00PM, 8:30PM-11:00PM; à la carte 3,500-4,500Pts. Specialties: Cordelito - Merluza à la vasca - Callos. **Credit cards** All major. **Pets** Small dogs allowed. **Nearby** In Laguardia: Paroquia de Santa Maria de los Reyes - Logroño - Agoncillo - Torrecilla de los Cameros - Villanueva de Cameros - Navarrete - Fuenmayor. **Closed** Christmas and Jan 15 - Feb 20.

The charm of Laguardia is plainly responsible for the appearance of excellent hotels, and the Castillo El Collado is surely the most attractive among them. Clearly passion, talent and imagination went into turning a small, 19th-century castle into an attractive hotel where various styles mingle successfully. It virtually leans against the town's ramparts, and it has been skillfully renovated. The reception desk and paneled dining room with wooden beams and decorated ceiling create a warm and cozy atmosphere. The food served here is refined. There are four rooms on the ground floor with interesting views. The most beautiful and luxurious ones, however, are upstairs; they include the *Doña Blanca* with superb shades of white and yellow, the *Sancho Abarca* with natural stone and a baroque-style bed, as well as the *Amor y Locura,* which is in the tower. In addition to being very sunny, it offers a view of both the ramparts and the valley. We prefer the one known as *Fabula* with its magnificent view and lovely bathroom done in South American *azulejos.* Not to be neglected is the charming *bodega* located in what was once the cellar.

How to get there *(Map 5): 17km northwest of Logroño.*

Posada Mayor de Migueloa

01300 Laguardia (Alava)
Mayor de Migueloa, 20
Tel. 941-12 11 75 - Fax 941-12 10 22
Sr Meri G. Huergo

Rooms 7 with telephone, bath, WC, satellite TV, minibar. **Price** Double 14,000Pts. **Meals** Breakfast 950Pts, served 8:00-10:00. **Restaurant** Service 1:00PM-4:00PM, 8:30PM-11:00PM; à la carte 4,000-6,000Pts. Gastronomic cooking. **Credit cards** All major. **Pets** Dogs not allowed. **Nearby** In Laguardia: Paroquia de Santa Maria de los Reyes - Logroño - Agoncillo - Torrecilla de los Cameros - Villanueva de Cameros - Navarrete - Fuenmayor. **Closed** Mid Dec - mid Jan.

Laguardia sits on a hill overlooking the peninsula separating the Río Ebro and the Cantabrian mountains. It was built in the 10th century by the King of Navarra to serve as a rampart against invaders. This explains its name. A jumble of small, time-worn streets converge in front of what was once the Palacio de la Viena and is now the Posada Mayor de Migueloa. After going through a huge door of solid wood, you go up one flight to the dining room. It should be said that this *posada* is best known and well-frequented for its gastronomic restaurant. Its charm comes from the low ceilings and the shortage of space between its limited number of tables. For this reason it is absolutely essential that you reserve if you plan to eat here. The rooms, with superb stone floors and huge comfortable beds, enjoy a special kind of atmosphere. You may also dine in the *bodega* located in what was once the cellar, accessible from the ground floor by an attractive vaulted gallery. The food is of the highest quality.

How to get there *(Map 5): 17km northwest of Logroño.*

Hotel Lopez de Haro

48009 Bilbao
Obispo Orueta, 2 and 4
Tel. 94-423 55 00 - Fax 94-423 45 00 - Sr Luís José Guillamón
E-mail: lh@hoellopezdeharo.com

Category ★★★★★ **Rooms** 53 with air-conditioning, telephone, bath, WC, satellite TV, minibar; elevator. **Price** Single 22,250Pts, double 29,500Pts, suite 36,125-43,125Pts. **Meals** Breakfast (buffet) 1,650Pts, served 7:00-11:00. **Restaurant** Club Nautico, service 1:00PM-3:30PM, 8:00PM-11:30PM; closed Sat lunch, Sun and National Holidays; buffet (lunch) 3,500-4,000Pts, mealtime specials 5,300-6,300Pts, also à la carte. **Credit cards** All major. **Pets** Small dogs allowed. **Facilities** Garage (2,100Pts). **Nearby** In Bilbao: Guggenheim Museum and Fine Arts Museum - Nuestra Señora de Begoña - Campo de la Bilbaina golf course and Neguri golf course (18-Hole). **Open** All year.

This superb hotel occupies the former headquarters of the republican newspaper, *El Liberal*, but behind the very classical and almost austere facade, a real jewel is hidden. The reception hall is particularly attractive with marble alongside green ivy, which makes for a remarkable effect. The caisson ceilings of the restaurant, the dainty tables with their pink linen and lamps, the elevator with its sparkling brass or the very English bar with its soft club armchairs– all the details are carefully thought-out. Yet however luxurious it may be, the hotel still keeps its warm character. In the bedrooms the walls have been left bare of any decoration, and the effect is very successful; very comfortable, they have very beautiful bathrooms. In the kitchens a French chef is in charge, and on the tables one finds Limoges porcelain and Bohemian crystal glassware. The welcome is always attentive and stylish, to crown the overall effect. An excellent base from which to visit the magnificent new Guggenheim Museum designed by the very talented Frank Gehry.

How to get there (Map 5): In the town center.

Mendi Goikoa

48291 Axpe (Bizkaia)
Barrio San Juan, 33
Tel. 94-682 08 33 - Fax 94-682 11 36

Rooms 12 with telephone, bath or shower, WC. **Price** Single 8,925Pts, double 13,125Pts. **Meals** Breakfast 900Pts, served 7:00-11:00. **Restaurant** Service 1:00PM-3:30PM, 8:30PM-10:30PM, closed Sun evening and Mon; mealtime specials 2,500Pts, also à la carte 5,000-6,000Pts. Basque cooking. **Credit cards** All major. **Pets** Dogs not allowed. **Facilities** Parking. **Nearby** In Bilbao: Guggenheim Museum and Fine Arts Museum - Durango - Abadiano - Elorrio. **Closed** Dec 22 - Jan 8.

You leave Bilbao on the coastal highway, and reaching Durango, you head inland for the green pastures of the Atxondo Valley. The village of Axpe is typical of this region, and it is in two former sheep-folds dating from the 18th century that Iñaki has his restaurant along with a few rooms. Here, a truly rural atmosphere reigns with thick interior walls of stone and very rustic floors. The rooms have solid wooden furniture, and there are attractive engravings of mountain plants and flowers. Each is spacious with a fine view, our favorites being Rooms 4, 7 and 11. The dining room overlooking the valley is rarely empty, and it offers excellent regional food. A truly charming hotel, one that is well worth leaving the beaten path to enjoy if, for example, you are going to Bilbao to visit the Guggenheim Museum.

How to get there *(Map 5): 39km east of Bilbao via E70, exit Durango towards El Orrio; then turn right on the road towards Atxondo, Axpe and Mendi Goïkoa.*

Hotel El Puerto

48360 Mundaka (Biskaia)
Portu Kalea, 1
Tel. 946-87 67 25 - Fax 946-87 67 26 - Sr Jaon Ercilia

Rooms 11 with telephone, bath, WC, TV, satellite TV, minibar; elevator. **Price** Single 6,500-8,500Pts, double 8,500-10,500Pts. **Meals** Breakfast (buffet) 900Pts, served 8:00-10:00. **Restaurant** See p. 319. **Credit cards** All major. **Pets** Dogs allowed. **Facility** Garage (600Pts). **Nearby** In Bilbao: Guggenheim Museum and Fine Arts Museum - Nuestra Señora de Begoña - Campo de la Bilbaina golf course and Neguri golf course (18-Hole). **Open** All year.

Mundaka is one of the typical little seaports spread out along the Basque Coast. Only thirty minutes from Bilbao, the El Puerto is known to surfers from the world over. It should be no surprise, therefore, that in the summertime, its clientele is young and very much into sports. The hotel is part of a traditional old house on the port with a delightful little garden of plane-trees. The interior is tasteful and well-kept-up, and the rooms are altogether classical; the baths and showers are all excellent. It should be noted that the stairs leading to the rooms on the third floor are somewhat steep. The best rooms overlook the square. In addition, the hotel has a shady terrace where you can have lunch or a quiet drink, and enjoy the life of the village from a very convenient and sheltered hide-away. This is an excellent hotel.

How to get there (Map 5): On the coast, 33km north of Bilbao, towards Bermeo.

Hotel Obispo

20280 Fuenterrabia - Hondarribia (Guipúzcoa)
Plaza del Obispo
Tel. 943-64 54 00 - Fax 943-64 23 86 - Sr Victor
Web: www.hotelobispo.com

Category ★★★ **Rooms** 17 with telephone, bath, WC, TV, minibar; 1 for disabled persons. **Price** Single 10,000-13,900Pts, double 12,000-16,900Pts, suite 14,000-21,000Pts. **Meals** Breakfast 1,200Pts, served 8:00-11:00. **Restaurant** See p. 319. **Credit cards** Amex, Visa, Eurocard, MasterCard. **Pets** Dogs allowed on request. **Nearby** San Sebastián; San Sebastián and Jaizkibel golf courses (18-Hole). **Closed** Christmas.

This new hotel is in one of the beautiful Renaissance houses that resisted the siege by the Prince de Condé in 1638. Indeed, Fuentarrabia does not lack for history and qualities. This charming town, only some twenty kilometers from San Sebastián, no doubt takes advantage of the proximity of the Basque coast to attract a clientele who prefer to get away from the tourist crowd in the summer months. Inside the hotel the austerity of the stone and wood, traditionally used in the regional architecture, has been well exploited. The decoration creates a warm and even snug atmosphere; everywhere the pale wood furniture, the flowery fabrics, parquet floors and large cord carpets form a rustic environment in good taste. The amenities have not been forgotten, while the welcome and service are professional.

***How to get there** (Map 6): 18km southwest of Saint-Jean-de-Luz.*

Hotel Pampinot

20280 Fuenterrabia - Hondarribia (Guipúzcoa)
Calle Mayor, 5
Tel. 943-64 06 00 - Fax 943-64 51 28 - Sra Alvarez
E-mail: informacion@hotelpampinot.com - Web: www.hotelpampinot.com

Category ★★★ **Rooms** 8 with telephone, bath, WC, TV. **Price** Double 13,000-16,000Pts, suite 16,000-19,000Pts. **Meals** Breakfast 1,200Pts, served 8:00-11:00. **Restaurant** See p. 319. **Credit cards** All major. **Pets** Dogs allowed. **Nearby** San Sebastián; San Sebastián and Jaizkibel golf courses (18-Hole). **Open** All year.

This was a private home during the 18th century in the heart of the very pretty town of Hondarribia. The lobby, with its walls of bare stone, displays carefully chosen antiques. You will find a staircase with attractive columns leading to the rooms upstairs. Decorated more simply but all personalized with taste, the rooms are comfortable and offer all the amenities. A quiet hotel offering a friendly welcome, where the absence of a restaurant adds to the peaceful impression.

How to get there (Map 6): 18km southwest of Saint-Jean-de-Luz.

Hotel María Cristina

20004 San Sebastián-Donostia (Guipúzcoa)
Calle Oquendo, 1
Tel. 943-42 49 00 - Fax 943-42 39 14
E-mail: hmc@sheratom.com - Web: www.sheraton.com

Category ★★★★★ **Rooms** 136 with air-conditioning, telephone, bath, WC, satellite TV, minibar; elevator. **Price** Single 23,900-45,000Pts, double 34,700-74,500Pts, suite 56,000-391,700Pts. **Meals** Breakfast 2,900Pts, served 7:00-11:00. **Restaurant** Service 1:30PM-3:30PM, 9:00PM-11:30PM; à la carte 6,700Pts. Regional and international cooking. **Credit cards** All major. **Pets** Small dogs not allowed. **Nearby** Bilbao: Guggenheim Museum - Visit to cider cellars in winter - Monte Ulia - Monte Urgull - Monte Igueldo; San Sebastián and Jaizkibel golf courses (18-Hole). **Open** All year.

This hotel evokes all the charms of the *Belle Epoque*, but it has been entirely renovated to satisfy a wealthy and refined clientele who appreciate luxury and comfort. There is a tribute paid to tradition in the pseudo-Louis XV and Empire decors of the lounges and bedrooms. Contemporary efficiency is present elsewhere, as can be seen in the quality of amenities in the bathrooms and the immense kitchens. Its situation in the heart of the city is not the least of its advantages. Most of the rooms have their own small balconies overlooking the Urumea River, and offer a fine view of the Victoria Eugénia Theater that hosts the International Cinema Festival each September. Beaches and casinos abound, and there are pleasant side trips to be made in the Basque countryside. All of this makes San Sebastián a capital of the region's tourism. Visitors attending conferences will be only a few short steps away from the Kursaal.

How to get there (Map 5): In the city center.

Hotel Mercure Monte Igueldo

20008 San Sebastián-Donostia (Guipúzcoa)
Paseo del Faro, 134
Tel. 943-21 02 11 - Fax 943-21 50 28 - Sra Pascual
Web: www.la-concha.com/mercure

Category ★★★★ **Rooms** 125 with telephone, bath, WC, satellite TV; elevator. **Price** Single 13,600-14,800Pts, double 17,000-18,500Pts; extra bed 5,500-6,000Pts. **Meals** Breakfast (buffet) 1,200Pts, served 7:30-11:00. **Restaurant** With air-conditioning, service 1:00PM-3:00PM, 8:30PM-11:00PM; mealtime specials 2,400Pts. Specialties: fish. **Credit cards** All major. **Pets** Dogs allowed (+3,000Pts). **Facilities** Swimming pool, parking. **Nearby** Monte Ulia - Monte Urgull - Monte Igueldo; San Sebastián and Jaizkibel golf courses (18-Hole). **Open** All year.

Built in 1967 on the top of a hill overlooking San Sebastián, this hotel is above all appreciated for its exceptional location as its lounge and dining room have huge bay windows with splendid views of both the city and the sea. Some of the rooms are quite ordinary, but nearly all of them have balconies, and those on the corners are sunnier. They offer a panoramic view of San Sebastián with, in the background, the low peaks of the Pyrenees and, on a clear day, Biarritz in the distance. It is all superb! On the large roof-terrace is a beautiful swimming pool and a self-service restaurant, much appreciated in summer. True, there is a small amusement park close by, but it closes down at sunset.

How to get there *(Map 5): 5km west of San Sebastián, towards Monte Igueldo; a funicular railway ascends from the "Ondarreta" beach to the amusement park.*

Hotel de Londres y de Inglaterra

20007 San Sebastián-Donostia (Guipúzcoa)
Zubieta, 2
Tel. 943-42 69 89 - Fax 943-42-00 31
Sr Uriarte

Category ★★★★ **Rooms** 133 with air-conditioning, telephone, bath, WC, satellite TV, safe, minibar; elevator. **Price** Single 14,900-17,400Pts, double 18,600-21,600Pts, double with sitting room 23,000-26,000Pts; extra bed 3,000Pts. **Meals** Breakfast (buffet) 1,400Pts, served 7:00-11:00; half board +3,450 Pts, full board +8,050Pts (per pers.). **Restaurant** Service 1:00PM-3:30PM, 8:45PM-11:15PM; mealtime specials 1,975Pts, also à la carte. Basque cooking. **Credit cards** All major. **Pets** Dogs not allowed. **Nearby** Monte Ulia - Monte Urgull - Monte Igueldo; San Sebastián and Jaizkibel golf courses (18-Hole). **Open** All year.

The Hotel de Londres y de Inglaterra enjoyed a glorious period when the Spanish royal family used to come to San Sebastián for the summer months. It overlooks the La Concha beach which was then very much in fashion. If fashion now appears to have have passed it by, the hotel has lost nothing of its splendor, and there is still something not unlike a show of pride in this historical edifice. The service cannot take too great care of its guests and the bedrooms are those of the classical grand hotel. Prices vary depending on whether your room overlooks the square or the ocean. Small boats are on hire from the hotel to cross to the small island of Santa Clara, always a pleasant way to spend an afternoon.

How to get there (Map 5): In the city center.

Hotel La Galeria

20008 San Sebastián-Donostia (Guipúzcoa)
Calle Infante Cristina, 1-3
Tel. 943-21 60 77 - Fax 943-21 12 98 - Sr Jose Maria Etxaniz
E-mail: hotelgaleria@facilnet.es

Rooms 23 with telephone, bath, satellite TV, minibar; elevator. **Price** Single 7,900-12,900Pts, double 11,900-15,900Pts. **Meals** Breakfast included, served 8:00-11:30. **Restaurant** See p. 319. **Credit cards** All major. **Pets** Dogs not allowed. **Nearby** Monte Ulia - Monte Urgull - Monte Igueldo - San Sebastián and Jaizkibel golf courses, 18-hole. **Open** All year.

Well away from the city center and very close to the Ondarreta Beach, this hotel is in a 19th-century Neo-Classic building. The residential neighborhood surrounding it is delightfully calm, offering a welcome summertime haven. The rooms cannot be called large, but all of them are comfortable with sober decoration. The solid-color fabrics are enlivened by painted moldings, and almost all have attractive wooden floors. Your best choice would be among those on the upper floors with a view of La Concha Bay. The lobby and its surroundings are modern and elegant. In addition you are very nicely welcomed. A pleasant and chic address in an interesting city.

How to get there *(Map 5): Near the Ondarreta beach.*

Hotel Jatetxen Urrutitxo

20400 Tolosa (Guipúzcoa)
Kondero Aldapa, 7
Tel. 943-67 38 22 - Fax 943-67 34 28
Sr Blanco Gordo

Category ★ **Rooms** 10 with telephone, shower, WC, TV. **Price** Single 5,500-6,500Pts, double 8,000-8,500Pts. **Meals** Breakfast 675Pts served 8:00-10:00. **Restaurant** Service 1:00PM-2:30PM, 8:30PM-10:30PM, closed Sun; à la carte 2,500-4,000Pts. Regional and international cooking. **Credit cards** All major. **Pets** Dogs allowed except in restaurant. **Facilities** Parking. **Nearby** Monte Ulia - Monte Urgull - Monte Igueldo; San Sebastián and Jaizkibel golf courses (18-Hole). **Closed** Dec 22 - Jan 10.

An all-white-and-red house, completely Basque in the midst of the country: such is the Hotel Jatetxen Urrutitxo. The house was built in 1920 and restructured into a hotel in 1987. Both decoration and atmosphere have a lot of charm, with a small touch of French style. The bedrooms lack any great embellishments but are all in good taste. The bathrooms lack no amenities. The restaurant is also good and the welcome friendly. This is a good place to discover in a part of the Basque country that should be explored.

How to get there (Map 5): 27km south of San Sebastián via N1.

Andorra Park Hotel

Andorra la Vieja (Principality of Andorra)
Les Canals
Tel. 376-82 09 79 - Fax 376-82 09 83 - Sr Antoni Cruz
E-mail: hotels@hotansa.com - Web: www.hotansa.com

Category ★★★★ **Rooms** 40 with telephone, bath, WC, satellite TV, minibar; elevator. **Price** Single 11,400-13,225Pts, double 15,600-17,650Pts. **Meals** Breakfast (buffet) 1,700-1,800Pts, served 8:00-11:30; half board +23,700-26,150Pts (3 days min.). **Restaurant** Service 1:30PM-3:30PM, 9:00PM-10:30PM; à la carte. **Credit cards** All major. **Pets** Dogs not allowed. **Facilities** Swimming pool, tennis, golf practice. **Nearby** Skiing - Walking. **Open** All year.

The Andorra Park Hotel is a real oasis in this city suburb recently converted into a vast commercial center. The hotel is excellent for a short visit if you are on the way to Barcelona, or if you want to ski in the small resorts of the Principality. The result of an attractive restoration, three types of rooms are available, and prices vary as to whether they have terraces or views over the valley. The decor is in the classical style of a grand hotel, but modern and luxurious. The park surrounding the hotel is magnificent: carefully mown lawns, an admirable swimming pool carved out of the rock itself, the mountains as a back-drop, tennis, practice range, etc. Everything is done so that you get to know the "outdoorsy" side of this town. There is also the restaurant opening wide and directly onto the long terrace and garden. Those who are unconditionals of modern consumerism can also be reassured - the hotel could not resist having its own direct access to the "Pyrenees" department store!

How to get there (Map 8): 220km of Barcelona.

Hostal San Pere

El Tarter/Soldeu (Principality of Andorra)
Prat dels Nogués
Tel. 376-85 10 87- Fax 376-85 10 87
E-mail: hstpere@andornet.ad - Web: www.hstpere.andornet.ad

Rooms 6 with telephone, bath, WC. **Price** Double 10,000-15,000Pts. **Meals** Breakfast included, served 8:00-10:00. **Restaurant** Service 1:00PM-4:00PM, 8:30PM-11:00PM; closed Sun night and Mon except in summer; à la carte 5,000Pts. Specialties: Meat dishes. **Credit cards** All major. **Pets** Dogs allowed except in restaurant. **Facilities** Parking. **Nearby** Skiing - Walking. **Closed** May 3 - 31.

Half way between the French frontier at Pas de la Casa and Andorra la Vieja, the Hostal de San Pere is a genuine mountain establishment, magnificently sited at the foot of the Tarter ski runs. Here one can enjoy peace and quiet with a view of the summits. The house has been well restored and provides many small corners for sitting undisturbed by the open fires, or even at the bar to enjoy the view over so much nature. Very rustic and very warm, the restaurant lets you discover the specialties of Andorra, and more particularly its grilled meats. The rooms are in the same style: with beams, timbered, some with sloping ceilings - each is different and comfortable. This is a charming and welcoming inn.

How to get there *(Map 8): 220km of Barcelona.*

Xalet Ritz Hotel

Sispony-La Massana (Principality of Andorra)
Prat dels Nogués
Tel. 376-83 78 77- Fax 376-83 77 20
Sr Joan Fernández

Rooms 50 with telephone, bath, WC, TV; elevator. **Price** Single 8,500-13,800Pts, double 12,000-19,600Pts. **Meals** Breakfast included, served 8:00-11:00; half board 8,500-12,300Pts (per pers.). **Restaurant** Service 1:00PM-3:30PM, 8:00PM-10:30PM; mealtime specials 3,000Pts. **Credit cards** All major. **Pets** Dogs allowed except in restaurant. **Facilities** Swimming pool, paddle-pool, garage, parking. **Nearby** Skiing - Walking - Seu d'Urgell. **Open** All year.

Here is an opportunity to leave the hustle and bustle of the Andorran capital and discover the snow-topped peaks of the Pyrenees along with forests and paths winding their way among picturesque streams. The Xalet Ritz, located at the head of the Valerá Valley, is an ideal spot for those who enjoy mountainous surroundings. The hotel is of stone construction typical of the region, and offers numerous forms of relaxation along more or less athletic lines. You can use it as a base camp for mountain hiking or, in a mere quarter of an hour, go on a ski trail, sacrificing momentarily the swimming pool and the hotel's attractive garden. The comfort and decor found in the rooms suggest the best in Alpine hotels. A fine choice at very reasonable prices.

How to get there (Map 8): 220km of Barcelona.

El Elefante

03730 Jávea (Alicante)
Cami Cabanes - Partida Cap Sades, 19
Tel. 96-646 00 09 - Fax 96-646 00 09
Sra Frith

Category ★★ **Rooms** 5 with bath. **Price** Double 7,000Pts, suite 9,000Pts. **Meals** Breakfast included, served 8:30-10:30. **Restaurant** Service 7:00PM-11:00PM; mealtime specials 1,995Pts, also à la carte. International cooking. **Credit cards** Visa, Eurocard, MasterCard. **Pets** Dogs not allowed. **Facilities** Parking. **Nearby** Cabo de San Antonio - Cabo de la Nao - Costa de Azahar to Valencia - Tosalet golf course (9-Hole). **Open** All year.

After spending fifteen years in the Middle East, John and Nadia Frith bought this house, which had had the privilege of receiving Alfonso XIII when it was the only lodging house in the region. But why the "Elephant"? Because in front of it there is a small mountain that looks strangely like such an animal. The owner has for a long time collected elephant-like objects, now scattered around the house. The greatest activity comes from the restaurant, and on the second floor five pleasant rooms, including that of the King with its private terrace, await you with their reasonable prices. Sun worshippers will relish the large terrace-solarium on the roof and can then refresh themselves in the swimming pool just close by and surrounded by lawns. The cozy restaurant and bar have bar have been through many also an evening that finished far too late, for this place is much appreciated. This is a hotel that does not give itself airs, and the welcome is very warm.

How to get there (Map 22): 87km north of Alicante on the coast; before Jávea, turn right, then Benitachell and the first on the left towards Cabo de la Nao.

Huerto del Cura

03203 Elche (Alicante)
Porta de la Morera, 14
Tel. 96-545 80 40 - Fax 96-542 19 10 - Sr José Orts Serrano
E-mail: h.huertocura@alc.es - Web: www.huertodelcura.com

Category ★★★★ **Rooms** 80 with air-conditioning, telephone, bath, WC, satellite TV, minibar. **Price** Single 14,000Pts, double 18,000Pts, suite with sitting room 22,000Pts, suite with 2 bedrooms 42,000Pts. **Meals** Breakfast 1,500Pts, served 7:30-11:00; full board +7,000Pts (per pers., 2 days min.). **Restaurant** Service 1:00PM-4:00PM, 8:30PM-11:00PM; à la carte. Specialties: fish. **Credit cards** All major. **Pets** Dogs not allowed. **Facilities** Swimming pool, tennis (1,000Pts), sauna (1,000Pts), parking. **Nearby** The palm forest, fiesta Aug 14 - 15 in Church of Santa Maria - Natural Park of Parje del Hondo Alicante - Santa Polar - Orihuela - Altea - Calpe. **Open** All year.

In the heart of Elche, a town known for its Paleolithic site and its celebrated "Lady", the Huerto del Cura (the "Curate's garden") will prove an agreeable stop on the road to southern Spain. The garden is a true oasis, particularly luxuriant, and constitutes the main attraction of this parador which offers accommodation in individual bungalows. The decor is contemporary but without excess, and the guest finds many services appropriate to this type of hotel, with everything contributing to its relaxed atmosphere. The bedrooms are all quiet, well-equipped, and decorated with contemporary furniture that is simple and in good taste. Your best choice is a bungalow slightly away from the swimming pool which offers greater quiet. The restaurant features food that has received good press from Spanish critics, and much can be said about the pleasure of lunching in the shade of the giant palms. What is truly extraordinary is the Huerto del Cura garden where countless varieties of lush plant life and palm trees thrive.

How to get there *(Map 21): 19km southwest of Alicante.*

Hotel El Montiboli

03570 Villajoyosa (Alicante)
Tel. 96-589 02 50 - Fax 96-589 38 57
Sr José Manuel Castillo

Category ★ ★ ★ ★ ★ **Rooms** 53 with air-conditioning, telephone, bath or shower, WC, satellite TV, minibar; elevator. **Price** Single 11,500-17,200Pts, double 19,600-29,600Pts, suite 25,200-40,600Pts, bungalow 27,600-42,800Pts. **Meals** Breakfast (buffet) included, served 8:00-11:00; half board +4,500Pts, full board +7,350Pts (per pers., 3 days min.). **Restaurant** Service 1:00PM-3:30PM, 8:30PM-11:00PM; mealtime specials 4,500Pts, also à la carte. Specialties: fish and regional cooking. **Credit cards** All major. **Pets** Dogs allowed except in restaurant (3,000Pts). **Facilities** 2 swimming pools, tennis (900-1,000Pts), hairdresser, fitness club, sauna, garage (2,750Pts). **Nearby** Alicante - Guadalest - Don Cayu de Setea golf course (9-Hole). **Closed** Jan - Apr.

Facing full onto the sea, the Montiboli is a hotel "de luxe" on a promontory and enjoying a very lovely site. A pretty path in the stone itself leads down to a first panoramic swimming pool, and then to a second one on the level of the semi-private beach itself. Near this one, a small restaurant serves paellas and seafood at lunchtime. Spacious, very bright, and with pretty bathrooms, the rooms all have terraces. Most attractive are the bungalows with a private staircase, lounge and open fireplace facing the sea. In the main building you will find a very cozy lounge, with its beams visible and very light colored furniture, next to a reading room. The reasonable number of rooms allows for an attentive welcome on the part of the hotel staff, and you will be very much at ease here. You will certainly appreciate the lifestyle as you wake up looking at the sea, then lunch on the beach, and go to sleep in peace having dined under the stars.

How to get there *(Map 22): 32km north of Alicante via A7, exit Villajoyosa.*

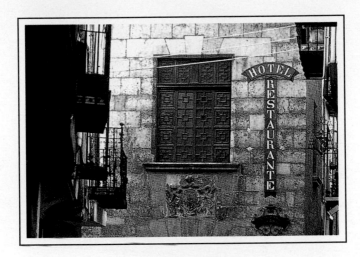

Hotel Cardenal Ram

12300 Morella (Castellón)
Calle Cuesta Suñer, 4
Tel. 964-17 30 85 - Fax 964-17 32 18 - Jaime Peñarroya Carbo

Category ★★★ **Rooms** 19 with telephone, bath or shower, WC, satellite TV, minibar, safe. **Price** Single 5,500Pts, double 8,500Pts, suite 10,500Pts; extra bed 2,000Pts. **Meals** Breakfast 850Pts, served 8:00-11:00; half board +2,250Pts (per pers.). **Restaurant** With air-conditioning, service 1:00PM-3:30PM, 8:00PM-11:00PM; mealtime specials 1,750Pts; also à la carte. Specialties: Sopa morellana - Croquetas morellanas - Ternasco trufado. **Credit cards** Visa, Eurocard, MasterCard. **Pets** Dogs not allowed. **Nearby** In Morella: castle, Basilica Santa Maria la Mayor, museum - Morella la Vella - San Mateo - The southern villages in the Maestrazgo Range. **Open** All year.

Morella is an extraordinary medieval village in the province of Castellón, to be found the famous Maestrazgo mountain range. Its strategic location on the border of the Kingdom of Valencia was prized not only by the Arabs and El Cid but also by the Carlists. Old walls still surround this small city which has preserved numerous architectural gems like the Church of Santa Maria Mayor. Another is the Cardenal Ram Palace still bearing the noble family's crest. It became a hotel in 1993, and its spacious ground-floor area has a lounge with an impressive vaulted ceiling. The restaurant is made up of three adjoining dining rooms. Their wooden floors and beams along with elegant rustic furniture create a fashionable atmosphere where you can enjoy the renowned cooking of the region. The large original stone staircase leads to the rooms, which are spacious and very comfortable while marked with a certain Spanish austerity. This is a refined hotel well off the beaten track.

How to get there (Map 15): 98km north of Castellón de la Plana toward Alcañiz.

Palau dels Osset

12310 Forcall (Castellón)
Plaza Mayor, 16
Tel. 964-17 75 24 - Fax 964-17 75 56

Category ★★★ **Rooms** 20 with air-conditioning, telephone, bath, satellite TV, minibar, safe; elevator - Wheelchair access. **Price** Single 6,500Pts, double 7,500-8,500Pts; extra bed 2,000Pts. **Meals** Breakfast 850Pts, served 7:30-11:00. **Restaurant** Service 1:00PM-3:30PM, 8:00PM-11:00PM, closed Mon and Tues; mealtime specials 1,700Pts, à la carte. **Credit cards** All major. **Pets** Dogs not allowed. **Nearby** In Morella: castle, Basilica Santa Maria la Mayor, museum - Morella la Vella - San Mateo - The southern villages in the Maestrazgo Range. **Open** All year.

Not far from Morella, Forcall is an interesting medieval village half way between the Sierra de Teruel and the province of Castellón. The Palau dels Osset is located in a 16th-century palace on a large square, its noble architecture, sober and austere with windows and arcades. Friezes are their sole decoration, reminding visitors of the hotel is historical origin. The same nobility is present inside; the vast lounge is overlooked by beams and the doors have beautifully sculpted frames. The decoration is up-to-date with comfortable sofas covered in attractive colors and very pretty lamps enhancing the atmosphere. The rooms are well-furnished and equally up-to-date. The best are on the third floor, especially no. 36 with its unadorned beams and no. 32 where you look out on the arcades of the hotel's facade. When the restaurant is closed, the *Mesón de la Vila* is a nearby and friendly alternative. A good address to know for a stop-over.

How to get there (Map 15): 115km north of Castellón de la Plana.

Hotel Reina Victoria

46002 Valencia
Calle Barcas, 4
Tel. 96-352 04 87 - Fax 96-352 27 21 - Sr Joaquin Calvo
E-mail: hrcinavictoriavalencia@husa.es

Category ★★★★ **Rooms** 97 with air-conditioning, telephone, bath or shower, WC, satellite TV, minibar; elevator. **Price** Single 11,800-13,250Pts, double 14,200-21,000Pts, suite 30,500Pts. **Meals** Breakfast 1,250Pts, served 7:00-11:00; half board +3,400Pts (per pers.). **Restaurant** Service 1:00PM-3:30PM, 8:30PM-11:00PM; mealtime specials 2,150Pts, also à la carte. Regional cooking. **Credit cards** All major. **Pets** Dogs not allowed. **Nearby** Valencia: Cathedral, Palazo Generalidad, la Lonja della seda, Ceramic Museum. City of Arts and Sciences - La Huerta de Valence - Porta Coeli charterhouse. **Open** All year.

The hotel has a nice location, close to the Town Hall on an attractive avenue lined with palm trees. A lovely 19th-century structure, it may seem slightly pompous but it is certainly in keeping with the style associated with international hotels. While the interior has lost some of its luster, a guest may wander comfortably through its spacious downstairs areas. The decoration is somewhat plain, with the exception of the hallways leading to the rooms that have a subtle and comfortable feel. They are at the same time large and modern, the most interesting giving on the street. We particularly recommend those on the corners. The rooms to avoid are plainly the ones giving on the interior courtyard. In Valencia, the Reina Victoria is a sure bet in a city where the choice of hotels is very limited.

How to get there *(Map 22): Near the Plaza del Ayuntamiento.*

R E S T A U R A N T S

A N D A L U S I A

ARCOS DE LA FRONTERA

El Convento, Marqués de Torresoto 7 - Tel. (956) 70 32 22 - Delicious regional cooking in a 15-century house: *cordero con hierbas aromaticas, tocino de cielo*. - Pts 3,000.

CÓRDOBA

El Churrasco, Romeno 16 - Tel. (957) 29 08 19 - Closed Sunday evenings and Mondays in winter. Closed Sunday evenings and Mondays in winter. A gastronomic institution offering flamenco in the basement. Excellent food: *ajoblanco en jarra, carne a la brasa, merluza al horno*. - Pts 3,000-4,000. – **La Casona**, Avda de El Brillante - Tel. (957) 27 18 02 - Another address in Córdoba not to be missed; charm and excellent food. - Pts 3,000-4,000. – **Astoria**, El Nogal 16 - Tel. (957) 27 76 53 - Closed Sundays in August. Matías Montes and his son Julio offer carefully prepared local specialties that are greatly appreciated by local residents. - Pts. 4,000-5,000. – **El Caballo Rojo**, Cardenal Herrero 28 - Tel. (957) 47 53 75 - Elegant and refined, traditional cuisine with specialties such as *rabo de toro* (bull's tail) and *salmorejo*. – **Almudaina**, Campo Santo de los Mártires - Tel. (957) 47 43 42 - Closed Sundays. Close to the Juderia and the Alcazar gardens. - Pts 5,000. – **Mesón El Burladero,** Calleja la Hoguera 5 - Tel. (957) 47 27 19 - A simple *Taverne* with a very correct *Manolete* menu. Some tables in the patio in summer.

BODEGAS AND MESONES NEAR THE PLAZA TENDILLAS

Bodegas Campos, near the Plaza del Potro. – **Casa Rubio**, Puerta de Almodóvar 5. – **Mesón de la Luna**, Calleja de la Luna.

CADIZ

El Faro, San Felix 15 - Tel. (956) 21 10 68 - Welcoming decor, fish and seafood. - Pts 4,000. - **Ventorrillo del Chato**, Playa de Cortadura - Via Augusta Julia - Tel. (956) 25 00 25 - Closed Sunday - Pts 3,500. In an old charming house with equally inviting food.

SAN ROQUE

Los Remos, Finca Villa Victoria - An elegant gastronomic treat. Specialty: *tortilla de camarones*. Excellent wine selection. - Pts 5,500.

GRANADA

Horno de Santiago, Plaza de los Campos 8 - Tel. (958) 22 34 76 - Closed Sunday evenings. Highly successful cooking offering modern versions of regional dishes. Elegant dining room, fine bodega. - Pts 4,500. – **Carmen de San Miguel,** pl. de Torres Bermejas 3 - Tel. (958) 22 67 23 - Closed Sunday, 15-30 August. In Alhambra, beautiful view on Grenade. – **Cunini**, Pescaderia 9 and Capuchinas 4 - Tel. (958) 25 07 77 - Closed Mondays. Good fish restaurant. At the bar, a large variety of seafood tapas. - Pts 3,500. – **Mesòn Andalus,** Elvira 17 - Tel. (958) 25 86 61 - Typical decoration. – **Sevilla,** Oficios 12 - Tel. (958) 22 12 23 – Correct cuisine, big tapas bar. Reservation needed. – **Mirador de Morayma**, Pianista Garcia Carillo 2 - Tel. (958) 22 82 90 - Closed Sundays. Noted for its fine view of the Alhambra and superb terrace in summer. – **Ruta del Veleta**, road to Sierra Nevada (5km from Cenes de la Vega) - Tel. (958) 48 61 34 - Closed Sunday evenings. Very good cuisine, grilled meat specialties, *carnes à la brasa*, and salted fish. - Pts 4,000. – **Zoraya,** Panaderos 32 - Tel. (958) 29 35 03 - Beautiful terrace in Albaicin.

JAÉN

Los Maricos, Nuerva 2 - Tel. (953) 25 32 06 - Delicious shellfish. – **Mesón Vicente**, Arco del Consuelo 1 - Tel. (953) 26 28 16 - Closed Sundays evenings. Regional cuisine, tapas bar and friendly dining room. – **Casa Vicente**, Francisco Martín Mora 1 - Tel. (953) 23 22 22 - Closed Sunday evenings. Meals served in the bar, the dining room and in the patio. Reservations recommended for the latter in summer. – **Asador Salvado**r, Ctra del Castillo de Santa Catalina - Tel. (953) 23 05 28 - Closed Sunday and Monday evenings. Excellent cooking in a charming house near Jaén Castle. - Pts 2,500.

JEREZ DE LA FRONTERA

La Mesa Redonda, Manuel de la Quintana 3 - Tel. (956) 31 00 69 - Closed Sunday evenings and holidays. Fine decor, friendly welcome and local specialties nicely prepared by José Antonio Romero. - Pts 4,500. – **Gaitán**, Gaitán 3 - Tel. (956) 34 58 59 - Closed Sunday evenings. Andalusian cuisine and some Basque specialties. - Pts 3,300. – **Venta Antonio**, road to Sanlúcar, km 6 - Tel. (956) 14 05 35 -Closed Mondays. Banal and functional decor but good and well-cooked fish specialties. – **Tendido 6**, Circo 10 - Tel. (956) 34 48 35 - Closed Sunday evenings. Beautiful andalous patio. - Pts 3,500.

TABASCOS AND MESONES IN THE SAN MARCOS QUARTER

Maypa, near the Plaza des

Angustias - The best known. – **Venezia-Faustino,** near the Place de l'Arenale.

MÁLAGA

Santa Paula, Avenida de la Guindos - Tel. (95) 223 94 45 - Fish, sea food, meat. Join the crowds at Málaga's most popular bodega. – **Café de Paris,** Paseo Maritimo - Tel. (95) 222 50 43 - Closed Sunday evening in winter. Good cooking. - Pts 3,500-5,000. – **Adolfo,** Paseo Maritimo Pablo Ruiz Picasso 12 - Tel. (95) 260 19 14 - A small restaurant, intimate and elegant with simple and refined food. - Pts 4,000. – **Antonio Martín,** Paseo Maritimo 4 - Tel. (952) 22 21 13 - Closed Sunday evenings. One of the oldest restaurants of Málaga. Fish, paella, on a beautiful terrace over the ocean. – **La Taberna del Pintor,** Maestranza 6 - Tel. (95) 221 53 15 - Specializes in good meat dishes served in a rustic decor. - Pts 3,000-4,000. – **El Boquerón de la Plata,** Alarcón Luyán 6 - The best bar for tapas and *gambas.*

FLAMENCO

Teatro Cervantes, a breeding ground of flamenco.

MARBELLA

La Fonda, Plaza del Santo Cristo 9 - Tel. (95) 277 25 12 - On one of the prettiest squares in town, in an 18th century house, one dines on a marvellous patio. Very chic. - Pts 6,000. – **Mesón del Pasaje,** Pasaje 5 - Tel. (95) 277 12 61 - Closed at midday in summer. Victorian decor in the small dining rooms, international cuisine. Attractive and not very expensive. – **La Tricycleta,** Buitrago 14 - Tel. (95) 277 78 00 - Closed Sundays and from January 15 to February 15. One of the best known restaurants in Marbella. Specialty, *Tricycleta brochettes.* – **Casa Eladio,** Plaza Naranjos 6 - Small and pretty ceramics-decorated patio.

TAPAS BARS

Bar Ana Maria, Plaza Santo Cristo - Closed Mondays. If not afraid of noise and a crowd.

CARMONA

San Fernando, Sacramento 3 - Tel. (95) 414 35 56 - Closed Sun evenings and Mon. The best address in this historic center. - Pts 4,000.

MIJAS

El Padrasto, Paseo del Compás - Tel. (95) 248 50 00 - Beautiful view of Fuengirola and the coast. Classic Spanish cuisine. - Pts 3,500.

NERJA

Pepe Rico, Almirante Ferandis 28 - Tel. (95) 252 02 47 - Very pleasant in summer. - Pts 2,500-3,000. – **De Miguel,** Pintada 2 -

Tel. (95) 252 29 96 - Open the night Oct to Mar.

FLAMENCO

El Colono, Granada 6 - Flamenco in a typical Andalusian house. One can also dine here.

RONDA

Don Miguel, Pl. de España 4 - Tel. (95) 287 10 90 - Closed Sundays from June to September. The restaurant is rather expensive but an attractive bar for having a glass and tapas. - Pts 2,500. – **Pedro Romero**, Virgen de la Paz 18 - Tel. (95) 287 11 10 - 'Bullfighter chic' ambiance, specialty *tocino del cielo al coco*. - Pts 3,000. – **Mesón del Escudero**, Marcos de Obregón 14 - Tel. (95) 287 13 67 - Closed Sunday evenings. A tavern not well known to tourists. Sergio prepares excellent and inventive regional specialties. - Pts 3,500. – **Mesón Santiago**, Marina 3 - Pleasant *taverne* in Andalusian style.

SANLUCAR DE BARRAMEDA

Mirador Doñana, Bajo de Guia - Tel. (956) 36 42 05 - Fish and seafood. - Pts 3,000. – **Bigote** - Tel. (956) 36 29 96 - Fish, on the Bajo de Guia beach.

SEVILLE

Casa Robles, Dr Pedro de Castro - Tel. (95) 456 32 72 - A true institution in the Andalusian capital. - Pts 4,000. – **Casablanca**, Zaragosa 50 - Tel. (95) 422 46 98 - Closed Sunday evenings. Very tasty food. - Pts 4,000. – **El Burladero**, Canalejas - Tel. (95) 422 29 00 - Closed in Aug. The favorite restaurant of the bullfighter. - Pts 3,500. – **La Albahaca**, Plaza Santa Cruz 12 - Tel. (95) 422 07 14 - Closed Sun. Beautiful Andalusian house of the famous architect Juan Talavera. Spanish and French cuisine. - Pts 4,500. – **Egaña Oriza**, San Fernando 41 - Tel. (95) 422 72 11 - Closed Sat midday, Sun and in Aug. Well situated above the Murillo gardens, a new restaurant appreciated by the Sevillians. Modern decor, gastronomic cuisine. - Pts 5,000. – **San Marco**, Cuna 6 - Tel. (95) 421 24 40 - Situated in a small palace with a delightful decor. Cooking favors the Italian style. - Pts. 3,500. – **Don José**, calle Pedro de Castro - Tel. (95) 441 44 02 - Closed Sundays. Good food served family style in a somewhat ordinary setting. – **Hosteria del Laurel**, Plaza Venerables 5 - Tel. (95) 422 02 95 - Very touristic but well situated in the Barrio Santa Cruz. One dines on a terrace on the square, pretty house. – **Taberna del Alabardero,** Zaragosa 20 - Tel. (95) 456 06 37 - In a old Palais. - Pts 4,000-7,000. By reservation. – **La Dehesa,** Luis Morales 2 - Tel. (95) 457 94 00 - Specialties: Meals. – **Rio Grande**, Betis - Tel. (95) 44 27 39 56 - Big terrace on the river. **Enrique**

Becerra, Gamazo 2 - Tel. (95) 421 30 49 - Closed Sundays. Closed Sundays. Traditional cooking including *espinacas con almejas* along with tapas at the bar. - Pts 3,500. – **Rincòn de Casana**, Santo Domingo de la Calzada 13 - Tel. (95) 453 17 10 - Closed Sunday in July, August. - Pts 3,500-4,500. – **El Mero**, Betis 1 - Tel. (95) 433 42 52 - Closed Tuesday. Shell fish. - Pts 3,500.

TAPAS BARS

Alhucema, Carlo Canal 20 A. – **Cerveceriá Giralda**, Mateos Gago 1. – **La Estella**, corner of Calles Estrella and Pajarito. Savory tapas and not expensive. – **El Jovem Costalero**, Torneo 18. – **Casa Román**, Plaza de los Venerables. – **Cas Robles**, Alvarez Quintero 58 - Tel. (95) 456 32 72 - A Sevillian institution you shouldn't miss.

– **Casa Morales**, García de Vinuesa 11 - Unchanged since 1850, ideal for taking a *fino* (sherry). – **La Taquilla**, ideal for the bullfight days, facing the arena. – **Rincón San Eloy**, San Eloy 24. – **El Rinconcillo**, Calle Gerona 40 - The oldest bar in Seville (1670), tapas and *tortillas de bacalaó*. - **Tremendo**, just next door, Calle San Felipe - Good beer accompanied by codfish and dried *mohama* (tunnyfish). – **Carboneria**, Plaza de las Marcedarias - Rustic, pleasant patio. – **Bar Garlochi**, corner of Calles Boteros and Alhondiga - Kitsch *'Semana Santa'* decor. Visit in the evening.

More chic: **Abades**, Calle Abades, for cocktails. – **Bar of Hotel Alfonso XIII**, for tea.

FLAMENCO

El Arenal, Dos de Mayo 26 - Tel. (95) 421 30 75. – **Los Gallos**, Plaza Santa Cruza 11 - Tel. (95) 421 69 81 - One of the best known spots, in the heart of the Barrio Santa Cruz. – **El Patio Sevillano**, Paeso de Colón - Tel. (95) 421 41 20 - Very, and too touristy.

A R A G O N

ZARAGOZA

La Ontina, Costa 5 - Tel. (976) 22 19 01 - Closed Sundays. A gastronomic restaurant featuring traditional dishes. - Pts 6,500 – **Goyesco**, Manuel Lasala 44 - Tel. (976) 35 68 70 - Closed Sundays. Unfailingly good food. - Pts 4,500 – **Txalupa**, Paseo de Fernando el Católico 62 - Tel.

(976) 56 61 70 - Closed Sunday and Monday evenings. A well frequented place offering a warm welcome, good food and fine service. Reserve in advance.

A S T U R I A S
C A N T A B R I A

GIJÓN

Casa Victor, Carmen 11 - Tel. (98) 534 83 10 - Closed Sundays. The best place in Gijón for fish specialties. Enjoy the bodega and its *sidra*. - Pts 4,000 – **Parrilla El Suelve**, Domingo Garcia de la Fuente 12 - Tel. (98) 514 57 03 - Closed Wednesday evening and Sundays. The best *parrilla* for Asturian meat. - Pts 3,000 Pts.

OVIEDO

El Raitàn, Plaza Trascorrales 6 - Tel. (985) 21 42 18 - Closed Sundays in summer. Ideal for sampling regional specialties. No menu but 9 dishes regularly served. - Pts 3,500. – **Casa Conrado**, Argüelles 1 - Tel. (98) 522 39 19 - Closed Sundays. A good family-style restaurant. - Pts 3,500 – **Faro Vidio**, Cimadevilla 19 - Tel. (98) 522 86 24 - Restaurant and *sidreria* producing very good cider along with local specialties. – **Del Arco**, Pl. de America - Tel. (98) 525 55 22 - Closed Sunday and August. - Pts 3,500-5,000. – **Cabo Peñas**,

Meaquiades Alvarez 24 - Tel. (98) 522 03 20 - Typical restaurant. - Pts 2,500-3,500. – **Casa Fermin**, San Francisco 8 - Tel. (98) 521-64 52 - Closed Sunday evenings. Sophisticated decor and refined traditional cooking. - Pts 4,000.

SANTANDER

Cañadio, Gòmez Oreña 15 - Tel. (942) 31 41 49 - Closed Sundays. Tapas and local specialties. - Pts 2,000 – **Machinero**, Ruiz de Alda 16 - Tel. (942) 31 49 21 - Closed Sundays. A good address located over the bar. - Pts 1,750-3,500. – **Cúpula del Rhin**, avenida de la Reina Victoria 153 - Tel. (942) 27 43 00 - A new address favored for its creative cooking. - Pts 4,000.

B A L E A R I C
I S L A N D S

MALLORCA
PALMA DE MALLORCA

Koldo Royo, Gabriel Roca 3 - Tel. (971) 73 24 35 - Closed Saturday noon and Sundays. A pleasant bodega and dining room plus excellent cooking. - Pts 5,000. – **Es Parlament**, Conquistador 11 - Tel. (971) 72 60 26 - Chic clientele with politicians that coming for the *paella del ciego*. Closed Sunday and in August. - Pts 3,000-5,000. – **Rififi**, Avda. de Joan Miró 182 - Tel. (976) 40 20 35 -

Closed Tuesdays. A friendly place noted for the freshness of the fish and sea food. - Pts 3,500. – **Porto Pi**, Joan Miró 182 - Tel. (971) 40 00 87 - Closed Saturday midday and Sundays. Old Mallorcan house. Basque 'nouvelle cuisine'. - Pts 4,000. – **Abaco**, C/ San Juan 1 - Baroque ambiance in a Manor-bar where you can drink cocktails with an atmospheric classical music. – **Bar Celler S'Antiquari**, Plaza Santa Cataline Tomás - Local clientele.

DEYA

Ca'n Quet, Carret. de Valldemosa, km 1.2 - Tel. (971) 63 91 96 - Closed from October to April, and Mondays. Pretty view of the mountains. - Pts 4,000.

IBIZA

IBIZA

Ca n'Alfredo, Paseo de Vara de Rey, 16 - Tel. (971) 31 12 74 - A traditional restaurant in Ibiza. - Pts 2,500-3,500. – **El Cigarral**, Fray Vicente Nicolás 9 - Tel. (971) 31 12 46 - Very well-prepared food including *judiónes con almejas, higos al licor de hierbas ibicencas*. – **S'Oficina**, Avenuda de España 6 - Tel. (971) 30 00 16 - Closed Sundays. The entrance is not very elegant but pleasant interior with patio. Basque cuisine. Pts 4,000. – **Bar San Juan**, Calle Montgri 8 - Tel. (971) 31 07 66 - Bistro style. Good fish. – **La Masia d'En Sord**,

Carret. de San Miguel, km 6.5, Apartado 897 - Tel. (971) 31 02 28 - Open from Easter till October. Old house, art gallery. - Pts 4,000.

SANTA EULALIA

Cás Pages, Carret. de San Carlos, km 10, (Pont de S'Argentara) - Closed Tuesdays and in February. Savory cuisine in this rustic old farmhouse.

SAN JOSÉ

Cana Joana, road Ibiza-San José, km 10 - Tel. (971) 80 01 58 - Closed Sunday evenings, Mondays except in summer, from October 15 to December 29. Very pleasant setting in this old country house. Try the *riscalos* (mushrooms) and the *escallopinos de pato* (minced duck). Reservation advisable. - Pts 4,000-6,000.

CASTILLA-LEON

AVILA

El Almacén, Ctra de Salamanca 6 - Tel. (920) 21 10 26 - Closed Sunday evenings and Mondays. Up-dated local specialities and an especially fine bodega. - Pts 3,500-4,500. – **El Molino de la Losa**, Bajada de la Losa 12 - Tel. (920) 21 11 01 - Closed on Mondays in winter. Former 15th century mill in the middle of the River Adaja. Service in the garden on fine days. – **Mesón del Rastro**,

Plaza Rastro 1 - Tel. (920) 21 12 18 - In the wing of a medieval palace. Specialties: *El barco*, lamb and beans. - Pts 3,000-4,000.

BURGOS

Asador de Aranda Papamoscas, Llana de Afuera - Tel. (947) 26 81 41 - Closed Sunday evening. A typical *mesòn castillan*, good food cooked on an open fire: *cordero asado* and *chuletillas*. - Pts 3,000. – **Casa Ojeda**, Victoria 5 - Tel. (947) 20 90 52 - Closed Sunday evening. A ritual address of Burgos. - Pts 4,000-6,000. – **Mesón del Cid**, Plaza Santa Maria 8 - Tel. (947) 20 59 71 - Closed Sunday evenings. Well situated in a 15th century house. From the dining room on the upper floors, superb view of the cathedral. Good traditional cuisine. - Pts 3,500.

LÉON

Casa Pozo, Plaza San Marcelo 15 - Tel. (987) 22 30 39 - Closed Sunday evenings, from July 1 to 15. Simple and welcoming atmosphere under the attentive eye of Pin, the patron, who keeps his house well run. - Pts 3,500-4,000. – **Adonias**, Santa Nonia 16 - Tel. (987) 20 67 68 - Closed Sundays, 15 days in August. Regional cuisine in a rustic and lively setting. - Pts 3,000-5,000. – **Formela**, Avda. de José António 24 - Tel. (987) 22 45 34 - Closed Sundays. Very fine food in a

modern setting. - Pts 2,000-4,000.

BAR

Prada a Tope Bar, on corner of the Plaza San Martin - Tasting of regional wine from Bierzo.

SALAMANCA

Chez Victor, Espoz y Mina, 26 - Tel. (923) 21 31 23 - Closed Sunday evening and Mondays. Castillian cooking with a French flavor. Truly gastronomic. - Pts 5,000. – **Chapeau**, Gran Via 20 - Tel. (923) 27 18 33 - Closed Sunday evenings. - Pts 3,500. – **Gasteiz**, Puerte de Zamora 4 - Tel. (923) 24 18 78 - A family atmosphere with Basque charm.

BAR

Café Las Torres, Plaza Mayor 26 - One of the best known bars on the square.

SEGOVIA

Mesón de Cándido, Mesón de Cándido - Tel. (921) 42 59 11 - Closed in November. All the personalities come here. An institution in Spain. - Pts 3,000-4,000. – **Mesón de José Maria**, Cronista Lecea 11 - Tel. (921) 43 44 84 - Closed in November. Equal with, and some say better than, its historical competitor. - Pts 3,000-4,000. – **Mesón Duque**, Cervantes 12 - Tel. (921) 43 05 37 - Intimate decoration and atmosphere for this other good restaurant of the town. – **Maracaibo**, Ezequiel Gonzàlez

25 - Tel. (921) 46 15 45 - Offers a traditional menu.

BAR

La Conceptión, Plaza Mayor 15, close to the cathedral - An ideal lunch stop with a terrace upstairs and a bodega in the basement.

SORIA

Maroto, Paseo de Espolón 20 - Tel. (975) 22 40 86 - The two Maroto brothers produce highly original dishes using local produce that include truffles and duck liver. – **Mesón Castellano**, Plaza Mayor 2 - Tel. (975) 21 30 45 - Closed January 15 to 31. Traditional restaurant. Specialties: *Chuletón de ternera, migas*. - Pts 2,500-4,500.

VALLADOLID

Mesón la Fragua, Paseo Zorrilla 10 - Tel. (983) 33 87 85 - Closed Sunday evenings, Mondays, in August. Luxurious, very expensive, frequented by the royal family. One of the best known restaurants of Castille. - Pts 3,500-5,000. – **Santi**, Correo 1 - Tel. (983) 33 93 55 - Closed Sundays except on holidays. Authentic Castillian cooking served in the restaurant or in the bodega of a splendid old house. - Pts 1,500-2,500. – **Fátima**, Pasión 3 - Tel. (983) 34 28 39 - Closed Sunday and Mondays evenings. The *bacalao* at the Fátima is a true marvel served in a place of equally genuine charm.

CASTILLA – MANCHA

TOLEDO

La Lumbre, Real del Arrabal 3 - Tel. (925) 28 53 07 - Closed Sundays. Up-to-date Castillian cooking. - Pts. 4,000-5,000. – **Assador Adolfo,** Granada 6 and Hombre de Palo 7 - Tel. (925) 22 73 21 - Closed Sunday evenings. Major classic regional specialties such as *perdiz estofada toledana* and *delicias de màzapan*. Good wines selection. - Pts 4,000-5,500. – **Venta de Aires,** Circo

Romano 35 - Tel. (925) 22 05 45 - On the outskirts of town - Good meats and generous Rioja wines. - Pts 3,000-4,000.

BAR

In one of the small lanes south of the Plaza Zocodover, you will find numerous bars and small restaurants open on the sidewalks: these were used as decor in 'Tristana' by Luis Buñuel.

CUENCA

Figón de Pedro, Cervantes 15 - Tel. (966) 22 45 11 - Closed Sunday evening, Mondays. One of the best known restaurants in Spain. Excellent regional cuisine. - Pts 3,000. – **Mesòn Casa Colgadas**, Canònigos - Tel. (969) 22 35 09 - Very beautiful view on the valley. - Pts 4,000. – **Rincón de Paco**, Hurtado de Mendoza 3 - Tel. (969) 21 34 18 - Invariably good at reasonable prices. - Pts 4,000 - 5,000.

PUERTO LAPICE

Venta del Quijote, El Molina 4. - Closed Thursdays and in September. Facing the church. Products of La Mancha in an ancient inn. Pleasant atmosphere, traditional and family cuisine. - Pts 3,000-4,500.

C A T A L U N Y A

BARCELONA

In the town center.

La Cuineta, Paradis 4 - Tel. (93) 315 01 11 - Typical restaurant in a bodega (17th-century). - Pts 3500-6,000. – **Senyor Parellada**, Argenteria 37 - Tel. (93) 310 50 94 - Closed Sundays and holidays. The atmosphere of a traditional *fonda* with charm

and fine cooking. - Pts 4,000. – **Los Caracoles**, Escudillers 14 - Tel. (93) 302 31 85 - Opened in 1835, this restaurant has kept all

its charm intact. Specialties: *caracoles* (snails), of course, and *paella de mariscos*. You are advised to observe Spanish eating hours to avoid waiting too long for a table. – **Can Ramonet**, Maquinista 17 - Tel. (93) 319 30 64 - Closed August. - Pts 3,500-4,500. – **Ca La Maria**, Tallers 76 bis - Tel. (93) 318 89 93 - Closed Sunday evening, Monday, August. - Pts 2,500. – **Agut d'Avignon**, Trinitat 3 - Tel. (93) 302 60 34 - Pts 4,000-6,000.

Agut, Gignas 16 - Tel. (93) 315 17 09 - Closed Sunday evenings, Mondays and in July. In the Gothic quarter, an old house (since 1924) always offering well cooked Catalan specialties. Good wines selection. – **15 Nits**, on the Plaza Real. One of the most

charming place in Barcelona, very busy, it's better to go late for avoided to stand in line. – **Egipte**, Jerusalem 12 - Tel. (93) 317 74 80 - Behind the Boqueria market. Small restaurant on several floors serving regional cuisine at very affordable prices. 'Plat du jour' at midday.

South

Ca l'Isidre, Les Flors 12 - Tel. (93) 441 11 39 - Closed Sundays and July 15 to August 15. A classic of Barcelona, Catalan cuisine, chic ambiance. Go there by cab in the evening, the hot quarter. - Pts 4,600-5,600. – **El Tragaluz,** 1 passage de la Concepciò 5 - Tel. (93) 487 01 96 - Closed Sunday. - Pts 5,500. Design decoration, at the first floor Japanese-grill, at the second floor traditionnel cooking under a beautiful glass roof. Fashion and society ambiance. – **La Tramoia**, Rambla de Catalunya, 15 - Tel. (93) 412 36 34 - "in", tapas and catalonian cooking. – **Els Pescadors**, plaza Prim 1 - Tel. (93) 309 20 18 - Closed Easter, Christmas, New Year. Shell fish. - Pts 5,000. – **Rias de Galicia**, Lleida 7 - Tel. (93) 424 81 52 - Fish. - Pts 4,000-5,000. – **Font del Gat,** passeig Santa madona Montjuic - Tel. (93) 424 02 24 - Closed Monday. - Pts 4,500. – **El Cellar de Casa Jordi**, Rita Bonnat 3 - Tel. (93) 430 10 45 - Closed Sunday and August. - Pts 2,000-3,000.

North

Botafumeiro, av. Gan de Gracia 8 - Tel. (93) 218 42 30 - Closed in August. Specialties fish and sea food. - Pts 4,000-6,500. – **El Asador de Aranda,** Avenida Tibidabo 31 - Tel. (93) 417 01 15 - Closed Sunday evenings. Traditional atmosphere, decoration and cuisine. - Pts 4,000. – **La Venta,** Plaza Doctor Andreu (at Tibidabo, served by the blue tramway) - Closed Sundays. Good fish and superb view of the city and sea. - Pts 4,200-5,000. – **A la Menta**, passeig Manuel Girona 50 - Tel. (93) 204 15 49 - Closed Saturday evening, Sunday in Juni to September. - Pts 3,000-4,000.

Port Vell and La Barceloneta

Les Set Portes, Passage Isabel II 14 - Tel. (93) 319 30 33 - The 7 doors in fact total 11 ! Paellas, rice in cuttlefish ink. Always lots

of people. - Pts 3,000-4,500.
– **Salmonete,** Playa de San
Miguel 34 - Tel. (93) 319 50 32.
– **L'Arrosejat,** Playa de San
Miguel 38 - It is a Barcelona
institution to go and eat paella
and seafood on the Barceloneta
beach.
– **Barceloneta**, L'Escar 22, Moll
del Pescador, Port Vell - Tel. (93)
221 21 11.

A gastronomic address under the
leadership of the famous Catalan
cook Mey Hofmann. The superb
ocean liner-style decor is by
Estrella Salietti. Not to be
missed!
– **Merendero dei Mari**, Palau de
Mar du port Vell, plaça Vila 1 -
Tel. (93) 221 31 41 - Closed
Sunday evenings. Also decorated
by Estrella Salietti. Tapas with
fish. When you leaving, stop at
the café Magatzem just near. - Pts
4,000.

– **Casa Costa-Cal Pinxo**, beach
of Barceloneta Baluard 124 - Tel.

(93) 221 50 28 - A good cooking
(fish) served in a very pleasant
dining room or terrace.

'XAMPANYERIAS'
Tapas bar Basque, often closed
Sunday evenings and Monday.
La Cava del Palau, Verdaguer i
Callis 10 - Closed Sundays. Near
to the Palau de la Música. Large
choice of wines, champagnes and
cocktails with sampling of patés
and cheeses. – **El Xampanyet,**
Montoada 22 - Closed Mondays.
A lot of atmosphere in this
'xampanyeria', certainly one of
the nicest in Barcelona, close to
the Picasso Museum. – **Euskal
Etxea** (opposite) Placete
Moncada - Pintxos, cider, keep
your small stick for the addition
– **Café du Musée du Textile**,
Montoada 28 - Drinks and snacks
available in the delightful
courtyard of the museum.

TAPAS BARS
Estrella de Plata, Pla de Palau 9
- Tel. (93) 319 82 53 - Closed
Sundays and Monday at lunch. A
large selection of very good
tapas. - Pts 3,000. – **Cal Pep,**

Plaza de las Ollas 8 - Tel. (93) 310 79 61 - Closed Sundays and Monday at lunch. Tapas at the bar from 8 to midnight plus a small menu of sea food specialties you can enjoy in the dining room beyond the bar. – **Bar Rodrigo,** L'Argeneria 67 - Closed Wednesday evenings and Thursdays. Near to Santa Maria de Canaletas church. One samples tapas with *vermut*, house specialty. – **Cervecería Baviera,** Ramblas 127 - Sampling of tapas and seafood, at table or standing at the counter. – **Can Paixano**, Reina Christina, after the Plaça de Palau - Famous for its good 'cave' and tapas. Very modest prices.

CAFES

Café de l'Académie, Lledo 1 - Fermé samedi, dimanche et jours fériés. Près du Generalitat. Un beau cadre, une bonne cuisine de marché

– **Els Quatre Gats,** Carrer. Montsio - Closed Sundays. Very famous café in a building (1896) of Josep Puig i Cadafalch, where Picasso had his first exhibition. Careful ! A modern version is next to the old bar.

– **Bar del Pí,** Plaça del Pí - Very popular 'Art-Deco' bar. Very popular Art Déco bar where on Sundays artists display their work.

– **La Fira**, Provenza 171 - Decorated with slot machines, bumper cars… "in".

– **Marsella**, San Pau 65 - One of the most famous night bar in the town.

– **Café de l'Opera,** Rambla dels Caputxins - A 'Belle Epoque' café with an authentic decor. The *café cortado* is excellent.

– **La Torre de Avila**, Poble Espanyol - Open the weekend from midnight to 4 a.m. The favorite nightclub of the yuppies in a Mariscal decor.

– **La Paloma**, Carret. del Tigre 27 - Open Thurdays to Sundays

from 9Pm. Vast rococo dance hall, surrounded by two tiers of seating where one finds all generations and social classes mixed together, rock and tango dancers.

– **Bar Mundial**, Plaça Santa Agusti Vell 11 - Closed Mondays. Very popular local bar for evening tapas. The back room serves *zarzuelas* and welcomes a more 'with it' clientele. Other specialty: peach liqueur (*melocotón*).

LA BOQUERIA

On the Ramblas, 89, don't forget to go for a stroll at the Boqueria market. – Just by side, the **Casa Guinart** for the salt specialties.

The famous pastrymaking-tea room of **Christian Escriba**,

Ramblas 83. Specialties: cakes with pine nut.
– **Vincon**, passeig de Gracia 96, near Pedrera.

NEAR TO BARCELONA

MONTSERRAT
Montserrat, Plaça Apostols - Open only at lunchtime.

SITGES
Vivero, Paseo Balmins - Tel. (93) 894 21 49 - Seafood. - Pts 2,300-4,500. – **La Nansa**, Carreta 24 - Tel. (93) 894 19 27 - Closed Tuesday evenings and Wednesdays in winter. Local dishes and bodega. - Pts. 3,000.

GERONA
Albereda, Albereda 7 - Tel. (972) 22 60 02 - Closed Sundays. Pts 3,500-5,400. – **La Penyora**, Nou del Teatre 3 - Tel. (972) 21 89 48 - Closed Tuesdays. A small, traditional restaurant. - Pts 4,000. – **Isaac el Sec**, beside the museum - Tapas.

FIGUERAS
Ampurdán, Carretera de Olot, km 1.5 - Tel. (972) 50 05 62 - Very good Franco-Catalan cuisine. - Pts 4,500-6,000.

CADAQUÉS
Galiota, Narcis Monturiol 9 - Tel. (972) 25 81 87 - One comes here for the fish and the Dali drawings on the walls. – **Casa Anita**, Carrer Miguel Roset - Tel. (972) 25 81 71 - This address is the must of Cadaqués she's stornm in summer between 8 and 10 p.m.

Cafe de la Habana, Carrer Bartomeus - It's a chic café for have a drink the evening. – **L'Hostal**, Rambla - A bar-disco, "in".

ARTIES
Casa Irene, Mayor 3 - Tel. (973) 64 43 64 - Closed from October 15 to December 1 and Mondays in winter. Delicious food in a marvellous setting. - Pts 4,000-6,000.

TORTOSA
San Carlos, Rambla Felip Pedrell 19 - Tel. (977) 44 10 48 - The decor is without interest but do not be put off. The fish specialties such as *rosseyat*, fish from the Ebro delta, or *romasco de rape*, arc excellent. – **Raco de Mig-Cami**, route Simpatica, 2.5km - Tel. (977) 44 31 48 - Closed Sunday evenings, Mondays. - Pts 2,550-3,500.

PUIGCERDÀ
La Vila, Alfons I. 134 - Tel. (972) 14 05 04 - Closed Mondays. Very good cuisine. - Pts 3,500. – **Madrigal,** Alfons I. 1 - Tel. (972) 88 08 60 - Bar-restaurant serving tapas and some house specialties: snails, cuttlefish.

LLIVIA
(6km from Puigcerdá)
Can Ventura, Plaça Mayor - Tel. (972) 89 61 78 - Closed Sunday evenings, Tuesdays, in October. One of the good restaurants in the Puigcerdá area for its decor and cuisine. Reservation necessary.

MARTINET
(on the road 26km from Puigcerdá)
Can Boix - Tel. (973) 51 50 50 - Gastronomic restaurant with French and Catalan specialties. Good and expensive. - Pts 5,000.

EXTREMADURA

CACERES
El Figón de Eustaquio, Plaza San Juan 12 - Tel. (927) 24 81 94 - Small restaurant very popular at lunchtime (reservation), well prepared traditional cuisine, one of the best addresses in the region. - Pts 2,500-3,300.

TRUJILLO
Hostal Pizarro, Plaza Mayor 13 - Tel. (927) 32 02 55 - Convivial atmosphere in this small restaurant; Two sisters have taken over this family business. Keen to promote regional specialties such as stuffed chicken (*gallina truffada*). – **Mesòn La Troya**, plaza Mayor 10 - Tel. (927) 32 13 64 - Tipical restaurant. - Pts 1,800.

GALICIA

LA CORUÑA
El Rápido, La Estrella 7 - Tel. (948) 22 42 21 - Closed Sunday evenings except in summer and December 15 to 31. The shellfish are magnificent. Regular and elegant clientele. Reservation

advised. – **Coral,** La Estrella 2 - Tel. (981) 22 10 82 - Closed Sunday except in summer. - Pts 2,500-4,500.

SANTIAGO DE COMPOSTELA
Anexo Vilas, Avenida Villagarcia 21 - Tel. (981) 59 86 37 - Closed Mondays. Moncho Vilas is proud of having prepared the menu for Jean-Paul II's visit to St.-Jacques-de-Compastela in 1989. Good recipes from Galicia. - Pts 4,000-5,500. – **San Clemente,** San Clemente 6 - Tel. (981) 58 08 82 - Very good fish. Choose the more comfortable dining room. – **Bodega Abrigadoiro,** Carretera del Conde 5 - In the old town. Perfect for a lunch break (*chorizo* and *tortillas*).

PONTEVEDRA
Doña Antonia, Soportale de la Herreria 4 - Tel. (986) 84 72 74 - Closed Sunday. - Pts 3,000-4,000. – **Casa Solla**, in San Salvador, Carretera de la Toja, 2km - Tel. (986) 85 26 78 - Closed Thursdays and for Christmas. The two best addresses in Pontevedra.

LA GUARDIA
Bitadorna, Calvo Sotelo 30 - Tel. (986) 61 19 70 - Closed Sunday evenings. Modern local cooking. - Pts 2,000-4,000. – **Anduriña**, Calvo Sotelo 58 - Tel. (986) 61 11 08 - Fish and sea food. Terrace and attractive view. - Pts 2,500 - 3,500.

N A V A R R A

ARISCUN
Etxeverria, near to Frontón - Tel. (948) 58 70 13 - Pretty little inn in a former farm. Regional cuisine. Some pretty rooms.

PAMPLONA
Josexto, Principe de Viana 1 - Tel. (948) 22 20 97 - Closed Sundays except in May and during the San Fermín Feria, Josexto is considered the best restaurant in the city. Warm surroundings. - Pts 6,000-8,000. – **Enekorri**, Tuleda 14 bajo - Tel. (948) 23 25 47 - Closed Sundays – Pts 5,000-6,000. Excellent produce, especially fish which is very fresh. A fine bidega. – **Casa Amparo**, Esquiroz 22 - Tel. (948) 26 11 62 - Closed Sundays - Pts 3,000-4,000. Dishes straight from the market served in a delightful ambiance.

M A D R I D

MADRID
La Vaca Veronica, Moratin 38 - Tel. (91) 429 78 27 - Closed Sundays and Saturdays at lunch. A charming place. - Pts 4,000. – **Donde Marian**, Torpedero Tucumán - Tel. (91) 359 04 84 - Closed Saturdays at noon and Sundays. Good meat dishes. A nice terrace on summer days. - Pts 4,000. – **Chuliá**, Maria de Guzman, 36 - Tel. (91) 535 31 23

- Pts 3,500. A generous and plainly feminine style of cooking. – **Betelu,** Florencio Llorente 27 - Tel. (91) 326 50 87 - Closed Sundays and Mondays. A small friendly restaurant with specialties of Navarra such as *alubias rojas* and *cogote de merluza.* – **Sal Gorda**, Beatriz de Bobadilla 9 - Tel. (91) 553 95 06 - Closed Sundays. Particularly well-prepared meals. - Pts 4,000. – **Nueva Horna de Santa Teresa**, Sta Teresa 8 - Tel. (91) 308 05 90 - Closed Sundays, during August and during Holy Week. A friendly family-style restaurant. Pts 4,500. – **Don Sancho**, Bretón de los Herreros 58 - Tel. (91) 441 37 94 - Closed Sundays, holidays and Monday evenings. The *bacalao dorado* is a treat. - Pts 2,500-4,000. – **La Gran Tasca**, Sta Engracia 24 - Tel. (91) 448 77 79 - Closed in the evening on Sundays and holidays. A famous stew: *cocido madrileño.* - Pts 4,000. – **Posada de la Villa**, Cava baja 9 - Tel. (91) 366 18 80 - Metro: Latina - Closed Sunday evening, 24 July to 24 August. In a old posada. - Pts 6,000-3,000. – **El Mentidero de la Villa**, Santo Tomé 6 - Tel. (91) 308 12 85 - Closed Saturday lunch, Sunday, August. - Pts 4,000-5,000. – **Las Cuevas de Luis Candelas**, Cuchilleros 1 - Tel. (91) 366 54 28 - Pts 3,500-5,000. – **Café de Oriente,** Plaza de Oriente 2 - Tel. (91) 541 39 74 - Closed Saturday midday, Sundays and in August. Chic. In summer the most elegant terrace in Madrid to take a glass. One dines inside. Catalan cuisine. Basque cuisine on reservation. - Pts 5,000. – **La Bola,** Bola 5 - Tel. (91) 547 69 30 - Closed Saturday evenings, Sundays and in July and August. Cosy atmosphere. Traditional cuisine. - Pts 3,000-4,200. – **Botín,** Arco de Cuchilleros 17 - Tel. (91) 266 42 17 - The Guiness Book of Records names it the oldest restaurant in the world, made famous by Hemingway. Specialties: *cochonillo* and *cordero asado.* Reservation necessary. - Pts 3,000-5,000. – **Casa Lucio,** Cava Baya 35 - Tel. (91) 365 32 52 - Closed in August. 'Taverne' freqented by artists, intellectuals, bullfighter. Traditional cuisine, very good Jabujo ham, reasonable prices. – **Casa Paco,** Puerta Cerrada 11 - Tel. (91) 266 31 66 - Closed Sundays and in August. Atmosphere of a real *'mesón'* (Catalan 'taverne'). Steakhouse specialties. - Pts 2,000-4,000. – **Taberna Carmencita,** Libertad 16 - Tel. (91) 531 66 12 - Metro: Chueca - Closed in August. - Pts 4,000. – **El Pescador,** José Ortega y Gasset 75 - Tel. (91) 402 12 90 -Closed Sundays. Delicious fish specialties. - Pts 5,000.

TAPAS BARS

Bocaíto, Libertad 6 - Reputed to serve the best tapas in Madrid. –

Las Bravas, Alvarez Gato 6 - For its *papatas bravas*. – **Casa Alberto,** Huerta 8 - Tapas eaten standing at the bar in beautiful wine cellar. – **La Chuleta,** Echegaray 20 - Bullfighting atmosphere. – **La Dolores,** Plaza de Jésus 4 - In a noisy ambiance, the best beer in Madrid accompanies the tapas. A few tables. – **Mesón Gallego,** León 4 - For its *caldo gallego*. – **The Reporter,** Fúcar 6 - For its trellised terrace. – **La Trucha,** Manuel Fernandez y Gonzales 3 - The tapas are delicious.

BARS

Café Gijon, Paeso de Recoletos 24 - One of the best known cafés of the capital. – **Chicote,** Gran Via 12 - Immortalized in Hemingway works. – **Los Gabrieles**, Echegara 17 - Little known by tourists. – **Hermanos Muniz,** Huerta 29 - Typically Spanish.
– **Cervecería Alemana,** Plaza Santa Ana 6 - Closed Tuesdays. Another Hemingway refuge.

Tapas.
– **Café Commercial,** Glorietta de Bilbao 10 - Superb, go and have a *café solo o cortado* (black or with milk). – **Bar Cock,** Calle Reina 16 (corner Alcala and Gran Via) - Kitsch, to the glory of the famous Madrid barman, Don Chicote. – **Viva Madrid,** Calle Manuel González y Fernandez 7 - Old 'azuleros', tapas. – **Circulo's,** Alcala 42 -Magnificent 19th century café, base of the 'Cercle des Beaux-Arts' club. Frequented by artists and intellectuals.

FLAMENCO

EL Andalus, Capitan Hayas 19 – **Café de Chinitas,** Torija 7 - Tel. (91) 248 51 35 - One of the best known and most touristy. Dinner served. – **Corral de la Pacheca,** Juan Ramon Jiménez 26 - Tel. (91) 458 11 13 - Less touristy, more reasonable prices.

NIGHT BARS

Teatrix, hermosilla 15. Open night and day. Decor by Starck for this old theater. A lot of ambiance in this bar-restaurant – **Joy Eslava**, Arenal 11 - An another theater changed in a nightclub, open until 5 a.m. – **Viva Madrid**, Manuel Fernandez y Gonzalez 17 (near plaza Santa Ana) - Tapas-bar very frequented until 2 a.m. – **Chocolateria San Gines**, at the end of Joy Eslava - The appointment of the reveller for the breakfast.

PAIS VASCO

SAN SEBASTIÁN

Arzak, Alto de Miracruz 2 - Tel. (943) 27 84 65 - Closed 3 weeks in June and 3 weeks in September. The reputation of the cuisine of Juan Mari Arzah has gone beyond the frontiers. Delicious Basque cuisine, delicious pastries. – **Salduba,** Pescaderia 6 - Tel. (943) 42 56 27 - Closed Sundays and June 10 to July 10. - Pts 3,000-4,000. – **Bodegon Alejandro,** Fermin Calbeton 22 - Tel. (943) 42 11 58 - Closed Sunday evenings, Mondays, November 15-30, in February. - Pts 2,800-4,600.

BILBAO

Goizeko Kabi, Particular de Estraunza 4 - Tel. (94) 441 50 04 - Closed Sundays from July 25 to August 14. A big and elegant restaurant, it is Bilbao's choice for the city's fish specialties. - Pts 4,000-6,000. – **El Asador de Aranda Egaña** 27 - Tel. (94) 443 06 64 - Closed Sunday evenings from July 25 to August 14. - Pts 3,500. – **El Viejo Zorti,** Licenciado Poza 54 - Tel. (94) 441 92 49 - Closed Sundays. A friendly bistro. - Pts 3,000. – **Guggenheim Bilbao,** Abandoibarra Etorbidea 2 - Tel. (94) 423 93 33 - Closed Sunday evenings and Monday. A fine place to visit after the Museum, of course.

MUNDAKA

Portu-Ondo, Barrio de Portu-Ondo - Tel. (94) 687 60 50 - Closed every evening except Friday and Saturday. A small, charming restaurant with a view of the Mundaka River. - Pts 2,500.

FUENTARRABIA

Ramón Roteta, Villa Ainara Irun - Tel. (943) 64 16 93 - Closed Thursdays and Sunday evenings except in summer. Very good cuisine served in summer in the garden of this beautiful old villa. – **Zeria,** San Pedro 23 - Tel. (943) 64 27 80 - Closed Sunday evening, Thursday (except in summer), November. -Pts 3,500-4,000. – **Kupela,** Zuloaga 4 - Tel. (943) 64 40 25.

SANTANDER

Posada del Mar, Juan de la Cosa 3 - Tel. (942) 21 56 56 - Closed Sunday, 10 September to 10 October. - Pts 4,000. – **Bodega del Riojano,** Rio de la Pila 5 - Tel. (942) 21 67 50 - Closed Sunday evenings. Lots of charm and atmosphere in this former wine cellar. Seasonal and market cuisine. – **La Sardina,** Dr Fleming 3 - Tel. (942) 27 10 35 – Closed Sunday evenings, Tuesdays except in summer. - Pts 3,700-5,600.

VALENCIA

VALENCIA

Civera, Lerida 11 - Tel. (96) 347
59 17 - Closed Sunday evenings,
Mondays and in August. Great
specialist in grilled, poached and
salted fish. Delicious but
expensive. Reservation advised. -
Pts 4,500. – **El Timonel,** Felix
Pizcueta 13 - Tel. (96) 352 63 00
- Closed Mondays, Holy Week
and in August. Very good fish
cooked simply. - Pts 3,500-5,000.

MORELLA

Mesón del Pastor, Cuesta Jovani
3 - Tel. (964) 16 02 49 - Closed
Wednesdays. Savory cuisine. –
Casa Roque, Segura Barreda 8 -
Closed Mondays and from
February 1 to February 20. - Pts
3,000-3,500.

INDEX

INDEX

HUNTER RIVAGES

4TH EDITION

HOTELS AND COUNTRY INNS
of Character and Charm
IN ITALY

• WITH COLOR MAPS AND PHOTOS •